THE ART OF WORLD LEARNING

THE ART OF WORLD LEARNING

COMMUNITY ENGAGEMENT FOR A SUSTAINABLE PLANET

Richard Slimbach

Foreword by Brian Whalen

Sty/us

STERLING, VIRGINIA

Sty/us

COPYRIGHT © 2020 BY STYLUS
PUBLISHING, LLC.

Published by Stylus Publishing, LLC.
22883 Quicksilver Drive
Sterling, Virginia 20166-2019

All rights reserved. No part of this book may be
reprinted or reproduced in any form or by any electronic,
mechanical, or other means, now known or hereafter
invented, including photocopying, recording, and
information storage and retrieval, without permission in
writing from the publisher.

Library of Congress Cataloging-in-Publication Data
The CIP for this text has been applied for.

13-digit ISBN: 978-1-57922-965-8 (cloth)
13-digit ISBN: 978-1-57922-966-5 (paperback)
13-digit ISBN: 978-1-57922-967-2 (library networkable
e-edition)
13-digit ISBN: 978-1-57922-968-9 (consumer e-edition)
Printed in the United States of America

All first editions printed on acid-free paper
that meets the American National Standards Institute
Z39-48 Standard.

Bulk Purchases

Quantity discounts are available for use in workshops
and for staff development.
Call 1-800-232-0223

First Edition, 2020

*To a grace-filled Earth. Our very essence
and future existence depend on you.*

*To intrepid global learners everywhere.
Risking discomfort to mine the genius of
other ways of life, you inspire hope for a
better humanity.*

CONTENTS

FOREWORD

LIKELY IN MANY historical periods the pace of change in the world has seemed rapid and almost overwhelming. But the challenges of our current age of globalization appear more daunting. How are we to adapt to a planet that is suffering from overpopulation, urbanization, climate change, a fragile ecology, economic disparity among people, and vanishing cultural and linguistic traditions?

Humanity evolves to adapt and thrive, and so too must our systems of thought and practice in various fields of endeavor. When environmental conditions force us to change, we look to new ideas and perspectives that can reshape our understanding and our actions.

Such a revolution is needed to shift the foundations of global education in order to make it relevant to and valuable for our contemporary world. Nothing less than a reconsideration of the field's very form and function is needed to impact every level of global education activity. We need to reimagine the big picture, the "why" of global education, as well as the designs and the practices that we take for granted in our everyday work. To accomplish this it is necessary to be led by bold revolutionaries who have a thorough knowledge of the field and the environment in which it functions, a creative impulse to dream of the future and what the field might become, together with no fear of breaking through convention.

Kuhn's well-known argument of the "structure of scientific revolutions" as a series of paradigm shifts aptly applies to the field of global education. For the past twenty years global education has focused largely on functional topics that are geared toward process and policy and not toward the content of learning. Evidence abounds in the main topics of decades of global education conferences: increasing student participation; demonstrating value through the assessment of student outcomes; research that improves programs; diversification of every aspect of the field; supporting students to make their global education experiences as successful as possible; and implementing best practices and standards. Has this paradigm now run its course? If so, what are the next "big ideas" that will shape our field, and where will they come from? How do we decide on new foundational principals and new designs for global education?

Shifting paradigms is not easy, nor is it for the faint of heart. It requires upheaval, serious and sometimes contentious debate, out-of-the-box thinking, genuine controversies, and a welcoming of outside perspectives, fresh ideas and new approaches. These are not always comfortable discussions to have, and they rarely seem to make their way into conference and meeting agendas.

The reformulation of a field should be both broad and deep, impacting the personal, interpersonal, and global dimensions of life. Those who work in and benefit from global education need to have their minds opened up and transformed; they need to relate to others in new, mutually beneficial ways; and they need to be motivated to think and act to make the world a better place. Such an undertaking as this is more an art than it is a science. It requires leaders who have the sensibilities and expertise of master artists, composing a visionary painting that inspires others to look differently at themselves, at others, and at the world. It requires leaders like Richard Slimbach.

For centuries travelers have sought out great works of art and architecture to contemplate their beauty and meaning and to open their minds to new ways of seeing and understanding the world and its cultural richness. Art in all its expressive forms has always been an important part of the global education learning experience. Therefore, it is apt to use the metaphor of global education-as-art-form to understand how we create and curate our global education programs. Designers and practitioners of these programs, and anyone engaged in the art of global education, will be inspired by the canvas that they encounter on the following pages.

Brian Whalen
Chief Academic Officer and Dean of Education
Atlantis

ACKNOWLEDGEMENTS

THIS BOOK'S GESTATION traces to a series of absorbing conversations and conference presentations related to global learning and the common good with some truly wise colleagues: Paul Hertig, Shuang Frances Wu-Barone, Dan Waite, Scott Blair, Viv Grigg, Chip Peterson, Cynthia Toms-Smedley, Adam Weinberg, Eric Hartman, Bruce La Brack, Todd and Junia Podrifka, Anthony Ogden, Roland Hoksbergen, Andrew Law, and Bernhard Streitwieser, among others. I am immensely grateful for their friendship, encouragement, and intellectual inspiration.

Many of the ideas in this book owe their existence to conceptual mentors I've never met: Dorothy Day, Margaret Mead, Jane Jacobs, Erich Fromm, Reinhold Niebuhr, Ivan Illich, Paulo Freire, E.F. Schumacher, John Dewey, Gustavo Gutierrez, Jack Mezirow, Ernest Boyer, Parker Palmer, David Kolb, Erving Goffman, Clifford Geertz, Harry Wolcott, Robert Chambers, Martha Nussbaum, Alan Fowler, Wendell Berry, and Kwame Anthony Appiah. In their writings I discovered, quite unexpectedly, that their primary interest was not in changing the world, but in seeing it clearly and living in it truthfully. Their gift to me was an appreciation of community-engaged learning as a sensibility, a certain way of being in the world.

I am indebted to those who have strengthened my faith in the public value of a global education. To the hundreds of inquiring students who, over the years, have inspired me by their pure curiosity and bold embrace of the ideas in this book. To the many families and grassroots organizations who generously supported these students in their intercultural living and learning. And to the many distinguished practitioners who have unfailingly enriched my professional life through meetings of the Association of American Colleges & Universities (AAC&U), The Forum on Education Abroad, and GlobalSL. If this book is a useful reflection of what dedicated colleagues have helped me understand about the art of world learning, I hope it returns something of what they graciously shared.

Special thanks to John von Knorring at Stylus Publishing for taking on this project, and for his splendidly acute editorial eyes; to Leslie, my life partner of 36 years, for anchoring and patiently supporting me; and to Robert Slimbach for producing the typeface (Garamond) that graces these printed pages. This book is dedicated to our two children, Justus and Destinae, whose generation must initiate the profound transformations needed to address the multilevel crisis of modern civilization.

INTRODUCTION

For years, my commute to and from work between the cities of Monrovia and Azusa, both in Los Angeles County, was on the 187 bus. One of the great things about bus riding is the chance to witness a kaleidoscope of humanity. On any given trip, there would be riders of all types—text-messaging businessmen; caregivers; house cleaners; mothers with children in strollers; students quietly reading textbooks, buds in ears; frail, elderly people with shopping carts; full-throated yakkers broadcasting unsolicited personal opinions; and at least one wheelchair user planted in the spot specially reserved for them. On cold, late-night rides, one or two homeless persons would be fast asleep on a seat in the rear of the bus. The 187 was a world on wheels.

In this curious company I often found myself contemplating the quality and strength of America's social fabric. How might different people, each with their own particular identity, occupying public space together, learn to live well with one another? I was familiar with the sweeping verdict of media pundits and political leaders: that building genuine community across deep differences was more and more inconceivable. The economic, racial, political, and religious divisions were just too sharp, especially as the inflammatory and polarized language of respect-seeking groups worsened.

Furthermore, I was aware of the growing evidence suggesting that we have entered a phase of passive segregation, be it in our media feeds, neighborhoods, or schools. Race and class, it seems, are on everybody's mind, and for good reason. By almost every empirical remeasure—income, wealth, employment, education, incarceration, and housing—the racial and economic gap has yet to close. Ideologically as well, more and more people seem to be stuck in their own "truths." Liberals accuse conservatives of being climate doubters and indifferent to the poor. Conservatives accuse

1

liberals of being unpatriotic, irreligious, and indifferent to family values. Both accuse the other side of impoverished moral thought. Given that so many groups have concluded that society does not recognize and respect their innermost self, it's increasingly difficult to imagine what it is, exactly, that binds us together.

There are two kinds of integration, *objective* and *subjective*. The former is about putting together people of different colors, creeds, countries, cultures, and classes in the same classroom, office, or neighborhood. The latter is about forming emotional bonds of connection that combine a positive sense of group pride with an overall "we-ness." Achieving subjective integration, of course, requires something of us—a psychological and social shift. Instead of seeing "us" immutably stuck in opposition to "them," we come to see and embrace "them" as part of what Martin Luther King Jr. (1986a) described as an "inescapable network of mutuality" and "a single garment of destiny." Moving from a parochial to a cosmopolitan mind-set is no longer a luxury on a small, interconnected, and warming planet; it has become a necessity. But for most of us that requires a bit of a journey from where we are now.

In this book, I've assigned myself the task of presenting a set of ideas and practical tools to guide us on this journey. Thankfully, over the past several decades a powerful set of vehicles have been developed to help bridge and repair the great rifts of humanity, whether within, between or among nations. These include study away/abroad, service-based learning, community research, field ethnography, diversity programming, environmental education, and social justice education (see Musil, 2009). Despite differences in social setting and content emphasis, each of these world-learning strategies supports three distinct yet interconnected tasks, each of them crucial to artfully addressing the fractures that imperil an equitable and sustainable future.

The first (personal) task is that of *stretching learners' minds*. All of us are tattooed at birth with tribal outlooks and beliefs. "We are all acolytes of our own realities, prisoners of our own perceptions, blindly loyal to the patterns and habits of our lives," explains anthropologist Wade Davis (2007, p. 12). Even so, our natural parochialism is not the end of the story. A potent antidote exists. Signature world-learning pedagogies aim to guide us, gently but resolutely, out of our respective bubbles and into active encounters with those who look and speak and think and believe unlike ourselves. World learning is all about establishing safe spaces for people to relate across their deep differences. The core assumption is that the Other's world has something to say to Our world.

To take any alternatives seriously, however, we must first experience them. As we do, our minds become more limber and inclusive. We begin to imagine ourselves living another's life. Perspective-taking helps us to not only more fully know ourselves in ration to the wider world but also recognize that our way of life is just one way of being human (especially if we've been told that our way is the greatest, most evolved, and most envied way on the planet). Different models of reality also enable us to consider a fuller range of alternatives to the global predicaments sketched out in chapter 1 of this text.

The second (interpersonal) task of world learning responds to the human proclivity toward Us/Them-ing by *turning strangers into neighbors, if not friends*. Fostering a culture of civility in pluralistic societies requires both good laws *and* good habits. We have a negative duty to do no harm to other people. But we also have an affirmative duty to do good, whether we like the Other or not. World learning, at its best, arranges opportunities for the kinds of meaningful encounters and active perspective-taking that break down stereotypes and build social trust. By replacing diatribe with dialogue, we can hope to discover common ground for the common good. "We should learn about people in other places, take an interest in their civilizations, their arguments, their errors, their achievements," writes moral philosopher Kwame Appiah (2006a) "not because that will bring us to agreement, but because it will help us get used to one another" (p. 78).

That said, it is also true that mere physical proximity to difference is not enough to consider how someone else may think or feel about something. In *To Kill a Mockingbird* (Lee, 1960), Atticus Finch, a lawyer in a small Southern town who is defending a Black man falsely accused of attacking a White woman, gives his six-year-old daughter, Scout, some sound advice:

> If you can learn a simple trick, Scout, you'll get along a lot better with all kinds of folks. You never really understand a person until you consider things from his point of view—until you climb into his skin and walk around in it. (p. 39)

Seeing things from the angle of someone in circumstances far removed from our own requires real relationship, especially if they are on the other side of some racial, cultural, national, or ideological divide. We must draw near to them, meet their gaze, get to know them, and share common tasks. The effect of such encounters is generally to convince us that others, despite a thousand differences, are simply altered versions of ourselves: vulnerable, uncertain, flawed beings who likewise crave love and wrestle with the dilemmas of childhood, education, family, work, love, aging, and death.

World learning, then, aims at minimum to help us overcome our natural blindness toward differently situated others. However impossible it might be to fully empathize with another human being, especially if their opinions and manners contrast our own, we can learn to cultivate an ethic of mutual charity based on cultural understanding and moral respect. Emotionally-intelligent world learning equips us to critique ideas and behaviors rather than to stigmatize persons. A secular progressive from the United States, for instance, should be able to tell a conservative religionist in Uganda that some of their beliefs about sexuality are misguided and unjust. And vice versa. But that is not the same thing as calling the other person a bigot or a pervert.

Learning to move out of relative sequestration and to engage difference as open-minded (though not empty-headed) individuals nourishes a collective state of consciousness that affirms the shared fate of Us and Them. This, as King (1964 December, 11) remarked during his Nobel Peace Prize lecture, is

> the great new problem of mankind. We have inherited a big house, a great "world house" in which we have to live together—black and white, Easterners and Westerners, Gentiles and Jews, Catholics and Protestants, Moslem and Hindu, a family unduly separated in ideas, culture, and interest who, because we can never again live without each other, must learn, somehow, in this one big world, to live with each other.

This brings us to the third (academic) task of world learning: *using interdisciplinary learning to better the world*. Here the learning objective is to comprehend the world truly, overcoming the complacent ignorance that often comes with economic and cultural privilege. The academic task maps by two questions: *What* and *how* should we learn? And having learned, *for what* should we use what we know? Knowledge by itself is morally ambiguous: It can remain inactive and indifferent or, if mobilized, it can serve either constructive or harmful ends. Much depends on the accuracy of the knowledge, together with the will to act in ways compatible with that knowledge. The head and the heart must be educated together.

The intellectual side of world learning invites learners to use direct experience and interdisciplinary study to think *systemically* about world realities. A group of education majors travel from a U.S. or UK university to teach English among Creole-speaking slum dwellers in Port-au-Prince, Haiti. Though earnest and well-intentioned, they will not automatically comprehend *why* so many people are destitute, *why* the infrastructure is so battered, and *why* the state is so hopelessly ineffectual. To think systemically in this situation would require that learners witness firsthand the pervasive deprivation, ideally by living and working directly with the people affected by it. Seeing it for themselves then becomes the experiential basis for theoretical study that seeks to unpack the tangled institutional roots of the problem. Inquiry and insight necessarily precedes position taking and advocacy.

Plan of the Book

These three goals—stretching learners' minds, turning strangers into neighbors, and thinking systemically about the world—delineate the artistry detailed in *The Art of World Learning*. Nevertheless, learning any craft—be it pottery making, carpet weaving, wood working, or clinical medicine—requires two masteries: the mastery of *theory* and the mastery of *practice*. To become a skilled general physician, I would need to acquire a comprehensive knowledge of the human body, along with the ailments and diseases that afflict it. But theoretical knowledge alone would hardly qualify me to practice medicine. Only after years of real, informed practice could I hope to master the art. Theoretical knowledge and experiential insight must become one. This text is written to reflect world learning as a way of knowing *and* a way of making.

Every field of practice, including global education, emerges and matures by fundamental ideas that are endlessly examined, discussed, debated, and reformulated by networks of scholars and practitioners. Global educators are no exception. In fact, we are, in the words of Michael Vande Berg (2012), "in the midst of a long, drawn-out, and now accelerating reappraisal about how we conceive of learning abroad" (p. 7). Or learning at home for

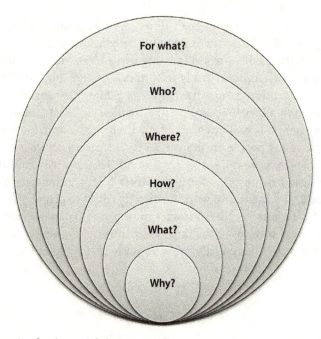

FIGURE I.I.   Six fundamental design questions.

that matter. The most important thing in this rethinking process is to find
new ways of conceiving definitive questions.

As backdrop to our reappraisal, chapter 1 portrays the great canvas upon
which world learning as art making takes place. A number of urgent and
intersecting crises challenge global learners to reject indifference, to grasp
complex realities, to stretch their imaginations, and to act pedagogically in
ways that help repair the world.

The chapters 2 through 7 correspond to six fundamental design questions (Figure I.1).

Chapter 2 asks: *Why* should we organize programs that help students
better understand the world? We explore a response through a complex set
of mandates—political, economic, educational, and ethical. While acknowledging the legitimacy of each driver or rationale, the case is made for defining a socially relevant global education in terms of the public good.

Chapter 3 casts a broad vision of student development, knowing that
the truest character of art depends on the quality of the self that infuses
each thing. Here we ask: *What* kind of person do we seek to shape, and for

what kind of world? Our response delineates the singular character of *global artists*—those who, through empathetic engagement with the world around them, develop a set of braided arts or competencies that support creative action in the world.

Chapter 4 follows as an extended inquiry into the formation of such persons. *How* might learners participate in the world in ways that truly transform consciousness and choice? What pedagogical perspectives, principles, and procedures can best shape the persons we need for the future we want? A response is framed in terms of a *worldly* vision of global learning that is immersed, emotional, and transformative.

Chapter 5 considers *where* we should expect the most powerful, life-changing learning to take place. Somewhat controversially, we argue in favor of a radical remapping of the geography of world learning to support a tactical progression of the nearby ("doorstep") to the faraway ("planet") in learners' global education.

Chapter 6 poses an oft-neglected question: Global learning for whom? *Who* is involved in and profits from a globalized education? Historically, students have been regarded as the primary, if not exclusive, beneficiaries of global-learning programs. This chapter presents an alternative "reciprocity model" aimed at balancing the benefit between students and the local families, groups, and organizations that host them.

Finally, chapter 7 probes the transformative potential of community-engaged learning by asking: World learning *for what*? Our discussion inquires beyond sincere but often romanticized accounts of having had a "life-changing" experience to contemplate the concrete and indispensable work of remaking local communities through the right application of affection, knowledge, and sustainable practice.

These inquiries have global educators in mind, especially those with support and supervision responsibilities: academic leaders, faculty leaders of short-term domestic and international programs, and program directors.

Community-Engaged Global Learning

Perhaps the best phrase to describe the distinct model of education expounded in *The Art of World Learning* is *community-engaged global learning*. The phrase denotes an ecology of learning that is learner-centered and experience-driven, locally-situated and globally-oriented, rooted in relationships and guided by academic insight. Scholarly work is done *with* communities, not just *in*, *to*, or *for* them. Knowledge is created through the community, rather than only flowing outward from the university.

Many colleges and universities are part of an expanding civic or community engagement movement within higher education (Saltmarsh & Hartley, 2011). Community engagement is portrayed by a diverse language: experiential, global citizenship, socially responsible, public, entrepreneurial, service-based, missional, participatory, asset-based, organic, and democratic. Despite important distinctions, each label expresses a common commitment to grapple with quality-of-life issues directly affecting human and natural communities. Budgets may be squeezed, and schools may be under intense pressure to demonstrate return on investment. Yet more and more schools and universities are effectively "deschooling" themselves by providing opportunities for multiple community groups and settings to become hosting spaces for a wide variety of human-to-human learning experiences (Slimbach, 2016). A growing number of students rightly believe that their capacity to develop new knowledge and skills can be enhanced by forming organic connections with local or distant families, community groups, government agencies, large businesses, or any number of social service organizations. Such alliances not only impart real-world relevance to classroom learning but also instill a fresh vision of how higher education's teaching, service, and research missions can support healthy, thriving community life (Figure I.2).

Community-engaged global learning is thus an artful appeal to a positive future. It urges a rising generation to think and feel and act in the gap between *what is* and *what can and should be*. This space between is both creative and fearsome. And it is what finally sets community-engaged global learning apart from more routine and individualistic forms of community service or study abroad.

The model contains several core principles and values, all of which run through this text.

Community

David Brooks (2016), cultural commentator for *The New York Times*, asks: "What's the right level to pursue social repair? The nation may be too large. The individual is too small." Brooks, along with other communitarian conservatives, reminds us that humans are social animals, designed for relationship. We need and want to be enmeshed in particular families, neighborhoods, traditions, moral virtues, and ecologies. In terms of global

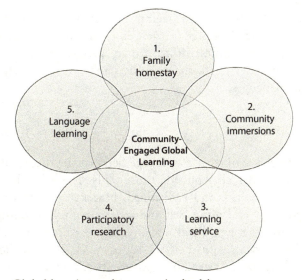

FIGURE 1.2.   Global learning and community health.

learning, the geographic or social *community* right-scales lived experience, along with collective responses to the technological, economic, cultural, and environmental accelerations that are reshaping the world. Local communities are close enough to people to understand and respond to their needs. They are also nimble and apolitical enough to effectively mediate between the concerns of private and public. "Community alone," writes Kentucky essayist Wendell Berry (1993), "can raise the standards of local health (ecological, economic, social, and spiritual) without which the other two interests will destroy one another" (p. 118). That's because a healthy community depends on cooperative relations with others, common patterns of thinking and doing, memory of the past, hope for the future, and love of place.

Throughout this text, *community* is used to denote a people living together in a place or sharing particular interests or quality-of-life concerns. They may be small farmers or factory workers, nursing home residents or an encampment of displaced persons. Also included in community membership is everything on which humans depend: soils, forests, watersheds, air, and all native creatures. Such communities are distinct from the public world where large institutions dominate, and where people pursue their own interests as workers and consumers, largely indifferent to other people and places. True community depends on one giving to another, whether in friendship, in marriage and family life, or within a kaleidoscope of human groups having their own membership and conceptions of the good. As global learners enter into relationship with community groups, they witness how ordinary people use local knowledge and practical intelligence to better understand and creatively act upon their shared challenges.

Engaged

Engaged forms of learning offer a bridge between the theory of the classroom and the lived reality outside those walls. The educational process is embedded, embodied, and envisioned. It seeks to unite what is typically divided: body and mind, self and society, being and doing, campus and community. Through direct, socially meaningful experience, learners form emotional bonds with their subject of study *and* with those having insider knowledge of it. Instead of passively absorbing information, learners position themselves in direct relationship with the phenomena under study.

Sustained exchanges can take place in households or small businesses, civic organizations or religious bodies, government agencies or family farms. The ordinary structures of community life offer innumerable opportunities to engage in what academic commentators call *high-impact educational practices* (Kuh & Schneider, 2008). These include foreign language study, family stays, volunteerism and service-learning, clinical placements, ethnographic fieldwork, environmental field schools, action research projects, and various forms of technical assistance. Rooting in actual communities, learners build a bridge with the living world they commonly study at arm's length. This enables them to acquire the virtues, intelligence, and ethical vocabulary needed for what Czech philosopher Vaclav Havel (1997, as cited in Elshtain, 2000) described as "the richest possible participation in public life."

Global

The global reflects an empirical reality—a world order where people, goods, ideas, and capital flow freely. In a globalized world we are always already interconnected. Because populations continuously overflow national borders, few groups on Earth remain culturally homogenous and spatially bounded. This reality renders sharp distinctions between the West and the rest, and among developed and developing countries, increasingly obsolete.

Similarly, the *global* in global learning can no longer be exclusively associated with the international. Study abroad has long existed as the exclusive face of global learning. If high school or college students wished to broaden their life horizons, they left their homeland, crossed an ocean or geopolitical border, and studied or worked in a far-away place. Today, this is a luxury in both time and money that precious few students can afford. Of the 18 million undergraduates enrolled in U.S. institutions, a quarter are older than 25. A similar percentage are single parents. The new normal is to be a student of color from a low-income family, working at least 20 hours a week. Precious few of these nontraditional students can afford to live on campus, much less quit work, leave their family, and pay thousands of dollars in program fees to live for a semester (or less) in Bolivia or Ghana. How will the global-learning needs of this *new majority* be met?

Fortuitously, difference and dilemma are no longer out there, in distant or exotic sites; they are right here, at our doorstep. Indeed, what we regard as global problems—like climate change and vanishing biodiversity—are ultimately rooted in the ways we choose to eat and drink, work and recreate, house and transport ourselves. Highly localized practices intertwine with global forces. What does this mean for a globalized education? Learners need opportunities to comprehend the local through the broader forces of history, politics and economics; and then to recognize the global through local practices, and predicaments. Without dissolving the traditional domestic–international divide, the global emphasizes the interplay of the close by and the far away, the micro and the macro, operating simultaneously, for good or for ill.

Learning

Conventional classrooms typically focus on setting up emotionally safe spaces for students to ingest disciplinary knowledge and acquire useful skills, removed from what many students call without apparent irony the "real world." The process of learning sketched out in the following chapters flips this model on its head. Global learners are expected to take risks by subjecting their bodies and minds and emotions to realities that are sometimes disturbing and other times inspiring. Despite the challenge—and arguably *because* of it—the learning that results can, and often does, surpass that produced by conventional methods. The value of global learning is best demonstrated by its outcomes: intellectual and practical skill development, formal knowledge of the human and natural world, and active engagement with complex problems and diverse communities.

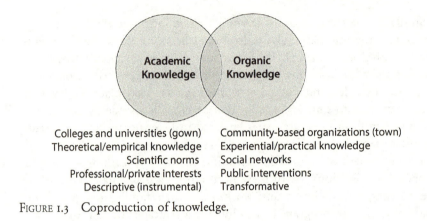

Colleges and universities (gown)   Community-based organizations (town)
Theoretical/empirical knowledge   Experiential/practical knowledge
Scientific norms   Social networks
Professional/private interests   Public interventions
Descriptive (instrumental)   Transformative

FIGURE 1.3   Coproduction of knowledge.

Moreover, learning isn't limited to students alone. At the center of our pedagogical model is *reciprocal learning*—the artful exchange of complementary knowledge. Universities contribute out of their store of tested methods, good theory, a scientific method, and orienting questions. What civil society, business, and government organizations bring to the table are an established local presence, organic knowledge born of extensive people-to-people experience, and vast social networks. Far from being incompatible, academic knowledge and organic knowledge derive vitality and direction from their connection to the other. Both realms overlap in a permeable space (Figure I.3).

Greater Good

Finally, and crucially, community-engaged global learning envisions a *good* that is greater than the instrumental ends that have come to dominate modern society. Ours is an age that celebrates and valorizes wealth, power, influence, and prestige. To ask "Global learning *for whom?*" and "Global learning *for what?*" is to probe beneath the enormous cult of the self for the larger meanings of and purposes for life. The good to which global learning aspires goes beyond professional credentials and earning capacity. Or even knowledge-for-knowledge's-sake. These are all important things when connected to a larger purpose, which is to say, when they raise the health of global communities.

Sir Albert Howard (2006) once called the "whole problem of health in soil, plant, animal, and man as one great subject" (p. 11). Derived from the same Indo-European root as "heal," "whole," and "holy," the word "health" is unifying and comprehensive, leaving nothing out. A healthy community is a place that is whole, where broken connections—social, economic, political, and ecological—are healed. (See Appendix C for an extended description of community health outcomes.) Global learners participate in local life in order to expand the greater good of community health as far as possible. This is the ultimate standard by which global-learning programs judge themselves.

Coming to Terms

Throughout the text, two phrases—*world learning* and *global learning*—are used interchangeably. Both phrases narrate forms of learning that engage human differences and quality-of-life challenges in ways that foster a mindful way of being in the world. The two phrases also blur the lines of what, historically, have been three distinct fields:

1. *Intercultural studies:* relations between and among social and cultural *groups*, primarily informed by anthropology, sociology, and intercultural communication
2. *International studies:* relations between and among *nations*, primarily informed by political science, economics, and foreign languages
3. *Global studies:* relations between and among transnational *systems*, which are informed by virtually every academic discipline

Global educators have traditionally made it their special business to promote communication between and among people of different cultures through direct, face-to-face encounters. These experiences promised to yield an educational bounty, variously described as "intercultural competence," "global citizenship" or "cosmopolitanism." Reflecting what was then known as the "intercultural relations" approach to world learning, anthropologist-linguist Edward Hall (1959) famously declared that "culture is communication and communication is culture" (p. 186).

The emphasis on intercultural communication across cultures markedly influenced not only global education but also international development, missions, and business. Intercultural communication theory offered professionals in each of these fields "simple, understandable, and immediately useful ways to facilitate communication across a wide range of cultures and contexts" (LaBrack & Bathhurst, 2012, p. 196). Yet, primary attention to microlevel operations of culture and communication tended to sideline broader analysis of macrolevel social arrangements shaping local life for billions of people. One needs only to imagine a pair of foreign students shopping on P.C. Hooftstraat in Amsterdam. Despite being able to communicate effectively and appropriately with salespersons, they may be blissfully ignorant to how the larger process of globalization tends to impoverish one place in order to be extravagant in another.

Overattention to values, expressive symbols, and languages can also easily overlook the fact that cultural meanings are often vigorously contested at the community level. Field settings in the modern world are invariably saturated with relations of racial, economic, and social power. These power dynamics "alter radically the nature of the social relationship between those who ask and look and those who are asked and looked at" (Geertz, 1988, p. 131). Underrating the entanglement of culture and power in social life prevents outsiders from developing critical awareness of what is perhaps *the* main obstacle to bridging entrenched divides and promoting the greater good.

Finally, a narrow focus on interpersonal dynamics can easily eclipse powerful organizational and institutional forces in culture. While micro- and midlevel beliefs and behaviors *do* have consequences, they are both formed and fortified through powerful institutions and networks (Heclo, 2008). The market, the state, education at all levels, advertising and news media, national myths and symbols—these and other structures forcefully shape consciousness and action. They also account for the "wicked" or impossibly complex character of the world's stubbornest problems.

The Art of World Learning encourages a new generation to apprehend culture in its full complexity. By making connections among the intercultural, the international, and the global dimensions of life, learners come to respect human differences while also learning to think institutionally and systemically. This is the necessary foundation, competency-wise, for creating an artful life amid the deepening crises of our time.

THE WORLD CANVAS

This world is but a canvas to our imaginations.
— HENRY DAVID THOREAU, *A Week on the Concord and Merrimack Rivers*, 1849

W HEN HE WANTS his students to comprehend the dynamics of globalization, Noah Bopp, the director of the School for Ethics and Global Leadership in Washington DC, hands each of them a piece of chocolate. With a Hershey's Kiss or Mars Milky Way in hand, Bopp asks them three questions (Rosenthal, 2009). The first question is this: Where does the chocolate come from? The answer: The world's cocoa (along with many other food commodities) originates in distant and impoverished places—over half in Côte d'Ivoire, followed by Ghana, Indonesia, and Nigeria. A single country—Côte d'Ivoire—produces more than 35% of the world's cocoa crop.

Bopp continues with a second question: How is this chocolate produced? Answer: It was likely harvested on small farms by members of the grower's own family, together with waged labor and child laborers. In the 2013–2014 cocoa harvest season in Côte d'Ivoire and Ghana, over two million children (ages 5–17 years) worked in hazardous cocoa production; a substantial minority was trafficked from Mali, Burkina Faso, and Togo (Tulane University, 2015). The use of exploitative labor on cocoa farms occurs in a complex cultural context. Many cocoa growers do not own the land they farm. Instead, they sharecrop, handing over between 50% and 70% of their crop to the landowner. Forced to sell at rock-bottom prices, both sharecroppers and landowners reduce costs by using family members (including children) as their workforce. But this still isn't enough to meet growing demand, which is why young children are trafficked from poor countries and coerced to work without pay. Having little or no access to schooling, and working 80 to 100 hours each week, most of these children will never taste the final product of the labor.

The story of chocolate doesn't end once the cocoa bean leaves the farm. As beans are transported across international borders to huge processing plants, they are subject to various trade rules, tariffs, and taxes before being available to buy. This leads to Professor Bopp's third and final question: Who makes these economic rules? Answer: legislators (government officials), lobbyists (representatives of industry and labor), and development specialists working for international lending institutions like the International Monetary Fund and the World Bank. That is, powerful, influential people. Those rules, we're told, are a rational response to the demands of global trade for increased economic efficiency and decreased government spending. But when decisions are made, the rules invariably favor bigger and richer countries and institutions over smaller and poorer ones. Market forces may set international prices for commodities like cocoa, but large chocolate companies devise systems that allow them to work with, and even profit from, the market's rapid fluctuations. Small growers and share-croppers are simply unable to control the price they receive for their crop, especially when speculative trading, government corruption, and export taxes are factored in. In most cases, they must accept whatever price they are offered by middlemen dealers who buy up the cocoa and then resell it to processors and exporters.

At this point, Bopp invites students to eat the chocolate. As they do, they are asked to imagine the powerful economic interests, cultural realities, social inequalities, and constrained choices that are wrapped up in every piece. Some students are understandably left with considerable ambivalence: Do I eat the chocolate? Is it ethically permissible to buy and consume *anything* produced under these circumstances? What are my options, and how do I personally weigh the good against the harm involved in each?

Seizing the Actual World

"The trick of reason," Annie Dillard (1989) reminds us in *An American Childhood*, "is to get the imagination to seize the actual world—if only from time to time" (p. 143). Here Dillard succinctly captures the central task and emphatic standard of world learning. By joining mind and skin—that is, with firsthand experience interdisciplinary study—world learning aims to instill a devouring curiosity for the actual, historical world around us. The goal is to shape what political scientist Thomas Homer-Dixon describes as a prospective mind. The prospective mind thinks in ways that are simultaneously *systemic* (seeing the whole instead of isolated parts) and *participative* (drawing upon others' ideas and expertise). Learner consciousness is no longer confined to the unexamined assumptions and habit patterns of an inherited way of life. It is able to envision *alternative* ways of being human, each with its own set of adaptive responses to the challenges of living. Shaping a prospective mind is the educational basis for imagining the world not only as *it is* but also as *it might be*.

Clearly, the real world, along with our life choices, used to be much simpler. We once lived in smaller-scale communities where basic needs were met locally. The distance was short between producers and consumers. We knew where our food and other goods came from, who produced them, and at what human and ecological costs. Neighbors cherished and protected their farms and forests, watersheds, and ecosystems. The consequences of our choices were much more obvious.

Today, we passively rely upon governments and global corporations to produce and provide our food, clothing, education, and entertainment. Commodities are produced wherever the costs are lowest, and consumed wherever profits are highest. This system of production and consumption connects us to other people and places in increasingly complex relationships. Planetary scientist Carl Sagan (1998) illustrates:

> In North America we breathe oxygen generated in the Brazilian rain forest. Acid rain from polluting industries in the American Midwest destroys Canadian forests. Radioactivity from a Soviet nuclear accident compromises the economy and culture of Lapland. The burning of coal in China warms Argentina. Diseases rapidly spread to the farthest reaches of the planet and require a global medical effort to be eradicated. And, of course, nuclear war imperils everyone. Like it or not, we humans are bound up with our fellows and with the other plants and animals all over the world. Our lives are intertwined. (pp. 80–81)

In such an economically, environmentally, and culturally crisscrossed world, it has become extremely hard, if not impossible, to separate the interests of others from our own interests. To borrow a phrase from postmodernism, we are "always already" affecting other people and other places. We paint our lives on a world canvas. And it is that world which we must comprehend—its particularities and possibilities—before we can act intelligently upon it. There are, of course, situations and questions where our knowledge is dwarfed by what we do not and cannot ever completely know. But instead of mystery signaling retreat into a purely cerebral or interior world, we can allow it to create space for surprise.

The actual world also features a tangled mix of gains and losses. We live in the best of times and in the worst of times. The last 200 years of modern civilization has brought us truly astonishing innovations: the railway, the assembly line, the printing press, the corporation, the modern university, clean water, the women's movement, civil rights, the electric light, petroleum, plastics, penicillin, the airplane, open-heart surgery, and the Internet. These achievements have raised the quality of life for virtually everyone. In fact, as a species, we're arguably safer, healthier, more prosperous, less violent, better educated, and more tolerant than at any time in history (Easterbrook, 2018; Pinker, 2018). Opportunities abound for cultural exchange, higher education, and the kind of travel experiences that transform the way we think about our place in the world. For much of humanity, life has never been better. The international trade regime that Bopp so creatively illustrates has been shown to lower prices, expand economies, and lift tens of millions into the middle classes. For hundreds of millions of others, it has made the difference between mere privation and sheer desperation.

But the canvas also has a flip side. Paralleling the extraordinary feats of industrial culture is a set of complex demographic, climatic, environmental, economic, and social emergencies. Collectively, they are converging into what has been likened to a perfect storm (Sample, 2009). A rare combination of factors, though not immediately obvious in the normal course of our lives, threatens to result in potentially catastrophic outcomes. Although each of the global predicaments is distinct and potentially acute, the risk is that their *interaction* will create what Jonathon Porritt (2009), former chair of the UK Sustainable Development Commission, calls the "ultimate recession—one from which there may be no recovery." The severity of Porritt's assessment calls us as global educators to help learners comprehend the greatest threats to global flourishing as the essential canvas for imagining a preferred future (Figure 1.1).

Peak Population: Overburdening the Earth

We begin with a familiar though menacing demographic truth: The world is getting much more crowded. Before the invention of agriculture 12,000

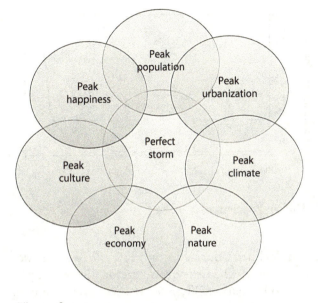

FIGURE 1.1.   The perfect storm.

years ago, there were 1 million people on Earth. People foraged and hunted the land, living in small mobile clans. It took another 12,000 years (until about 1800 AD) for our numbers to grow to 1 billion. Then population took off. Our second billion arrived in 1930 (only 130 years later); our third billion just 30 years later, in 1960; our fourth billion in 1975 (only 15 years later); our fifth billion in 1987; our sixth billion in 1999; and sometime in 2014 we reached 7 billion. Every four and a half days we add another million people. According to a frequently cited United Nations model, we will swell to 8 billion by 2025 before leveling off at 9 or 10 billion people somewhere around 2050 (Figure 1.2).

We may not notice the numbers in North America and Western Europe, where fertility has fallen below replacement level (the so-called "demographic transition"). But in places like South Asia and Africa, population continues to peak. In fact, nearly all of the population growth from now until 2050 will take place in poor countries. Currently birth rates are above 5 children per woman in 35 countries, including Bangladesh, Pakistan, Nigeria, Afghanistan, India, Ethiopia, Haiti, and China. Population growth in poor countries will more than counter-balance the falling population in rich countries.

What accounts for all this explosive growth? It's a lot like our bank accounts—a matter of deposits and debits. People are "deposited" through

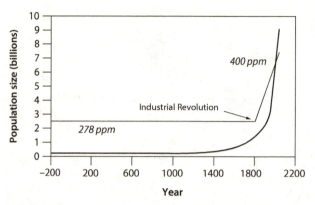

FIGURE 1.2.   Human Population, 0–2050 AD.

birth rates and "debited" through death rates. When the two are equal, the earth holds steady; when they converge or diverge, population rises or falls. It used to be that fertility rates *and* death rates were high, mostly due to famines, warfare, poor sanitation, and the lack of antibiotics or vaccines: Mothers had a lot of babies but few survived to old age. By the nineteenth century, however, mechanized food production reduced famine deaths and local warfare largely disappeared. "Miracle" medical procedures and life-saving drugs appeared, enabling life expectancy to nearly double.

That said, the real population problem is not too many people. (The global fertility rate has steadily declined every year since 1965, from nearly 5 births per woman to 2.4.) And the problem certainly isn't too many poor people, who have a barely noticeable effect on global natural resource use and pollution. Our basic predicament surrounds rising incomes *and* the increased demand for carbon-intensive goods. The burgeoning consumer class across the Global South wants what their Northern counterparts already enjoy: meat-rich diets, private automobiles, and homes equipped with wide-screen TVs and air conditioners. But the potential cost is unimaginable—a *doubling* or even *tripling* of the already breathtaking drawdown in critical natural resources on the planet. Alan Weisman (2013) issues a sober warning in *Countdown*: "In the entire history of biology, every species that outgrows its resource base suffers a population crash—a crash sometimes fatal to the entire species" (p. 39). Weisman is doubtful that the earth has the resources to service a planet of 10 billion residents.

Peak Urbanization: The New "Squatopolises"

Of the two billion more people to be added to the planet by 2050, virtually all of them will be born in cities—and overwhelmingly in stressed-out places like Karachi, Port-au-Prince, and Cairo. It's not just that so much of the world's population *lives* in cities; much of the world has *become* a city. A vast network of urban centers is the origin or destination of most of the world's commodities, foreign direct investment, ideas, product sales, corporate office locations, international travel, telecommunications, and diplomatic relations. Today, about 600 cities, containing only one-fifth of the world's population, generate 60% of global gross national product (GNP).

This dramatic aggregation of economic power is not the result of organic domestic conditions, but of a global institutional framework that emerged following the Cold War. Political choices favored deregulated high industry in communication, technology, finance, and banking. Almost all employment, investment, and development concentrated in cities. Neglected were the rural hinterland and agricultural industries. Rural populations, rendered surplus by the globalized economy, moved to the cities in record numbers. The pattern continues unabated today: Physically able poor people, fleeing overpopulation, devastated agriculture, unemployment, and intractable conflicts, stream toward their nations' crowded cities. And they do so at a stunning rate of 70 million people each year, 1.5 million people per week, and 130 people every minute (Saunders, 2012).

This mass movement into poor cities presents public officials with an immense challenge of providing basic shelter and essential services for newcomers. Lacking any legal options, most migrants are forced to homestead beside railway tracks, along riverbanks, and on tumbling hillsides. They build their dwellings piece by piece, as they can afford it. Dubbed "squatopolis" by journalist Robert Neuwirth (2004), these are urban spaces where there is little secure land to live on, little clean water to drink, and few jobs with any kind of future. The work that most find is disconnected from the formal world economy—as day laborers and street vendors, rickshaw wallas and garment workers.

If the fringe world of slums has an upside, it is to showcase humanity at its best, not worst. Most informal settlements are kilns of reverberating energy and impromptu social organization. They attract the young and resourceful, spawning innumerable micro-enterprises. Cities poor and rich are engines of growth, with the potential to also be the most environmentally friendly form of habitation. When people live cheek by jowl, they tend to use less electricity, less fuel oil, and less natural gas—all of which reduces carbon emissions.

Cities can thus be viewed as both triumph and tragedy. While clustering talent, technological innovation, economic activity, and institutional development, they also are ground zero of the emerging crises of population growth, underemployment, uncontainable sprawl, and ecological overshoot. For better *and* for worse, cities are the stage on which history will play. One of the great challenges facing this generation is to help shape a healthier, more just, and resilient urban existence.

Global educators can support this project through an interdisciplinary approach to city-focused study, research, and practical action. Learning might focus on the role of cities in the national and global economy; how cities are put together; how cities shape and are shaped by different human groups and the natural environment; how communities are created, destroyed, and revitalized; how urban problems like gentrification, housing affordability, economic inequality, criminality, congestion, and pollution generation arise and are addressed; and how urban design seeks to make cities work for all residents.

Peak Climate: A Warmer World

A surprising fact is that cities occupy just 2% of the Earth's landmass, yet their combustion of fossil fuels—for construction, electricity, cooking, transportation, and industrial production—is responsible for up to 70% of the climate-disrupting concentrations of dangerous greenhouse gases (UN Habitat, 2011). These gases act like a blanket, preventing some of the heat radiated by planet Earth from escaping freely into space.

The scientific community is a cautious bunch, slow to reach definitive conclusions out of the mountains of data. But their collective verdict is this: According to the Intergovernmental Panel on Climate Change (IPCC; 2013),[1] increases in the planet's global climate temperature due to excessive greenhouse gas emissions risk "severe, pervasive and irreversible impacts for people and ecosystems." Of the hottest years on record, 15 out of 17 have come since 2000. The year 2016 was the hottest year since modern recordkeeping began in 1880 (NOAA National Centers for Environmental Information, 2017). Under current policies and practices, scientists almost unanimously predict a 4°C (7.2°F) warming by the end of the century (World Bank, 2012).

The consequences of the collective carbon load are clear cause for alarm, as international investigative journalist Christian Parenti (2011) documents in *Tropic of Chaos*:

> [E]ven if all greenhouse gas emissions stopped immediately—that is, if the world economy collapsed today, and not a single light bulb was switched on nor a single gasoline-powered motor started ever again—there is already enough carbon dioxide in the atmosphere to cause *significant* warming and disruptive climate change, and with that considerably more poverty, violence, social dislocation, forced migration, and political upheaval. Thus we must find humane and just means of adaptation, or we face barbaric prospects. (p. 226)

The world has already neared temperatures that threaten a catastrophic breakup of the Greenland and West Antarctic ice sheets. Although the actual melting would take centuries, it would be unstoppable. Sea levels would rise to levels that flood coastal cities from the United States to Bangladesh, rendering them uninhabitable, or at least uneconomic. The tropical Global South, in particular, would suffer increased frequency of extreme heat waves, mega-droughts, and torrential superstorms. Crop yields would be devastated, exacerbating hunger and poverty. Millions of climate refugees would be forced into already-overflowing slums. The result, if not complete anarchy, would be widespread suffering and violence.

"The hardest truth about climate change," writes McKenzie Funk in *Windfall* (2014), is that it is not equally bad for everyone" (p. 288). The richest 10% of humanity—the ones who produce a full half of Earth's climate-harming emissions—are best prepared to withstand its worst effects. The poorest half are responsible for approximately 10% of total greenhouse gas emissions, but they happen to live in flood-prone tropical coastal zones and dry rural areas of poor countries. These are places that are least likely to have the capacity to cope and adapt. In short, it is the world's most vulnerable people who must pay the highest price for the actions of those who are most secure (Oxfam, 2015).

Climate change and deprivation are clearly linked. Without a stable climate, years of progress to reduce acute poverty could stall or even be erased. And yet precise solutions are hard to imagine. Climate change adaptation on a global scale will require trillions of dollars of infrastructural investment in poor and medium-income countries. Tens of millions of people from Africa and Asia would need to be resettled.

The root of our predicament is easy enough to name: an energy-intensive, fossil-fuel-powered system that requires infinite expansion in a finite world. But no one seems to know how to turn the system off, or how to introduce the necessary reforms, without economic collapse. Today's college students will decide the fate of life on Earth and beyond. As we consider in chapter 7, the vocations and lifestyles they choose, and the policies they pass, will either change the trajectory of our planet, or not.

Peak Nature: Silent Ecocide

At this point in history, the task of securing a durable world for future generations faces off with some grim ecological realities. The cumulative impact of global consumption patterns is estimated at being responsible for between 50% and 80% of Earth's total land, material, and water use (Ivanova et al., 2015). This is pushing a fourth peak: the destruction of the planet's natural capital.

Throughout the world, water tables are falling and wells are going dry. Soil erosion has exceeded soil formation on one-third of the world's cropland. A quarter of the world's mangroves, critical to coastal fisheries in the tropics, are now gone. Furthermore, 80% of the planet's rivers do not support life anymore. Forests are shrinking by 13 million acres per year in order to produce lumber and paper and to clear land for agriculture. The world's ever-growing herds of cattle, sheep, and goats have converted vast stretches of grassland to desert. In the United States alone, despite four decades of environmental advocacy, we lose 6,000 acres of open space *every day* and 100,000 acres of wetlands every year.

With the destruction of habitats comes the threat of the massive kill-off of animal and plant species. Extinction is a natural phenomenon: It occurs at a natural background rate of about one to five species per year. But scientists estimate we're now losing species at 1,000 to 10,000 times the background rate, with literally dozens going extinct every day (Pimm et al., 2014). Further, 99% of currently threatened species are at risk from human activities. Overfishing has already reduced the total mass of large ocean predators such as tuna, cod, and swordfish by 90%. Extinction threatens a third of the planet's amphibians, and a quarter of its birds, mammals, and reptiles. Pulitzer Prize-winning journalist Elizabeth Kolbert (2015) terms the die-off of plant and animal life the *sixth extinction*. She writes:

It is estimated that one-third of all reef-building corals, a third of all fresh-water mollusks, a third of sharks and rays, a quarter of all mammals, a fifth of all reptiles, and a sixth of all birds are headed toward oblivion. The losses are occurring all over: in the South Pacific and in the North Atlantic, in the Arctic and the Sahel, in lakes and on islands, on mountaintops and in valleys. If you know how to look, you can probably find signs of the current extinction event in your own backyard. (p. 17)

Human beings are considered to be the most intelligent species on the planet, but we are engaged in the most unintelligent enterprise imaginable: the destruction of our own natural life-support system. Industrial culture has effectively deforested, plowed, dredged, drained, dammed, bulldozed, and paved over much of the earth's land surface. Humanity has yet to strike a balance with the earth it inhabits.

Like climate change, what's driving mass extinction is *affluence*, fueled by an economic paradigm of endless *growth*. As disposable incomes rise, upwardly mobile city dwellers readily exchange huts for houses, bicycles for cars, ceiling fans for central air-conditioning, fresh vegetables and fruits for factory-farmed meat, and an intensely local lifestyle for one that includes long-distance air travel. No one can be blamed for wanting to better their life. But the collective impact of nearly eight billion people (World-o-Meters, 2019), each wanting more of what modernity has to offer, is rapidly depleting precious resources and destroying planetary life. Bill McKibben (2010) puts it bluntly: "We're running Genesis backward, decre-ating" (p. 25).

Peak Economy: The Great Divide

Paralleling weather and ecological calamities has been grotesquely expand-ing gaps in income and wealth. Reports of dithering wage growth have become commonplace. The largest emerging economies—countries with at least 50 million people—continue to struggle against debts and deficits, along with the decline of both the quality and quantity of labor. Dozens of developed economies face a productivity crisis that threatens the hopes of improving their population's living standards. The United States, con-tends Nobel laureate economist Joseph Stiglitz, is no longer home to the American Dream, but to a "Great Divide" (2016) beset with stagnant wages, declining household income, and mounting national debt.

Over the past 40 years, the American middle class has been disappearing. Free trade deals have sent millions of manufacturing jobs overseas. Of those that remain, few are unionized. In their place has emerged a burgeoning *gig economy* where work consists of a series of temporary and on-call jobs. Workers are paid whatever they can get, without health benefits or job security. In fact, the majority of Americans now live paycheck to paycheck. Rising numbers are stuck in dead-end jobs, whether in retail sales, restaurant or hotel work, or in child and elder care. Poverty researchers Kathryn J. Edin and H. Luke Shaefer (2015) estimate that three million American children—1 in 25—now live in households with incomes of less than $2 per person per day. If they lived in Africa, they would be counted as extremely poor. But they are not in Africa; they are our neighbors in the most powerful nation on Earth.

These conditions are the cumulative result of economic policies and programs set in motion over the last half-century. In the 1970s, transnational elites undertook sweeping restructuring into a new globalized production and financial system. Free trade agreements and financial liberalization lifted state restrictions on cross-border trade and capital flows. Production facilities were relocated abroad—in places such as China, India, the Philippines, Indonesia, and Bangladesh—in order to escape higher real wages, unemployment benefits, and environmental regulations.

The offshoring and outsourcing of work helped dramatically reduce poverty in Asia. But financial integration also led to dire imbalances in the global economy. Wages declined. Working conditions deteriorated. Unemployment rose. Public services were either abolished or severely slashed. As of 2017, Oxfam reliably reports that, surreal as it sounds, the world's eight richest people possess among themselves as much wealth as the poorest half of the entire human race. *Eight* persons. This was down from 388 just six years earlier. Instead of trickling down, "wealth is moving rapidly to concentrate at the tippy, tippy top of the pyramid," reports Gawain Kripke, the director of policy and research at Oxfam America (Oxfam, 2017). The top one-tenth of 1% now owns almost as much wealth as the bottom 90%. And they are busily transferring that wealth to their children and grandchildren, often through offshore tax havens.

Contrasting this powerful plutonomy are the majority of the world's workers who face tenuous labor conditions across the occupational spectrum. This *precariat* (precarious proletariat) describes a burgeoning class of informal workers who lack legal regulation or social protection.

[They are] . . . the perpetual part-timers, the minimum-wagers, the temporary foreign workers, the grey-market domestics paid in cash . . . the techno-impoverished whose piecemeal work has no office and no end, the seniors who struggle with dwindling benefits, the indigenous people who are kept outside, the single mothers without support, the cash labourers who have no savings, the generation for whom a pension and a retirement is neither available nor desired. (Standing, 2015)

Some 1.5 billion people (46% of the world's workers) now experience insecure employment, exponentially expanded by the rise of robotic auto-mation. In Southern Asia and sub-Saharan Africa, precarity is already a fact of everyday life for over 70% of people, whether employed as teachers, taxi drivers, call-center workers, or field laborers.

But economic vulnerability is not limited to the Global South. In the United States, precariats now make up one half of the U.S. work force. They drive for Uber in Atlanta, build skyscrapers in Philly, harvest onions in Georgia, sew garments in L.A., teach as college or university adjuncts, and work as "associates" in thousands of regional Walmarts. Many work 10–12 hours a day, sometimes seven days a week, doing *anything* that can't be offshored or outsourced to other countries. Workers are not being exploited as much as discarded: They have little opportunity to organize, form unions, or bargain collectively for higher wages and better working conditions. Being structurally irrelevant, they are dispensable.

As troubling as this sounds, many analysts predict that the worst is yet ahead. The next wave of labor substitution, brought about by artificial intel-ligence and sophisticated robots, threatens to displace tens of millions of low-skilled jobs (Frey & Osborne, 2013). One of the encouraging lessons of history is that as technology displaces jobs, it creates new ones. But it isn't hard to imagine a dystopian future where jobs and wages for masses of assembly-line and factory workers, taxi and truck drivers, receptionists, cashiers, typists, and bank tellers don't recover. They simply are unable to migrate to occupations protected from automation. At that point, the two great aims of industrial-ism—the replacement of people by technology and concentration of wealth into the hands of a small plutocracy—will have come close to fulfillment.

Peak Culture: Vanishing Voices

As mentioned previously, much of the world is on the move. Ambitious young people the world over are forsaking their natal lands to pursue educational and job opportunities in modern cities. In most cases, they are changed for the better. They have access to modern medicines, decent schools, and many more options in relationships and livelihoods. Acquiring proficiency in a so-called "supercentral" language—such as English, Mandarin Chinese, Hindi, Spanish, or Arabic—opens up a wider world of communication and commerce. Having tasted the sweet fruit of civilization, few provincials can be persuaded that they were better off before.

But modernity's inarguable benefits come with a cost, not the least of which is the demise of ancestral tongues and unique ways of life. In addition to the global collapse of biological diversity, the world is experiencing a comparable contraction of cultural diversity. The key indicator is language, since virtually every major aspect of human culture is dependent on language for its transmission. Of the 6,000 or so languages spoken today, upwards of half teeter on the edge of oblivion (Nettle & Romaine, 2000). What is at risk and what is lost when a language goes silent? For most of us, the answer is very little. After all, why should a group of 50,000 people speak three or four different languages rather than a single global language? And why learn to grow or hunt food when everything imaginable can be had at a modern supermarket? For that matter, why learn to build or fix anything yourself when immigrant labor can do it cheaply and well?

In a modern age, tribal tongues and ancient skills thus appear as an anachronism. But consider for a moment what vanishing voices and cultures signify: the gradual disappearance of fully half of humanity's social, cultural, and intellectual legacy. "The voices of traditional societies ultimately matter," writes anthropologist Davis (2013), "because they can still remind us that there are indeed alternatives, other ways of orienting human beings in social, spiritual and ecological space." Different languages capture and construct different social realities, connecting people to each other and to a place. With every language and cultural tradition that is lost is one less incredibly rich way of being and thinking within a vast storehouse of cultural memory.

This isn't an argument for keeping traditional societies frozen in time and space as a kind of zoological specimen. Neither is it a call for moderns to return to a pre-industrial past. Change is a constant throughout human history. The pressing issue for this generation isn't to defend the traditional against the modern, but to find a way for all peoples—especially the most vulnerable—to benefit from the best of industrial culture without doing violence to their basic identity, cultural heritage, and moral distinctiveness. In other words, it's to make the world safe *for* and *from* modernity.

The Loba people of northern Nepal illustrate how complex this discernment process can be. For centuries, the ancient kingdom of Mustang, or Land of Lo, has existed on the high and windswept Tibetan Plateau, one of the most remote regions in the world. The Loba still farm with wooden plows and spend hours spinning prayer wheels and consulting Buddhist astrologers on every aspect of life (Wegner & Weidman, 2015). But this is rapidly changing. With a new highway now linking remote villages to China and Nepal, the Loba have electricity and the chance to pursue school or work elsewhere. At the same time, Loba elders have reason for concern about the fate of their language, religion, customs, and intimate knowledge of the land. The problem doesn't lie with the highway itself, or with the introduction of new technologies. (The Inuit of Alaska use snowmobiles and shop in supermarkets, but still manage to maintain their native language and traditional hunting practices.) The challenge across the globe is how to negotiate an aggressive global consumer culture increasingly dominated by powerful political and economic interests.

Consider the Ogoni people of Nigeria, who witnessed their once fertile soil gradually destroyed, not by water and wind erosion, but by pollutants from Shell oil operations. Or Borneo's Penan people, whose forest homeland was irreversibly destroyed by the unsustainable practices of Malaysian logging companies. Virtually all Penan now reside in shantytowns, trapped in squalor and reduced to servitude and prostitution as degraded replicas of so-called "civilized" people.

There is a fine line between embracing change within cultures and forcing change upon cultures. A critical outcome of global learning is thus *discernment*—the ability to decipher what should be *cherished* and what should be *challenged* within the economic-political system that encompasses us. Journeys elsewhere provide an opportunity for sojourners to bear witness, if only for a brief period of time, to alternative ways of being human. Those visions of life then become a lifelong resource for evaluating what modernity giveth and what it taketh away.

Peak Happiness: Misery Amid Plenty

One of the curious paradoxes of modern culture is that as material prosperity and technological sophistication have increased, self-reported happiness has not. The world's laudable success in reducing extreme poverty has created an unexpected divergence between economic growth and subjective satisfaction. Real per capita income has more than tripled since the late 1950s, but the percentage of people saying they are very happy has, if anything, slightly declined. Millions of Americans find themselves isolated and alone. Middle-aged divorce rates have doubled since the 1990s, along with substantial increases in substance misuse and depression, particularly among middle-age, lower-class Whites. In fact, clinical depression has become the world's greatest health problem. It is also the strongest risk factor for the one million annual suicides—a total that outnumbers deaths from war, natural disasters, and murder. Suicide rates in the United States alone, in every age group except older adults, have surged to the highest levels in nearly 30 years (Tavernise, 2016).

Despair, along with a detached mode of life, is especially prevalent among low-paid service-class workers and the blue-collar working class, constituting two-thirds of the American workforce (Edin, Nelson, Cherlin & Francis, 2019). Declining household income only partially explains the insecurity, despondency, and commitment-aversion they experience. In 2013, a Gallup poll revealed that 70% of Americans hate their jobs or have "checked out" of them (Lopez, 2013). What accounts for this? Is it the low quality of their work environment? The offshoring and accelerated automation of jobs? The deliberate undermining of everything from overtime pay to healthcare and union bargaining power? The sharp decline in their standing relative to their parents and to "creative class" workers? The precise factors affecting work conditions may be debatable, but the clear effects for growing numbers are rising levels of anxiety, insecurity, and even rage.

Politicians are fond of telling Americans that they live in "the best country in the world." But in terms of actual quality of life, the United States ranks an unremarkable 18th—just above Luxembourg and well below Costa Rica (Helliwell, Layard, & Sachs, 2019). Of course, felicity and misery involve complex variables reflected in various facets of human nature and social life. What we do know about high life satisfaction is that it is associated with health of mind and body, loving families, supportive friendships, a rewarding job, being a valued member of one's community, and novel experiences. By contrast, those who are buffeted by soul-numbing work, stagnating wages, consumer and student debt peonage, and underwater mortgages must settle for lives of quiet desperation.

Privileged college students are hardly immune to the modern malaise. Richard Louv (2005) relates at least some of their mental and emotional turmoil to what he terms *nature-deficit disorder*. Stuck within campus compounds and virtual worlds, collegians lose a sense of awe, physical activity, and creative imagination that wild places offer. To compensate for the losses, they find it all too easy to eat, drink, or smoke too much. Others seek temporary escape from the dullness of their lives through shopping, gaming, or constant binging of Netflix. Social networking is an especially seductive diversion. It not only encourages a preoccupation with image and social approval; but also, at a saturation level, diminishes one's capacity to be still, to look another in the eye with undivided attention, and follow what they're feeling. Empathetic connection is the necessary basis for making altruistic commitments.

Happiness may seem like an elusive study topic, but try to imagine a team of student researchers setting out to examine how different societies gauge life satisfaction. One might rightly expect average evaluations to differ across societies and over time. The remote Himalayan kingdom of Bhutan, for example, employs a fluid concept called Gross National Happiness (GNH) to measure the well-being of its citizens and natural environment. Every policy must pass a happiness test: Does it enhance the country's spiritual, physical, social, and environmental well-being? Cigarettes and plastic bags fail the test, so are banned (Royal Government of Bhutan, 2013). How then has Bhutan, one of the world's tiniest and poorest nations, become one of the happiest and ecologically sustainable countries on Earth? Is it the strong family structure and quality of human relationships? Its respect for the natural world? Good governance and peaceful coexistence with other nations?

The cross-cultural examination of happiness (and myriad other topics) offers world learners more than mere inspiration. It provides them a basis for serious thinking about how best to organize communities and systems in a world of unforeseeable disruptions. Should nations pursue economic growth to the point of environmental ruin, even when incremental gains in GNP do not increase collective happiness? Should self-enlargement be pursued at the cost of social trust and solidarity? What notion of "success" and "progress" can hope to balance the material, social, psycho-spiritual, and environmental dimensions of life? A global understanding of what makes for better lives is prerequisite to imagining ways to build a better world.

Conclusion

These seven global trends constitute much of the canvas upon which the history of the twenty-first century will be painted. Human population growth, the emergence of megacities, climate disruption, ecological breakdown, a disappearing middle class, the silent extinction of languages and cultures, and the declining mental health engulfing many affluent countries—these are just some of the wicked problems threatening the health and vitality of human civilization. Though each is relatively new, they are all growing in magnitude. Then there is the looming risk of a major nuclear exchange—a prospect that could lead to the shredding of the planetary environment and a literal liquidation of humanity.

As formidable as they appear, the critical challenges of today will not look the same 30 or 50 years from now. This generation of global learners will need to be prepared, not just for the complexity we face here and now, but for unforeseeable change in the future. As former Secretary of Education Richard Riley memorably put it, "We are currently preparing students for jobs that don't yet exist, using technologies that haven't been invented, in order to solve problems that we don't even know are problems yet" (cited in Fadel & Trilling, 2014, p. 3).

Seemingly intractable problems in the present often disguise great opportunities. If we are willing, those dilemmas push us to reconsider the myths and unstated assumptions about how the world works. World learning best serves our historical watershed by doing what it does best: opening students' minds to the distinctive genius of diverse ways of life. World cultures are living libraries, repositories of the human legacy and potential. If we can help this generation learn the lessons that other cultures teach, maybe, just maybe, a globalized education can help tip the current system in a more desirable direction.

Notes

1. This includes all the world's academies of science, including the National Oceanic and Atmospheric Administration, National Aeronautics and Space Administration, Environmental Protection Agency, American Geophysical Union, American Association for the Advancement of Science, American Meteorological Society, U.S. Geological Survey, and hundreds of the world's top universities.

GOOD FOR THE WORLD

The Art of Intention

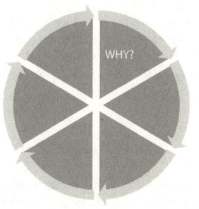

We have lived by the assumption that what is good for us would be good for the world. . . . We have been wrong. We must change our lives so that it will be possible to live by the contrary assumption, that what is good for the world will be good for us. And that requires that we make the effort to know the world and learn what is good for it.
— WENDELL BERRY, *The Art of the Commonplace*, 2002

NOT LONG AGO, a family friend that we'll call Laura visited our home after vacationing on the tiny Caribbean island of Barbados. When my spouse, Leslie, asked about the time, Laura nonchalantly replied, "It was alright. Nothing special." The next day, while mulling over the previous evening's conversation, Leslie remarked in a puzzled tone: "How could she regard a week in Barbados as 'nothing special'?" The answer, we speculated, had less to do with life on the island than with the outlook Laura carried to Barbados as unclaimed baggage.

33

"The pleasure we derive from journeys is perhaps dependent more on the mindset with which we travel than on the destination we travel to," writes Alain de Botton in *The Art of Travel* (2004, p. 246). The outer world is a reflection of our inner world of largely unconscious intentions and longings. Before we take a step forward, we anticipate it, order it. What we see in the world then shapes how we live in it. Consciously or not, we all act out of what philosopher Charles Taylor calls a *social imaginary* (2003). If the world appears to us disenchanted and meaningless, we will tend to live with a buffered self—disengaged, defensive, and cynical. Conversely, if we hope for a better future in this wide, wonderful, and wounded world, our everyday activity will be laced with meaning and purpose. Though our self-stories and self-images are rarely articulated, they lie at the center of personal and social change.

This chapter probes some of the stories we, as global educators and learners, tell ourselves about the value of intensive interaction with different people, possessed by different habits, ideas, and traditions. Our guiding question is this: *Why should we organize programs that help students better understand the world?*

The Power of Why

Students interested in educational travel customarily consult with either their academic or campus-based study away or service-learning advisers, or a third-party program provider. Following an exchange of pleasantries, the conversation typically turns to *where* the students want to go and *what* they want to do. Rarely is the question of *why* ever broached. Perhaps the answer seems fairly obvious. Students participate in service projects, research collaborations, or study away programs because they want to. The creative benefits are assumed, allowing community engagement to be routinely regarded as an end unto itself.

But mere knowledge *of* the world, however interesting, doesn't necessarily clarify what ends that knowledge serves. Community engagement *for what?* What is its raison d'être, its purpose for the world? Why should colleges and universities go through all the logistical trouble of inserting tens of thousands of young adults in unfamiliar and often hazardous community settings, whether domestic or abroad? Indeed, why should going *elsewhere* be accorded importance at all? Immanuel Kant, the great German philosopher, never traveled more than 100 miles from his birthplace in his entire 80-year life; Thoreau never left the United States; and Emily Dickinson was more or less housebound. Yet all of them wrote brilliantly of the wider world.

"Why?," says innovation expert Warren Berger (2014), is "a more beautiful question." It prompts us to be mindful, to make conscious the things that often get lost in unconscious mind wandering, which, according to researchers, constitutes as much as 50% of our waking hours. Posing the *why* question to anticipated world-learning ventures compels us to search our hearts for uncritically accepted motivations and expectations. We peel back the layers of taken-for-granted assumptions until we get to the heart of a matter.

I'm going to India.

Why?

To travel to another country with friends. Also, to earn academic credit.

But why?

Articulating the ultimate *why* necessarily precedes deciding *what* we want to do. Our natural impulse is just the opposite—to think and act and communicate from the outside in, from *what* to *why*. We go from what is most clear and concrete to what is fuzzy and ill-defined. The problem is that *what* we do—study, teach, volunteer, travel, conduct research—does not, in itself, reveal any defining *telos* or purpose.

Similarly, asking *why* paves the way for asking *how*. The *how* of program logistics and pedagogy is critically important: Passion and vision without structure and process is a recipe for failure. But when the practicalities of global learning—be it student recruitment, pre-field preparation, or health and safety concerns—dominate consciousness, they tend to push out the deeper and ultimately more important questions: *What principles and values define this journey? What goals can I articulate? How do they align with the kind of person I want to become, and the kind of world I want to see?* Hanging a question mark on things we've long taken for granted can spark the imagination and help motivate us in new directions.

The most fundamental question, then, is not *what* we are learning, nor *how* we are learning it, but *why* (Figure 2.1).

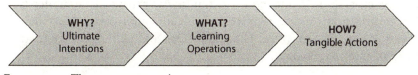

FIGURE 2.1.   Three-step progression.

Assume for a moment that you supervise a long and impressive list of global engagement activities, including study abroad, global service-learning, action research, international student recruitment, and strategic partnerships. If a professional guest were to inquire about the larger purpose, for example, for bringing international students to campus or sending national students abroad, what would you tell them?

- Is it to equip the nation with a world-class labor force?
- Is it to enhance the institution's international profile and brand?
- Is it to generate new revenue streams by expanding the school's tuition base?
- Is it to provide students a competitive edge in the job market?
- Is it to organize peak experiences that help students feel alive and even "find themselves"?
- Is it to deepen disciplinary or technical knowledge, or to advance research agendas?
- Is it to foster a new kind of citizen, one with global awareness and commitments?

Compelling arguments can be made to support each of these purposes. They tend to sort along private and public lines. On one hand, schools are under intense pressure to create clear pathways by which graduates can secure satisfying and well-paying jobs. Higher education as career preparation accents the instrumental or *private gains* ("good for us") that justify the high price tag of higher education (known as return on investment or ROI). College becomes a means to upward social mobility.

On the other hand, colleges are expected to be home for all sorts of *public goods* (i.e., good for the world). As an experiment in living (a theory put forth by John Stuart Mill), college introduces students to an intellectual culture where they become aware of new possibilities for thinking and living. This happens best when diverse groups of students get together and use their hivemind to think around issues that matter. Exchanges between people holding different perspectives formed by contrasting life experiences produce more limber and creative minds. An expanded circumference of cognitive inputs makes it more difficult for one to accept established answers to any given problem. The result is that a wider range of alternative ideas can enter public life.

Priority Purposes

The expansion of global-learning programs is commonly rationalized in terms of different priority purposes. These purposes roughly correlate with the assorted stakeholders—parents, campus administrators, education providers, community partners, prospective employers, and, of course, the students themselves. Each group has its own interests in and purposes for internationalizing student consciousness (Hudzik, 2011). Because stakeholder groups often inhabit parallel universes, sometimes those interests overlap, and at other times they diverge.

Five purposes are prominent enough to be considered drivers in the field of global education (Figure 2.2).

Political Driver: Cultural Diplomacy

Since World War II, higher education has been seen as an indispensable means in the broader work of international relations. Contrasting the hard power of military might and economic coercion, public or cultural diplomacy provides a source of soft power aimed at winning the hearts and minds of foreign audiences. Joseph Nye (2004), the Harvard political scientist who coined the term, explains *soft power* as "tangible assets such as an attractive personality, culture, political values, and institutions and policies that are seen as legitimate or having moral authority" (p. 6). Like pieces on a complex chessboard, these assets can be moved to achieve ultimate foreign policy objectives.

International education has long served as a diplomatic tool, and educators as political agents. Medieval universities brought students together

FIGURE 2.2.   Priority purposes: From private to public goods.

from across European countries for vocational training that could be used in service to the State or Church. During the colonial era, the British established universities throughout the Empire. Many of the most promising students (nearly all male) were sent back to England to be schooled in colonial administration (Pietsch, 2013). American soft power through higher education received its impetus in 1958, in the midst of the Cold War with the Soviet Union. During that year the National Defense Education Act was passed to build foreign language and world region studies programs, often with overseas field experience. The Peace Corps and Fulbright programs were also established to project a positive American image worldwide, mostly through people-to-people connections and scholarly collaboration.

Soft-power programs emphasizing intercultural exchange continue today. Each year, the United States sends over 300,000 winsome young American ambassadors abroad. In addition, American universities annually attract over one million foreign students, adding billions to the U.S. economy (Institute of International Education, 2016). As international students return to their home countries, the expectation is that they will champion all things American, including its institutions, political ideals, and foreign policies. International education promises to deliver a big bang for the international relations buck.

In recent years, however, a troubling gap has developed between rhetoric and reality. Interest in foreign languages and in-depth regional study is at an all-time low. And even though the number of American students studying abroad is on the rise, relatively few programs offer opportunities for serious, long-term cultural engagement. Trending is actually in the opposite direction—toward shorter and shorter field terms, many of them conducted as "island" programs in distant seas of otherness. Moreover, a disturbingly large percentage of students treat study abroad as a wild, semester-long spring break. The export of an indulgent American culture, claims Public Diplomacy Council member Martha Bayles (2014), betrays the cultural diplomacy mission and even puts the educational enterprise at risk. "It may be a blessing in disguise," says Bales, "that the percentage of studying abroad is rather low" (p. 224).

Further undermining international education's diplomacy mission is the deterioration of America's image abroad. Many other countries no longer see the United States as virtuous, heroic, and disinterested. In 2013, Win/Gallup International asked nearly 66,000 people in 68 countries a variety of questions about the world, including this one: Which country poses the greatest threat to world peace? By far, the United States was voted the biggest threat (Brown, 2014). The reasons were not hard to diagnose. They included destructive misadventures in Iraq and Afghanistan, with millions driven from their homes, and the exporting of pop culture products dominated by vulgarity, violence, and vitriol. A new U.S. Study Abroad Office housed in the Department of State is actively trying to reboot America's global image. Its mission, as articulated by former Assistant Secretary of State Evan Ryan (2015), is to foster "a global network of foreign citizens who understand the United States, and Americans who understand the wider world, all of whom can be partners in solving the world's challenges."

Economic Driver: Institutional Profit and Prestige

With the end of the Cold War in 1991, the emphasis within international education circles shifted from the political to the economic. Fierce competition within global higher education for resources, students, and faculty drove schools to adopt internationalization strategies that would enhance institutional profitability and reputational prestige. One such strategy was to aggressively recruit full-tuition-paying foreign students.

Similarly, many colleges and universities found that ventures abroad, from institution-owned-and-operated study abroad programs to branch campuses, could be significant revenue generators. Many of the collegians who study abroad each year are not outsourced to third parties or directly enrolled in foreign universities. They pay full tuition plus hefty program fees to their home institution, all the while freeing up bed space for other students. Muhlenberg College, a small residential school in Pennsylvania, sent nearly 200 (approximately 10%) of its students on semester-long education abroad programs one year. After accounting for all program costs, the school estimates saving nearly $560,000 (Alstete, 2014).

Today, cross-border education is a multibillion-dollar business, one of the 12 international tradable services in the General Agreement on Trade in Services (GATS). Universities and policy makers rightly emphasize the broadening value of world learning. However, the language to justify it has gradually become instrumental: "to prepare students to succeed in a highly competitive, knowledge-based, technology-driven global economy" (Standish, 2012, p. 2). Global engagement activities are expected to prepare students with the social and intellectual skills that employers need. When this is accepted as unquestioned orthodoxy, the intercultural experience itself is turned into a saleable commodity that is produced for, and sold on, the market. Tensions between academic values and financial concerns become inevitable. This is not an argument against world learning being responsive to the labor market's competence demands. But when know-how is divorced from know-why, the distinctive ends of fostering practical wisdom and forming lives of consequence tend to get buried under financial priorities.

Personal Drivers: Adventure and Advancement

The next driver is profoundly personal, energized by the individual quest for adventure elsewhere and, upon return, the promise of personal advancement. Adventure, as the first two syllables of the word suggest, speaks of movement toward something and someplace new. For most collegians, that movement entails what Paul Theroux (1975) describes as "pursuit and flight in equal parts" (p. 2). Both, I think, are characteristically human. We desire to get away, to chase curiosity, to discover new sides of ourselves. I've repeatedly heard travelers testify to never feeling "more fully alive" than when they exchanged the humdrum of daily routines for chance encounters and unconventional living. If life is indeed a blank canvas, it makes good sense to throw all the paint of new adventure on it that we can.

There was once a time when much of the world was a mystery. For fifteenth-century explorers like Vasco da Gama and Christopher Columbus, the Age of Discovery signaled a period when the thirst for new geographic knowledge coalesced with an imperial quest for fame and fortune. Then, from the sixteenth to nineteenth century, young British gents set out on treks of Europe's great cultural centers. Designed as mobile finishing schools in manners and customs, Grand Tours generally functioned as a hiatus between adolescence and adulthood, schooling and working. Mind you, travel at this time lacked the modern comforts of paved roads, hotels, international banks, and Wi-Fi connectivity. And as it happened, the young aristocrats proved far more interested in connecting with *des femmes blanches* in sleazy brothels than in soaking up the glories of ancient civilizations. Nevertheless, the Grand Tours proved hugely influential in terms of Britain's cultural evolution. From them emerged the mass tourist and modern education abroad industries, with meanings and motives ranging from exotic leisure and adventure to personal growth and education.

Global learners *adventure* in highly personalized ways. In terms of travel styles, the mass can be sorted into two main groups. The first group, the *culture vultures*, wants to experience it all. "They travel to worlds different from their own, to find excitement, to see new wonders and to have experiences of a lifetime. . . . The world is theirs for discovery, if not for the taking," explains Anthony Ogden (2008, p. 37). Whether it's bungee jumping the Nevis Highwire in New Zealand or rafting the glacier-fed Futaleufú River in Chile, culture vultures hardly look to be affected by the social realities or wisdom traditions of the regions they visit. Their goal, unabashedly, is to have the time of their lives.

Others set out on a journey of self-discovery. In her best-selling memoir *Eat, Pray, Love*, Elizabeth Gilbert (2007) narrates a year spent traveling in Italy, India, and Indonesia. With a surprising lack of irony, Gilbert writes: "It wasn't so much that I wanted to thoroughly explore the countries themselves; this has been done. It was more that *I wanted to thoroughly explore one aspect of myself* set against the backdrop of each country, in a place that has traditionally done that one thing very well" (pp. 30–31, emphasis added). For Gilbert, foreign places with rich histories and complex societies became instruments of self-realization.

A second group of sojourners, the *careerists*, calculate personal investments in world learning largely in terms of future monetary yields. Consistent with the cool consumerism promoted throughout the general culture, study away functions as a transaction: Students purchase the experiences and later judge whether they were worth the money. For the careerist, making a difference or pondering one's life is low priority. The main consideration is return on investment: Does my adventure look good on a resume and advantage me in the job market? Motivations are still instrumental rather than intellectual and intercultural. Though few careerists venture outside the foreigner bubble, they hope to convince future employers that their travels reflect a resourceful and risk-taking, even heroic, kind of person.

Once having fun, finding oneself, and getting ahead are accepted as primary purposes in world learning, the character of the enterprise swings from a potential public benefit to a private saleable good (Bolen, 2001). All too often, promotional images of program sites only accentuate the commercialism. Overseas destinations are typically "sold" as a travel fantasy of exotic landscapes, colorful natives, and endless fun. Unfortunately, this only helps to normalize a touristic gaze for understanding and acting upon the world.

Perhaps the easy, pleasing formula of education abroad has fallen vic-
tim to its own success. Subject to unregulated growth since the 1960s,
practitioners are understandably reluctant to acknowledge how a fun-in-
the-sun, success-in-the-global-economy approach to world learning may
actually operate at cross-purposes with ensuring a more humane and hab-
itable world for future generations. True, altruistic and egoistic motives
frequently coexist. But when self-centered purposes prevail, the flow of
benefits from study, research, and volunteering are almost always one-way—
from host communities to foreign visitors.

Educational Driver: Global Citizenship

There is a third group of sojourners whom I'll call *budding globalists*. For
them, adventure is less about conquering physical terrain than about sur-
rendering to it. They travel to not only be changed by the experience but
also to engage with perceived injustices, most often through voluntary
service within difficult, forgotten places. In contrast to nativists, budding
globalists believe that their moral responsibilities do not start and stop
at the borders of their homeland. They may reside comfortably in the
global 1%, but a key motive for travel is to discover how the other 99%
of humanity lives, and why. Toward that end, they stretch themselves,
physically and culturally, in an effort to learn how to think outside the
box of their inherited culture. *Global citizenship* is often used to describe the
educational ideal.

Would-be global citizens have their own distinctive worldview, playfully
captured by the acronym WEIRD—for Western, educated, industrialized,
rich, and democratic. They revel in difference and take a keen interest in
"creating a better world" through an education with wide horizons and
progressive ethical commitments.

The quest for more universal sympathies and allegiances is brilliantly
captured in Plato's famous allegory of the cave. Plato asks us to imagine
humans chained and imprisoned from birth in a dark, underground cav-
ern. Behind these unfortunate souls are puppet-showmen who, by flickering firelight, cast shadows of figurines on the wall. The shadows loom
suddenly and then vanish; they are the only reality the prisoners see and
know. In their quest for true liberation, the captive minds ascend "along
the rough, steep, upward way" into the light of the sun (the world as it is).
For a while, the outdoor light—far more brilliant than the dim, red glow

of the cave—prevents them from seeing a thing. They stumble forward, rub their eyes, and use their "cave knowledge" to find their way. In the end, they must abandon everything they think they know in order to make sense of a newly discovered world. Their unshackled consciousness prevents them from ever returning to the shadow-world.

Herein lies the promise of global citizenship: the chance to free the imagination from cave blindness. Our ties to family and land and nation, however valuable as springboards to life, can also become a straightjacket that binds us to our own perceptions. Journeys into other social worlds press us to see reality as larger and more complex than what we have known before. As we step out of the cave and into the sunlight, we come to see the shadow plays and cultural scripts for what they are.

Global citizenship would thus seem to be an ultimate end for world learning. The concept struggles, however, to overcome at least three character defects:

- *Formlessness.* Few seem to know what a global citizen actually looks like in practice, or how progress toward the ideal might be assessed. Much too often, global citizenship is cast as an almost guaranteed outcome of participating in world-learning programs, regardless of location, degree of immersion, length of stay, and other vital program characteristics (Woolf, 2010). Even as a metaphor, we are mostly left with a moral abstraction. The claim that all human beings belong to one community, not just particular local ones, says nothing about *where* we live (ecological conditions), *whom* we live there with (by race, culture, religion, and economic status), and *how* we are to live there. Love cannot be directed toward humanity or the global community in general. Fyodor Dostoyevsky (2015), in *The Brothers Karamazov*, declares, "It has always happened that the more I detest men individually the more ardent becomes my love for humanity" (p. 48). It's easy to love an abstraction, but it rarely inspires devotion or meaningful action.
- *Elitism.* The promise of global citizenship is mainly directed toward a very small population with the discretionary time and money to travel the world. Economic privilege carries with it an almost inescapable hazard: to view one's elite status as the just reward of higher intelligence and industriousness. To the extent this moral illusion takes root in consciousness, aspiring global citizens begin to imagine the world from the vantage point of frequent fliers,

easily entering and exiting different polities and social relations, armed with visa-friendly passports and credit cards, and largely unbothered about ethical considerations and social responsibility. Claims to cosmopolitan openness begin to sound like a self-serving cant coming from one who may love soul food or Vietnamese *pho* but would never live in or near a minority housing project. Safely sequestered within a bubble of affluence, the grand promise defaults to a kind of "merit badge in a strictly personal journey towards self-discovery and upward social mobility" (Zemach-Bersin, 2009).

- *Rootlessness.* The cosmopolitan impulse rightfully challenges parochial and exclusive attachments, whether to family, ethnic group, or nation. But doing so can set up a false binary of the local and the global. Invariably, global citizenship comes to be framed as an outcome of *international* experiences, and those within largely interchangeable world cities (e.g., London, Paris, Bangkok, and Dubai). When marketed to a generation *already* largely disconnected from place, the ideal unwittingly encourages young adults to stay on the move and put down few roots. They learn to invest little, know little, and care little for the immediate locale beyond its ability to gratify. To be sure, dancing the *syrto* all night in a Greek village or partaking in a traditional coffee ceremony with an Ethiopian family can prove quite broadening. But magical moments rarely generate new social connections, much less firm justice commitments.

World learning can help cultivate a competent public morality, but only if we disentangle attainable student learning and community development outcomes from metaphorical flourish and marketing hyperbole. Global citizenship must indicate something more than a fondness for travel, an enjoyment of cultural diversity, and a heartfelt hope for a more humane world (Streitwieser & Light, 2016).

Ethical Driver: Greater Good

For all their merits, the drivers discussed thus far fall short in one vital respect: They fail to adequately consider what is good for the world. In chapter 1 we charted a maelstrom of colliding factors that threaten to radically alter human life worldwide, especially for the most vulnerable.

Though perhaps not immediately obvious in the normal course of our lives, they represent a planetary emergency of unprecedented gravity. They urge us to create conditions on Earth that promote the flourishing of all life, biological and cultural.

A lived commitment to the greater good challenges the fatalistic assumption that the current system is inevitable or, in any case, lacks any real alternative. It also calls out what Pope Francis (2015) diagnoses as our root crisis: a *globalization of indifference*. Moderns, he writes, feel increasingly "incapable of feeling compassion at the outcry of the poor, weeping for other people's pain, and feeling a need to help them, as though all this were someone else's responsibility and not our own" (no. 54). This is fundamentally a crisis of solidarity, the breakdown of an "Us" consciousness. Once ensconced in the shadow worlds of appearance and consumptive pleasure, "all those lives stunted for lack of opportunity seem a mere spectacle; they fail to move us" (no. 54).

World learning challenges the culture of indifference with pedagogies of engagement. Beyond simply *imagining* what it would be like to be someone else, we enter into another's lived reality and learn to hear voices that speak from some place other than our own. More *inclusive loyalties*—the promise of global citizenship—depend on *empathetic encounters* with those we'd otherwise choose to avoid. We need not travel far. Some of the world's most stigmatized and vulnerable groups are right at our doorstep: Central American asylum seekers, Iraqi and Syrian refugees, teenage mothers, day laborers, and scores of homeless persons and prison inmates, many of them mentally ill. Society's stigmatized and cast off groups are not just "problems" to be managed. Each woman, man, and child is at least our neighbor in the human family, possibly brothers and sisters, and perhaps, in some mysterious way, the very face of God. "I'm telling the solemn truth," Jesus declared at the climax of a parable. "Whenever you did one of these things to someone overlooked or ignored, that was me—you did it to me" (Mt. 25:40, *The Message*).

This religious insight underscores a critical condition of global learning for the greater good: moral imagination. Humans are endowed with the unique ability to conceive of fellows as moral beings, not as objects whose value rests in mere utility. Moral imagination charges global learning with a passion for the common good. Love, compassion, and other "political emotions" open student hearts out toward others, allowing them to see the uneven and often unlovely destiny of human beings. They do so not with guilt or pity, but with the recognition of full and equal humanity in other persons. This is key to engendering and sustaining a justice-seeking, capabilities-rich commonwealth.

Models of moral imagination relevant to global learning draw upon major ethical and religious traditions.[1] Modern thinkers often use evocative language like the Great Work (Thomas Berry), the Great Economy (Wendell Berry), and the Beloved Community (Martin Luther King Jr.) to express an order higher than the sum of individual ends and interests. The idea takes in the whole of reality, "both known and unknown, visible and invisible, comprehensible and mysterious" (Berry, 2002, p. 221). In essence, the greater good is a story we tell about a world made right in the totality of its relationships (see Figure 2.3). A world where all individuals and institutions, families and peoples, the natural world in all its richness, and the transcendent powers that provide ultimate meaning for existence are knit together and fulfilled in mutual respect and delight.

Right relationship roots in the skillful practice of common values, including integrity, reverence, transcendence, solidarity, and self-restraint, all of which are necessary for individual and communal flourishing. Human

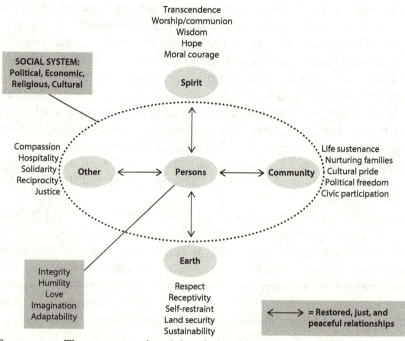

FIGURE 2.3.   The greater good as right relationship.

relations are no longer ruled by hierarchies, competition, and profit maximization. Domination, exclusion, and exploitation are overcome. Persons and families in the human community secure a life that is pleasurable, healthy, sustainable, contributive, and enduring.

We might be tempted to dismiss talk of a larger common good as hopelessly Pollyannaish. But all aspirational social and political values depend upon a compelling moral vision. Without it, society inevitably succumbs to what Erich Fromm called "the pathology of normalcy" (2010). Existence becomes unsubstantial and illusory. Lacking an ultimate reference point for "the good," world learning, too, loses its moral energy and transcendent purpose. Students are left without a North Star, a guiding authority in how to stand with culture, how to stand against culture, and how to stand in service of culture. They have only the utilitarian and the sensational.

Four axioms ground world learners in their efforts to advance the greater good:

1. *Everybody matters* (human dignity).

    Jesus once posed the quintessential cosmopolitan question: *Who is my neighbor?* (Luke 10:29, *New International Version*). Are we to view the Haitian or Honduran mother—distant from us geographically, socially, racially, economically, and emotionally—as our neighbor? What links us to children of war or women with fistulas a world away? For that matter, what implicates me in the fate of farm workers and refugees in my own society, my own neighborhood? Do all lives matter equally, or do some lives matter less than others? How we answer these questions reveals the extent to which we see ourselves bound to and indebted to each other. The implications, of course, are radically egalitarian and universalistic. All persons are of equal value and deserving of fair recognition, mutual respect, humane treatment, and equal opportunities for self-realization.

2. *Everything is connected* (interdependence).

    Humanity and nature are tied together in what Martin Luther King Jr. (1968a) described as "an inescapable network of mutuality." What affects one form of life directly, affects all indirectly. King used metaphors such as "the world house" and "the beloved community" to portray a world where all are implicated in each other's lives. Everything we do, everything we have, all that we are is dependent on people and lands far removed from our sight. We awoke this morning in a bed that someone else built. We turned on power and bathed in water that originated elsewhere. We put on clothes stitched by someone else's hands and consumed food that others grew, harvested, processed, packaged, and shipped. Our world is one of interdependent living beings. However indirect and tenuous our connections, we reside under a common roof.

3. *All life is precious* (intrinsic value).

The greater good regards all life, in all places, as unique, irreplaceable, worth understanding, and absolutely worth protecting. Life forms and ecosystems cannot be reduced to their market value. Nor can the sole consideration be the *private* good, where things are seen as either "for me" or "against me." Certain goods are intrinsically valuable; they morally and legally belong to everyone. Clean air, stable climate, productive land, seeds, groundwater, energy, the human genome, the Internet, cultural traditions, heritage sites—this is a "commonwealth" that should be governed on behalf of all. The greater good is thus grounded in skilled and reverent stewardship, not cost-benefit analysis; placed affection, not just productive efficiency; conviviality more than profitability; and ecological prudence over technical control. In a relentlessly private age, it seeks to create and protect the means by which everyone, everywhere, can sustain and better both lives and communities.

4. *Every human being has obligations to every other* (solidarity).

The greater good must ultimately be appropriated personally, as ethical choices that we make in relation to the wider world. In the Good Samaritan story, a traveler is beaten and robbed by bandits along the road from Jerusalem to Jericho. After two religious men pass by without offering assistance, a Samaritan stops, binds the stranger's injuries, carries him to an inn, and pays for his care. He directly encounters human need and responds with heart and hands. He displays public love through personal action.

While admiring the Samaritan's compassion, readers of the parable might demur: Do acts of charity—doing *for* others—go far enough in discharging our obligations? Might stopgap assistance effectively sidetrack the questions that actually implicate our lives? Consider the effects of climate change. Acts of charity that bring financial or material support to drought or typhoon victims might easily mask the basic *solidarity* question: Do we—the wealthy countries or corporations or persons (the major polluters)—have a right to create conditions in which the poorest and lowest-emitting people suffer? True solidarity requires that we look at the ways our lives are implicated in the injustices that make charity necessary. King (1967a) famously declared: "True compassion is more than flinging a coin to a beggar. It comes to see that an edifice which produces beggars needs restructuring" (pp. 187–188). World learning, at its best, helps shape a moral culture where persons strive together to find proximate solutions to what often appear to be intractable problems.

Conclusion

Considerations of the greater good shift the conversation about the ultimate *why* of community engagement away from an exclusive concern with *self-enlargement* (What's in it for me?) to *social responsibility* (How is my life implicated in the lives of others, and what do I do about it?). World learning moves from being a presumably innocent, morally neutral activity to a form of soul craft, imbued with moral meaning and ethical direction.

A final word of clarification: Although this chapter has considered different goods and potential ends separately, as distinct rationales, we need not regard them as rivals. Each has value. They reflect the multiple mandates of modern educational institutions and the complex motivations and expectations of learners. Instead of pitting one good against the others, our task is to *rightly order their relative worth and function*. The ultimate question is not: Which goal will direct global engagement to the exclusion of all others? It is this: Which purposes will "drive" our programs and which will "ride shotgun" *if* our collective purpose is to contribute to the health of the planet and the planet's peoples? Will we be market driven and mission sensitive or mission driven and market sensitive? By learning to do justly to wider interests than our own, we hold out the prospect of a holistically capacitated generation acting confidently to repair the world. It is to this hope that I turn in the next chapter.

Notes

1. The prophet Isaiah dreamed of the day when the wolf and the lamb would lie down together—when, in other words, the strong would no longer devour the weak. Mahayana, one of the two major strains of Buddhism, speaks of non-injury and

ahimsa (compassion) toward all life forms. In Islam, the idea of *tazkiyah* (wholistic development) refers to the growth of harmonious relations with God, with oneself, with other people, and with the natural environment. Ancient Israel imagined *shalom* as a social order of justice, harmony, and well-being. Plato and Aristotle introduced the beautiful idea of *eudaimonia,* or *human flourishing,* to indicate perfect well-being based on natural law and reason. Within the Christian tradition, the fullest human development was to be found in the *Imitatio Christi* (the "Imitation of Christ") and in the embrace of human life freed from the moral power of idolatry (the *kingdom of God*). Thomas Aquinas, a medieval Roman Catholic scholar, attempted to synthesize biblical and classical traditions with the language of the *common good,* understood as the sum total of the conditions of social life that allow people, whether as groups or individuals, to achieve the life that they value. Many nonreligious terms, current in the development literature, indicate a similar ideal state. These terms include *development, well-being, happiness, capabilities, sustainability,* and the *good society.*

THE GLOBAL ARTIST

Art Personified

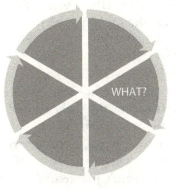

If you ask me what I came to do in this world, I, an artist, will answer you:
I am here to live out loud.
— EMILE ZOLA (1880)

IN VISUAL ARTWORKS such as painting, sculpture, and photography, artists will often make use of more than one traditionally distinct medium. Some will merge painting and sculpture. Others will work on a canvas that combines oil paint, newspaper collage, and glass. Rather than create a work in only one material—like oils for painting or clay for sculpture—their art will mix media in ways that defy previous genres. The result is great versatility in the content of art, as well as a rich viewer experience.

Similarly, cultural contexts reveal an unprecedented degree of mixing. In many regions of the world, the global fusion of media, markets, and migrations has produced a multilayered social canvas that is inescapably multicultural and transnational. Perhaps nowhere is this trend more

51

apparent than in 20-something Los Angeles. You wouldn't know it from the dystopian visions portrayed in Hollywood films like *Blade Runner* and *Elysium*. But in the contiguous borderland neighborhoods of Central Los Angeles, Spanish-speaking Black and Korean kids, all-White rap crews, and Chinese-Filipinos are bellwethers of a new, post-multicultural era. These kids show us that it is possible to eat at McDonald's, dress down in T-shirts and Levi's, mix hip-hop with disco and flamenco with techno-pop, speak English, and shuffle with a smartphone, and *still remain something else.*

This new, synthesized culture continues to be born within the world's great urban centers. From New York and London to Jakarta and Mumbai, diverse social groups and cultural communities are increasingly bound to each other in myriad complex, hybridized relationships, and without much consideration to racial or ethnic purity. Every time a Thai Buddhist family moves to Queens, and the son marries a Catholic Latina or secular Chinese, the products of their union bring to the American Experiment an accent and angle on the world never seen before.

Some might view this reality as a sign of irreversible social disintegration. However, for world learners the contemporary cultural mixing represents something of great beauty, the challenge and promise of our age. In common with visual artists who blend various media and ethnic influences to create original polycultural pieces, global artists look for opportunities to enrich their private and public worlds with influences from elsewhere.

The cosmopolitan age doesn't just reconfigure social relationships. It also creates new challenges, global in scale, that cannot be met by single nations or markets alone. Climate change. Energy scarcity. Ecological degradation. Infectious disease. Mass migration. Nuclear threats. Human trafficking. Terrorism. Transnational crime. Religious radicalism. Political gridlock. Soaring wealth inequality. These are among the daunting, supercomplex problems that threaten our planetary future.

In chapter 2, we discussed the significance of a globalized education and if it would ultimately be found in its ability to contribute to a more flourishing world, or if it would finally succumb to narrow economic factors—such as postgraduate income and employment rates. Students and families have good reason to worry about return on investment in college. But it is also true that "without significant precautions, education equips people merely to be more effective vandals of earth" (Orr, 1994, p. 5). The declining state of virtually all of the planet's life systems should be enough to convince us that the world doesn't need more "successful" people, at least not as we typically define it. What it needs are people who have learned to live well in their places, with self-restraint, prudence, and affection.

Against this backdrop, this chapter maps a model of mixed-media learning designed to form a certain kind of person—the global artist. Global artists bring together context, content, and process within their educational experience in ways that enable them to create a much more humane and fulfilling presence in the world. Against a sterile museum-like conception of artfulness hermetically removed from ordinary life, we consider how learners might find their full moral voice in a world more divided and depleted than ever before. At its core is deep change—that is to say, learning—within one's moral dispositions, intellectual capacity, world understanding, practical skills, and ethical commitments.

Our guiding question is this:
What kinds of learner-artists do we hope to fashion, for what kind of world?
Embedded within this "what" question are three subquestions:

1. What kind of alternative world do we see as possible (social vision)?
2. What kind of persons might help bring that world into being (competence)?
3. What kind of educational process can help develop those persons (pedagogy)?

The competency or expertise question is inseparable from the vision question. As pointed out in chapter 2, how we *see* the world inevitably shapes our sense of the kind of student needed *for* that world. If we perceive the world as essentially fair and sustainable, with free markets and technological miracles eventually restoring the earth's natural systems and enabling everyone to achieve the good life, we will expect learners to demonstrate outcomes that strengthen their prospects for success within the established order. However, if we believe that the planet faces compound crises, and that the well-being of tens of millions of persons depends on new ways of living on Earth, we will expect learners to demonstrate positive changes in their core values, their perception of themselves, and their personal lifestyle.

The expertise question should also not be abstracted from the pedagogy question. If a central educational goal is for students to see the world clearly (wisdom) and to feel it truly (compassion), we need a learning process that catalyzes deep change in personal values, perspectives, and life habits. That is the subject of chapter 4. Competency development, of course, is what higher education is all about. Yet, after decades of practice, global educators still lack empirically grounded evidence to judge which learning activities, in which social contexts, best develop the kind of person we need for the kind of world we want. If the emerging generation is to show humanity a better version of itself, their educational mentors will need to more precisely delineate the relationship between particular program experiences and the intended impact of those experiences on participants.

A related challenge is to align standardized assessments with both purpose and pedagogy. Colleges and universities typically adopt rationales and methods with pragmatics in mind: What can our budget afford? Who is available to lead or supervise the activity? What ventures promise to generate the most revenue and student satisfaction? How will we minimize risk to the institution? Often the last question to be asked is: What should learners actually be able to *do* as an outcome of their varied curricular and cocurricular experiences?

When pragmatics trumps purpose, "success" becomes a numbers game. How many international and American minority students can we recruit to campus? How many globally oriented courses and strategic partnerships can we list for accreditors? How much on-campus bed space can we free up by sending students abroad? Quantitative measures do focus needful attention on institutional *inputs* (e.g., financial resources dedicated to program development), as well as on *outputs* (e.g., revenue generated by international students). The problem comes when inputs and outputs eclipse student and community development *outcomes* as the primary locus of decision-making. At that point, we easily lose sight of the forest for the trees.

The Liberal Arts: Then and Now

The idea of a liberal arts education has roots in the Greco-Roman tradition. The original syllabus, formalized during the European Middle Ages, consisted of seven arts: a *trivium* of logic, grammar, and rhetoric, and a *quadrivium* of arithmetic, geometry, music, and astronomy. The *trivium* cultivated the arts of reading and composition, while the *quadrivium* taught the arts of observation and calculation. In ancient Rome, subjects like medicine and architecture were excluded from the liberal arts because they were too practical. Likewise, during the Renaissance, it was painting and sculpture that troubled the line between art and craft. Nevertheless, the basic idea of the liberal arts—to offer students the best in human thought in order for them to fully exercise their liberties as a free people—persisted.

By the nineteenth century the content of the liberal arts changed drastically. Especially in the United States, and corresponding to the creation of the modern university, the physical sciences (e.g., physics and chemistry) migrated from technical colleges to join the humanities, the social sciences, and the life sciences as a core curriculum. Eventually the idea of a general education emerged. In addition to competency in some specialized subject (a major), students were expected to acquire a body of wide-ranging knowledge. While educators could agree on the basic principle of depth and breadth in learning, endless debate surrounded *how much* general education was necessary, *what* foundational knowledge was essential, and *how* students might demonstrate that they actually learned what they were supposed to.

Today, the American model of the liberal arts, almost without exception, includes literature, history, languages, philosophy, mathematics, and science. It aims to graduate *educated generalists*—persons of intellectual breadth and depth who are able to think across disciplines and apply their knowledge in ways that improve the human condition. The liberal arts can thus be seen as foundational to the world of work, though distinct from specialized job training. Following political philosopher John Stuart Mill (1867), champions of the liberal arts draw a solid line between professional and general education: A liberal education, Mill insisted, "is not to make skillful lawyers, or physicians, or engineers, but capable and cultivated human beings."

Mill could not have imagined, 150 years hence, what a hard sell cultivating humanity would be. Today's college student enters a higher education system increasingly oriented toward technical knowledge and specialized skills that serve the needs of the business world. College is no longer perceived as a place to overcome ignorance, to cultivate an integrated self, to become a soul, and to learn how to repair the world. When students talk to each other, they don't inquire how each other's search for truth is going. They ask a single return-on-investment question: What do you plan to do with your degree?

The ascendant influence of market forces and commercial values in college life has signaled something of a crisis for the liberal arts. Most students view them as either dispensable courses they hope to get out of the way as soon as possible, or as an overpriced indulgence for the affluent few who can afford to invest in making a life rather than a living. Compounding the perception problem is a pedagogical oddity: The liberal arts are typically cloistered within campus compounds disconnected from real-world problems.

The sequestered study of great ideas may appear quite scholarly. But faced with a hyper-specialized economy, young adults have increasingly traded a broad exposure to the outlines of knowledge for practical knowledge with an immediate financial pay-off: education, business, nursing, social work, computer programming, engineering, and so on. With motivations decidedly instrumental, language like learning for learning's sake or taking social responsibility sounds increasingly anachronistic, like some throwback to the '60s.

At the same time, few faculty bodies can agree on an answer to the basic "what" question—*What should students actually know, be, and do?*

The irony in all this is that universities in other countries are embracing the liberal arts tradition at a time when U.S. schools are in the process of giving it up. This is especially true in India and East Asia where schools are joining broad multidisciplinary learning to specialized technical training in the so-called STEM fields: science, technology, engineering, and mathematics.[1] The classic liberal question—What is the nature and quality of a moral life?—is considered naturally inseparable from the expressly *il*-liberal question—What does morality require me to be and to do in the present world?

The Great Work

During their lifetimes, this generation will be called to do what those in their parents' generation failed to do. They will need to marshal sufficient competence, conscience, and care to

- stabilize world populations;
- eradicate extreme poverty;
- use water, energy, and materials much more efficiently;
- drastically reduce greenhouse gas emissions;
- protect biological diversity;
- repair, as much as possible, the damage done to the earth as a result of industrialization;
- discover and address the root causes of persistent mental distress;
- reweave the social fabric by turning strangers and enemies into friends and neighbors;
- reduce social and racial inequalities in access to education and health services;

- expand voting rights, women's rights, immigrant rights, LGBT rights;
- ensure affordable housing and a strong safety net for the most vulnerable; and
- address continuing inequalities in the criminal justice system.

In short, this generation will have to learn how to make a proper—that is to say, a psychologically sane, economically just, socially peaceable, and ecologically sustainable—home in the world. This is the Great Work of our time. If liberal education is to be responsive to this task, it cannot afford to exist in an ivory tower of timeless musings on abstract ideas. It must truly "liberate" learners to assume a caretaking role in the world, one that promotes and protects all forms of life. Toward this end, the liberal arts locates itself, concretely and directly, in real-world conditions and questions.[2]

The Global Liberal Arts

Intimations of a new Global Liberal Arts are apparent among a critical edge of students looking for an education that is responsive, not only to the wisdom of the ages but also to the challenges and opportunities of contemporary society. Biology and education majors are choosing to learn foreign languages, study abroad, and pursue interests in social and political issues. Artists and musicians are developing technical skill in computer graphics and engineering (perhaps inspired by Apple's elegant iThings). Students in the humanities are taking out minors in business and accounting. Ingeniously combining elements of professional programs with stock from the traditional liberal arts curriculum, they are quietly merging knowledge and skills from formerly polarized fields.

The emerging model coolly transcends the great books versus marketable skills debate. It artfully reconnects what has been fragmented into disciplines, sequestered within walled-and-gated campus compounds, limited to texts from a bygone era, and abstracted from a larger social purpose. Students have the opportunity to acquire the experiential and conceptual knowledge needed to support sustained, meaningful action in the wider world. In the process, higher education advances a greater good.

If a truly liberating education is to recover its moral and civic purpose, the deep roots of dualism must be cut. Twenty-first-century problems don't allow us to segregate mind from body, matter from spirit, the ancient from the contemporary, living from learning, culture from nature, and positive knowledge from practical action. The Great Work requires a balanced wholeness. Think of a hanging mobile, with crossbars and wires connected to an ensemble of hanging and rotating forms, each of them suspended in delicate balance. Similarly, the global liberal arts carefully relate the content (what?) question to questions surrounding the ultimate purpose (why?), beneficiaries (for whom?), locations (where?), and process (how?) of learning. What were once understood as binary opposites enter into a mutually enriching and purposeful alliance. Examples include

- the classical and the modern;
- the classroom and the community;
- the curricular and the cocurricular;
- conceptual, contemplative, and experiential modes of inquiry;
- the domestic and the international;
- the mind and the emotions;
- intellectual and moral/manual competence;
- diversity issues and global predicaments;
- human cultures and the physical world;
- civic engagement and global development;
- personal development and social and environmental responsibility; and
- individual choice and systemic change.

In a globally responsive liberal arts framework, permeable disciplinary boundaries replace fixed silos. "Only fluency across the boundaries will provide a clear view of the world as it really is," writes legendary biologist E.O. Wilson (1999, p. 14). Such fluency requires pedagogical structures that are fluid and flexible, reaching across the natural sciences, the social sciences, and the humanities.

Which brings us to the actual design of the global liberal arts, and to the kind of persons—global artists—whose hearts and minds will be formed by it. What temperaments, social habits, and intellectual abilities will they need to help repair and regenerate their corner of creation? A fuller response to this question is presented in Appendix A, but here is an initial sketch:

Global artists are persons with the ability to resist parochialism and remain open to a wider reality. They critically read classic and contemporary works as windows into human experience and world events. Although they have achieved a basic comfort with numbers and computer applications,

they regard direct, firsthand knowledge as the ultimate basis of the intellectual life. They enter directly into the unique histories and conditions
of other peoples, eager to converse about consequential issues. They cross
borders of difference, pay attention, and listen well, suspending personal
judgments long enough to truly hear a divergent perspective and allow its
truth to prevail against them. They learn how to see profoundly, think
deeply, care widely, and act wisely.

Global artists don't just happen. They are formed through the deliberate coordination of high-impact curricular and cocurricular experiences
that, together, cultivate the capacity to understand and act on issues of
global significance across human differences. A set of interlocking "arts"
evokes the desired wholeness in this sweeping vision of student development (Figure 3.1).

Intellectual and Moral Arts

One of the great paradoxes of higher education is that young women and
men invest tens of thousands of dollars to be tutored in a wide array of
academic disciplines, but with scant consideration of *how* that knowledge
might actually improve the human condition. Intellectual development is
largely severed from moral action. This was not always the case. In the view

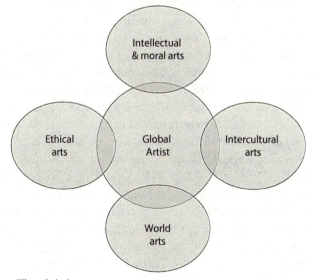

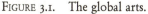

Figure 3.1.   The global arts.

of the ancients, the intellectual arts and the moral arts were inseparable in human development. Cicero spoke of *liberal learning* (1971) as the ability "to restrain the passions and to make the appetites amenable to reason" (p. 128). Aristotle (2004) defined it as the mean between extremes of excess and deficiency in order "to engender a certain character in the citizens and to make them good and disposed to perform noble actions." The primary purpose of education was expressly *not* to make as much money as possible; it was to teach individuals how to live well in their places.

The intellectual arts bring hungry minds into intimate relationship with the world of ideas. Students explore their deepest questions across disciplinary boundaries. They learn to reverence truth wherever it discloses itself—in classic literature, in social and political theory, in the thinking of those inhabiting other cultures, but also in the continuous stream of normal life activity. "Truth is everywhere," writes A.G. Sertillanges (1998) in *The Intellectual Life*, discoverable in classic texts, as well as in "conversations, chance occurrences, theatres, visits, strolls" (p. 73). The omnipresence and interconnectedness of truth ultimately connects all fields of study to each other.

As with any craft, the intellectual arts require considerable discipline to optimize energy and output. Proper diet, regular exercise, and sufficient sleep are important allies with concentrated, methodical study. The typical American college student is not just deficient in all three; many also try to ease the overwhelming stress of school with binge drinking, fast food, gaming, and other energy and motivation killers. Commentators regularly accuse Gen Y-ers and Z-ers of rarely reading books and being generally disaffected from the world of big ideas (Bauerlein, 2009; Twenge, 2017). A recent experience of mine overhearing casual conversation between five college students at a local Starbucks would seem to support this judgment. For over two hours, the group talked about other people, random parties, travel experiences, and assorted frivolities (clothes, cars, movies, and celebrities). Not once did talk turn to current topics of real consequence—such as border policy, hate crimes, the automation of jobs, or ecosystem collapse.

"We are drowning in information, while starving for wisdom," observed sociobiologist E.O. Wilson (1998, p. 294). Staggering amounts of information are at our fingertips, yet we may be less informed and less knowledgeable than ever. Broad knowledge and the capacity to seek truth and think critically grounds ethical action in the world. Intellectual understanding is not enough. For good thinking to translate into doing well, character must be valued as much as smarts. Truth and virtue, the intellectual arts and the moral arts, are indivisible. Whereas the intellectual arts help them to *know* their social responsibilities, the moral arts compel them to *act* on that knowledge.

Not everyone is convinced that leading students to act well in the world is the proper business of higher education. Stanley Fish (2012), for one, believes that educators have "no chance at all . . . of determining what [student] behavior and values will be in those aspects of their lives that are not, in the strict sense of the word, academic" (p. 59). In other words, since there is little that educators can do to develop students' moral convictions and commitments, the task of beautifying souls is best left to religious congregations and psychotherapists. Knowledge, says Fish, ought to be valued for its own sake and not as a means for saving the world.

But is simply knowing something powerful enough to dislodge ingrained habits of mind and to spur right action? Few, I imagine, would dispute the idea that all people should be treated fairly. But how many of us actually embrace our moral duties toward others? Historian Michael Ignatieff (1984) opines:

> The allegiances that make the human world human must be beaten into our heads. We never know a thing till we have paid to know it, never know how much is enough until we have had much less than enough, never know what we need till we have been dispossessed. We must be blinded before we see. Our education in the art of necessity cannot avoid tragedy. (p. 50)

Most of the world's biggest threats are largely unresponsive to more knowledge, more money, and more power. What they require is a *deepened humanity* that keeps small-mindedness and self-serving loyalties at bay. High-impact global learning deliberately arranges field experiences to open student minds to world predicaments and alternative points of view. What world learners see and hear reaches into their souls and arouses what Martha Nussbaum (2013) considers essential "political emotions"—empathy, temperance, solidarity with others, love, justice, and courage. "If distant people and abstract principles are to get a grip on our emotions," writes Nussbaum, "these emotions must somehow position them within our circle of concern, creating a sense of 'our' life in which these people . . . matter as parts of our 'us'" (p. 5). Through guided immersion in the triumph *and* tragedy of the world, learners connect the life of the mind to the passions of the heart. This lays the foundation for the application of intelligence and technical skill to projects aimed at fashioning more humane and ecologically resilient communities.

Intellectual Arts (learning to think well)

- *Intellectual inquiry*: Probing the "big questions" related to critical global challenges embedded in the humanities, natural sciences, and social sciences.
- *Information literacy*: Accessing and critically evaluating information as a means of self-education and freedom from indoctrination.
- *Rational deliberation*: Evaluating and synthesizing evidence, and making well-reasoned arguments.
- *Critical thinking*: Questioning ideological assumptions and conclusions through contrasting points of view and respectful dialogue.
- *Quantitative reasoning*: Using mathematical concepts and skills to better comprehend real-world problems.
- *Written and oral expression*: Clearly articulating a coherent line of thought in writing and speech.
- *Photography*: Recording and transmitting visual images onto a page or screen.
- *Presentation*: Transmitting complex information through visual images.

Moral Arts (learning to be good)

- *Transcendence*: Forging connections to the larger universe as a basis of meaning and hope.
- *Love*: Spontaneous, unmotivated actions to protect and conserve the people and things to which one is intensely attached.
- *Hospitality*: Befriending and tending strangers as part of a shared human project.
- *Empathy*: Connecting imaginatively with the sufferings and unique experiences of others.
- *Forgiveness*: Excusing the errors and faults of others.
- *Prudence*: Making wise judgments in complex trade-offs.
- *Justice*: Giving to each living thing—human and nonhuman—what they deserve.
- *Temperance*: Placing restraint and sustainable limits on patterns of consumption and waste.
- *Sacrifice*: Foregoing personal satisfactions in the name of someone or something else.

- *Solidarity*: Forging ties of obligation between those with more than enough and those with less than enough.
- *Courage*: Facing challenges and reversals without flinching or backing down.

Intercultural Arts

Being good and thinking well do not take place in a vacuum. Persons are social creatures, embedded in a complex web of relationships—social, cultural, and economic. True, in a global market system most of these relations are thin, as thousands of miles separate most producers from most consumers. Names and faces of our economic neighbor are not and cannot be known. This is the case even with strangers who are geographically proximate. Low-wage immigrant workers fill almost every local community and industry, from agriculture and construction to food and domestic services. But the mobile character of their labor only intensifies the impersonal nature of the economic relationships that now extend, in a structural sense, far beyond our kith and kin.

Globalization may render most of our economic ties indirect and impersonal, but those relations still have a profound impact on human and Earth communities. My own consumption habits, for example, rely heavily on the land, labor, and natural resources of poor countries. And my production of waste (in the form of CO_2 emissions) contributes to devastating weather events in those countries. I am connected, for better *and* for worse, to distant strangers.

What does a reasonable morality dictate under these circumstances? Any effort to determine our obligations must first take into account what moral philosophers call *special obligations*. Each of us is clothed in a particular skin, family history, and national identity. In contrast to the thin relations we share with geographically or socially distant peoples, our lives directly and personally touch the lives of family members, schoolmates, Facebook friends, colleagues, and gym buddies. These relationships thicken our social network significantly, and for a simple reason: They are private and proximate. As such, they naturally lay claim to our attention and sympathies in ways that farmers in Mozambique and street children in Manila do not.

For many years I was troubled by the unequal intensity of love I felt for immediate family members. Why should I not feel just as obligated to a suffering girl in South Sudan as I do for my granddaughter? Does some special relationship to my granddaughter ethically allow me to not care for them equally? Only gradually did I realize that the favoritism I felt toward the nearest and dearest in my life was quite natural, even desirable. Kentucky farmer-poet Wendell Berry (2003) helped clarify how devotion thins as it widens.

> I care more for my household than for the town of Port Royal, more for the town of Port Royal than for the County of Henry, more for the County of Henry than for the state of Kentucky, more for the state of Kentucky, than for the United States of America. But I do not care more for the United States of America than for the world. (p. 90)

As noted in chapter 2, the placed nature of human existence and commitment confounds the often idealized notion of global citizenship. Moral experience teaches the impossibility of loving the whole of humanity or nature in anything but an abstract and sentimental way. It's not that we believe that distant strangers don't matter at all; we simply don't believe they matter as much as "our own people." This isn't because we're callous and narrow-minded; it's just that we tend to love and protect what we know, and we can only know a small sliver of humanity—those who become "special" to us through repeated, up-close-and-personal encounters. Love cannot float in empty space.

So, while a globally integrated economy and long-distance air travel make it easier than ever before to encounter people from all over the world, it does not thereby turn strangers into neighbors. When I first began work on this chapter, thousands of unaccompanied refugee children were migrating from Central America to the United States to escape poverty and violence in their native lands. Instead of receiving safe refuge, they were cruelly warehoused and then transported past mobs of anti-immigrant extremists. Eventually they were deported back to life-threatening circumstances. Officials described the situation as a *border crisis*.

In fact, the crisis is ongoing and systemic. As early as 1754, Jean-Jacques Rousseau predicted that capitalist prosperity would come at the expense of widening social inequality. The prosperous few would impoverish themselves through luxury, vanity, and pity toward the poor, even as poor people would increasingly suffer unemployment (through the importation of machines), envy, and chronic unrest. Social solidarity would give way to the *neighbor divide*, a global society of strangers divided within and among themselves by suspicion, scapegoating, and power mongering.

That divide persists today, with profound implications for the intercultural arts. Inequalities of fortune tend to produce social chasms. Over time, economic "winners" and "losers" come to increasingly inhabit two different spatial and social worlds. The winners can afford to live in what political scientist Charles Murray described as social and cultural bubbles. In Los Angeles the bubbliest zip codes include Newport Beach, Santa Monica, and Pacific Palisades. They feature leafy neighborhoods guarded by private security forces and garnished with all the things that socially shield privileged inhabitants from the rest of their society: gated estates, fleets of sport utility vehicles, private schools and health clubs, self-selected associations, deluxe corporate offices, trendy cafés, and upscale shopping centers.

The world of the losers could not be more different. Their social reality includes public housing, crowded buses, failing schools, municipal parks, and underfunded emergency rooms. They often have children without marrying or, if married, are far less likely than winners to stay married and raise children in stable, two-parent households. Virtually every area of their lives contrasts that of the rich: where they live and work, what they eat and drink, how they earn their money, and how their kids are reared and schooled. With rich and poor each living in entirely different galaxies, it's little wonder they communicate with each other only when they have to.

The culprit here isn't ethnic diversity brought on by immigration; it's residential segregation. When people live apart from one another, they don't develop the kind of bridging ties that promote tolerance and trust (Uslaner, 2012). They find relational and ideological safety in a balkanized existence, surrounded by individuals and institutions that look and act and think like them. The result is that people simply know and value and care less and less about people unlike themselves.

How, then, are we to build an enriched common life across our deep and continuing differences? Apart from various policy prescriptions, individuals can work at expanding their circle of concern. They might choose to live in an integrated community (neighborhood or campus) and be intentional about making friends with those different from themselves. Outside of reciprocal relationship, most of us will simply not tune in to the experiences and feelings of others. Imaginative and empathetic engagement with others is the basis of understanding. It is also a prerequisite for any collaborative action aimed at reducing, for example, street violence or the levels of CO_2 in our atmosphere. The biggest problems facing this generation involve other people whose life experiences and perspectives are different from our own. Addressing these problems starts with making conversation with the people most affected by them. Dialogue trains us to transcend our natural proclivity to exclude the stranger from the beloved community of humans. This is especially critical within a growing culture of hate and violence, whether directed against Muslims, people of color, undocumented workers, or sexual minorities.

Table 3.1 maps some of the essential border crossings that define the intercultural arts. Categories of stranger include indigenous persons, sexual

TABLE 3.1. Seven Essential Border Crossings

People of the machine → People of the land	Encounters that enable students to *unlearn* a way of life based on expansion and extraction, combustion and consumption, and to *relearn* new patterns of desire, diet, resource use, and energy consumption
Native-born → Undocumented	Encounters that enable students to grasp the undocumented experience, and how law excludes immigrants from membership in the political community
Racial majority → Minority	Encounters that enable students to comprehend the social and historical causes, contexts, and costs of racial and ethnic inequality
Privileged → Poor	Encounters that enable students to comprehend the "other America"—the largely invisible people stuck in endless cycles of poverty, powerlessness, and despair
Copatriots → Enemy	Encounters that enable students to form friendships with those who their nation defines as *enemy*, while probing the myths and messages that serve to externalize evil and justify violence
Catholic/Protestant → Religious "other"/"none"	Encounters that enable students to participate in the ritual life of the religiously different as a basis for forming friendships, overcoming suspicions, and mining truths
Heterosexual → Gender-queer	Encounters that enable students to probe the relationships between sex, gender, and sexuality through friendship with lesbian, gay, bisexual, and transgendered persons

minorities, undocumented immigrants, devout religionists, and, especially for city dwellers, a systematically wounded environment. World learners are challenged to step into unfamiliar social and natural worlds, and through repeated experiential and intellectual encounters, to turn hostility into hospitality, estrangement into friendship.

World Arts

Border crossing may be the most personal means of building a stronger common life, but it still does not exhaust the goals of the global arts. Over the span of their lifetimes, this generation will need to do more than turn strangers into friends. They will need to figure out how to stabilize the climate, protect biological diversity, reduce fossil fuel energy inputs, feed 10 billion humans, distribute global resources more equitably, defuse terror and nuclear war, and safeguard the rights of the world's most vulnerable peoples. These transnational tasks are not primarily *cultural* (except in the broadest use of the term) and will not be resolved through intercultural understanding alone.

The intercultural arts and the world arts operate symbiotically, supporting each other to foster a multifaceted competence. Without reciprocal care established through authentic friendship, we lack the "Us" consciousness needed to work on problems that riddle the common good. But without public policies that promote the common good, we can't expect the social distance that erodes care and cooperation to narrow. The more sympathetic the relationships are between the powerful and the less powerful, the more sensitive the more powerful become to the problems that disproportionately affect less powerful groups.

Chapter 1 used the metaphor of a perfect storm to signify the convergence of seven global predicaments that threaten to destabilize huge populations across the Earth. When it comes to identifying the priority problems that might provide curricular structure for student engagement, a surprising consensus exists among leading scholars, professional associations, and development agencies (see Table 3.2). Some of the best analysis includes the work of Lester Brown (2009), J.F. Rischard (2003), M.N. Ahmed (2010), Thomas Homer-Dixon (2008), Paul Eurlich (2012), David Pimentel and Marcia Pimentel (2008), and Richard Heinberg and Daniel Lerch (2010). Their scholarship closely parallels the United Nations' Millennium Development Goals, the grand challenges developed by the National Academy of Engineers, and the Principles for a New Urban

Paradigm presented in the UN Habitat manifesto titled *The City We Need 2.0* (UN Habitat, 2016).

Although these issues have global scale and effects, they come together in the challenge of making cities sustainable. The essential meaning of the word *sustainable* is *able to be maintained over time*. Entrepreneur and author Paul Hawken (1993) simply describes it as a *golden rule*: "Leave the world better than you found it, take no more than you need, try not to harm life or the environment, make amends if you do" (p. 139). The question of whether modern society can be made sustainable will ultimately be answered not in the world's rural communities, but in its complex, human-dominated

TABLE 3.2.   Grand Challenges of the Twenty-first Century

Population	Fertility patterns, mortality patterns, aging, disease, migration, urbanization, slum proliferation, refugee flows
Ecology	Topsoil depletion, water shortages, degradation of forests and fisheries, desertification, energy scarcity, biodiversity loss, climate disruption, urban infrastructure
Health	Sanitation, clean water, hygiene promotion, infectious disease, immunization, fluoridation, maternal and child health services, improved nutrition, sexual health and reproductive services
Technology	Solar energy, virtual reality, computer intelligence, robotics, biotechnology rules, nanotechnology, trans-humanism, digital divide, social networking, Big Data, intellectual property rights, cyber-security, privacy and surveillance
Economy	Labor flows, international labor and migration rules, global patterns of production and consumption, trade-investment-competition rules, growing wealth inequality, criminal networks, foreign aid
Conflict	Proliferation of nuclear and biological weapons, state-sponsored terror, subnational conflict, peacemaking
Rights	Gender and equity issues; the rights of children; abuses based on ethnic, racial, sexual, or political identities; global food security; inadequate shelter, education, and healthcare
Governance	State actors, taxation, nonstate actors, failed states, multinational corporations, civil society organizations, international organizations (e.g., United Nations), social movements

cities. Toward that end, research universities like University of California, Los Angeles (UCLA), Princeton, and the University of Helsinki have committed themselves to grand challenge research programs. UCLA, for example, has adopted urban sustainability as its first university-wide Grand Challenges Initiative. Its expressed goal is to make the Los Angeles region 100% sustainable in water and energy without harming biodiversity by the year 2050 (UCLA, n.d.).

Sustainability is an integrative concept that draws on the intellectual resources of virtually all academic disciplines: ecology (carrying capacity, stewardship of land), economics (equitable means of distribution), political science (just world order), world geography (resource distribution), education (world languages and lifeways), nursing (health risks associated with industrialization), psychology (human avarice and aggression), history (sustainable ways of life), sociology (nonexploitive work relations), religion/philosophy (global ethics, models of flourishing), and science/ engineering (e.g., renewable energy, green building). The idea not only brings diverse fields of study into dialogue with each other but also gives them a common vocabulary for talking about an education that is more responsive to the world's vital signs (Orr, 1990; Weissman, 2012). Key educational leaders have gone so far as to mark sustainability as "the ultimate liberal art," summoning the academy to dedicate itself, across all disciplines, to the making of a better world, however incrementally (Rhodes, 2006).

Preparing students, competency-wise, for the next half century will require a global-learning curriculum that integrates direct border crossing with creative, level-appropriate inquiry into various sides of our human predicament (see Figure 3.1). Doing so links an *intercultural relations* approach to a *global studies* framework in an imaginative vision of global flourishing. An integrated model accounts for social goods related to other groups *and* for goods related to the planetary commons. The scale and complexity of modern society renders this highly demanding work, but there is surely no more urgent educational task. In the words of Carol Geary Schneider, past president of the Association of American Colleges & Universities (AAC&U, 2003):

> [W]e have begun to invent a form of liberal education in which the world's most significant challenges—contemporary as well as enduring—become a significant catalyst for new scholarship, new curricula, new sites for learning, and new applications of knowledge. (p. 3)

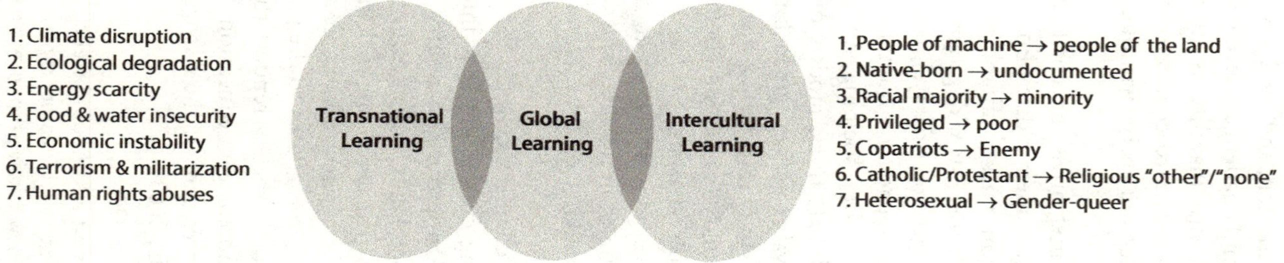

FIGURE 3.2.   Integrated model of global learning.

1. Climate disruption
2. Ecological degradation
3. Energy scarcity
4. Food & water insecurity
5. Economic instability
6. Terrorism & militarization
7. Human rights abuses

Transnational Learning

Global Learning

Intercultural Learning

1. People of machine → people of the land
2. Native-born → undocumented
3. Racial majority → minority
4. Privileged → poor
5. Copatriots → Enemy
6. Catholic/Protestant → Religious "other"/"none"
7. Heterosexual → Gender-queer

Ethical Arts

A fourth dimension of creative artistry expresses the ability of learners to put themselves imaginatively in the circumstances of others, and then to act in ways that enhance the quality of their lives. Our planetary predicament is fundamentally human and ethical. It involves personal judgments and moral choices on everything from the food we eat to the way we travel, how we occupy land, and what we buy. Given our capacity to harm or to heal, the ethical arts define matters of justice and social responsibility.

It merits repeating that making a beautiful life should not be confused with mere career development or with conventional markers of professional success—things like employability, earnings, acclaim, and power. In his 2007 commencement address at Bellarmine University, Wendell Berry sounds this note, profoundly:

> You will have to understand that the logic of success is radically different from the logic of vocation. The logic of what our society means by "success" supposedly leads you ever upward to any higher-paying job that can be done sitting down. The logic of vocation holds that there is an indispensable justice, to yourself and to others, in doing well the work that you are "called" or prepared by your talents to do.

This is the language of ethics—discerning what *ought* to be done on the basis of one's peculiar genius. The ethical arts teach us that we share a measure of responsibility, not only for our own future but also for the future of the world. There is a sweet spot that each of us is obliged to find—a place, in the words of Frederick Buechner (1973), where our deep gladness intersects with the world's deep hunger. Vocation is something much grander and more demanding than knowledge for knowledge's sake or job training for upward mobility. The ultimate dividend for aspiring global artists is to finally look beyond the immediate horizon of one's life to the world beyond, and to use one's talents to help create a better world for their children's children.

Social responsibility continues to be a source of contention within the academy. Some regard it as the lost mission in American higher education, while others consider it a tragic departure from dispassionate scholarship. Recall Stanley Fish's (2012) insistence that higher learning should stick with truth searching and leave extraneous concerns like world saving either to other agencies or one's spare time.

I don't dispute the central importance of academic inquiry to the global arts, at least in theory. There are certain things one must know in order to have a mind capable of understanding complex social realities and the alternative moral choices presented by them. Solid analysis necessarily precedes responsible action. But that is not the same thing as supposing that learning is an operation solely of our minds, rather than a work done through our lives. Education can't help but form character and direct human agency, whether by design or by default. "There is no such thing as a neutral education process," argues Richard Shaull (2000), drawing on Brazilian educator Paulo Freire.

> Education either functions as an instrument which is used to facilitate integration of the younger generation into the logic of the present system, encouraging conformity; or it becomes the practice of freedom, the means by which women and men deal critically and creatively with reality and discover how to participate in the transformation of their world. (p. 16)

The ethical arts aspire to unite the pursuit of truth with the practice of freedom. At its core is the belief that knowledge carries with it the responsibility to see that it is used well. If the twentieth century has taught us anything, it is that formal knowledge of Homer and Augustine, Plato and Tocqueville can easily exist independent of any concrete effort to *apply* their insights to one's social relationships, vocational choices, and personal lifestyles. I may heartily assent, for example, to the overwhelming factual evidence that we're marching into a dark, completely unprecedented climate environment, and even grieve its bleak consequences, but still not see myself as morally implicated whatsoever. The structural links between the privileges I enjoy and the harm I unwittingly inflict remain invisible to me. Rather artlessly I conclude the following: The world is unfair, with benefits and deficits unevenly distributed across the world. My lifestyle choices may contribute to a warming planet, rising sea levels, stronger storms, harsher droughts, and dwindling freshwater supplies. Widespread suffering and even death for the world's most vulnerable people may result. But combined with a billion other causes, rippling out into a trillion little effects over many years and all over the planet, how can I possibly be held responsible? Even if reliable accounting could be done, my impacts are miniscule and thus morally insignificant—so what's the use of changing my behavior?

The ethical arts act to clarify our moral obligations. They do this, first of all, by restraining the human tendency to deny or deflect personal responsibility and to drift into fear and complacency fueled by the highly fraught political moment. Speaking to the ethical challenge of our new climate predicament, philosopher Peter Singer (2004) "puts it in terms a child could understand" (p. 34). He writes:

> As far as the atmosphere is concerned, the developed nations broke it. If we believe that people should contribute to fixing something in proportion to their responsibility for breaking it, then the developed nations owe it to the rest of the world to fix the problem with the atmosphere. (p. 34).

Assuming responsibility and taking aggressive action—as individuals and as nations—is the moral antidote to remaining ignorant and indifferent.

Ethics, then, concerns *how* we use our time, talent, and treasure in the world, and to what consequence. Our actions have a personal and a social dimension. Individual lifestyle choices largely reflect the consciousness with which we experience life and perceive its ultimate meaning. Shifts in that consciousness, mobilized by masses of people, are what drive system reform. The personal *is* political. True, the vast majority of energy and resource consumption, along with pollution and waste production, is generated by commercial, industrial, corporate, agribusiness, government, and military entities—not individuals. But it is also true that the root cause of our existential crises arises from within ourselves: in the way we choose to eat, drink, relate, work, move about, and warm or cool ourselves. Nassim Taleb, in *Antifragility* (2012), insists that creating better systems of command and control cannot prevent the accumulation of global risks within an increasingly complex society. The only way to make global civilization less crush-prone or "antifragile" is by creating the capacity to absorb risks at their source: the level of personal action. The place to begin, then, is not with grand political or technological solutions. Borrowing from the language of the 12-step movement, we start with "a searching and fearless moral inventory of ourselves . . . admitting to ourselves and others the exact nature of our wrongs" (Twelve-Step Program, n.d.).

Personal action is also vitally important in moral terms. Not aligning our actions with our principles, or behaving in ways we obviously know are harmful to people or planet, are clear moral failings. Each person is obliged to do whatever they can to mitigate the damage caused by being a member of industrialized civilization. Unless we, as individuals, are willing to "be the change we want to see in the world," it's unlikely that we will devote the time and energy to act collectively around those issues at local or national levels. The integrity/hypocrisy gap is just too wide.

Personal and social responsibility thus act symbiotically. Change becomes sustainable when it is *socially owned* from the bottom up (individuals, households, and communities) and *legally protected* from the top down (government). Our particular social and geographic positions and life circumstances will obviously shape the actions we choose. But advantaged countries and their citizens are morally compelled to do *something* to maximize good and minimize harm in the world (Pogge, 2008; Singer, 2010; Unger, 1996). Choices, however small, matter.

Conclusion

In the 1880s, Sir Francis Galton popularized the composite photographic technique. By combining several distinct photographs from multiple persons, Galton was able to create a single blended image. Similarly, to create a profile of the essential traits and abilities of a global artist, we superimpose images of intellectual, moral, intercultural, world, and ethical competence. Appendix A offers this composite profile, a response to the question that opened this chapter: *What kind of student-artist do we hope to fashion, for what kind of world?* Carol Geary Schneider (2003) calls this montage of cosmopolitan competencies *integrative learning.*

> A shorthand term for teaching a set of capacities—capacities we might also call the arts of connection, reflective judgment, and considered action—that enable graduates to put their knowledge to effective use . . . to translate their education to new contexts, new problems, new responsibilities. (p. 1)

Integrative learning signals the ongoing liberation of head, heart, and hands toward a restorative presence in the world. A better future doesn't just happen. Fundamentally, it requires millions of small acts and restraints, undertaken by scores of people, and conditioned by a profound sense of responsibility for the fate of people and planet. Creating this shared vision of a desirable world, and furnishing the next generation with the requisite "arts," is the educational task of our times.

The next chapter considers the actual method that might energize this task.

Notes

1. Notable are Ashoka University (a new liberal arts institution located near New Delhi), Habib University (in Karachi, Pakistan), Peking University, Fudan University, Nanjing University, the University of Hong Kong, South Korea's Yonsei University, and the National University of Singapore.

2. The nearest articulation of a liberal education responsive to the Great Work comes from AAC&U (n.d.): "Liberal Education is an approach to learning that empowers individuals and prepares them to deal with complexity, diversity, and change. It provides students with broad knowledge of the wider world as well as in-depth study in a specific area of interest. A liberal education helps students develop a sense of social responsibility, as well as strong and transferable intellectual and practical skills such as communication, analytical and problem-solving skills, and a demonstrated ability to apply knowledge and skills in real-world settings."

A WORLDLY WAY
OF KNOWING

The Learning Arts

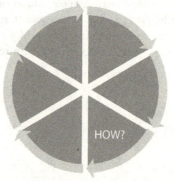

HOW?

*We receive three educations, one from our parents, one from our schoolmasters,
and one from the world. The third contradicts all that the first two teach us.*
— CHARLES LOUIS DE SECONDAT, Baron de Montesquieu

THE ECONOMIST E.F. Schumacher (1975) thought deeply about how education might catalyze the creativity, innovation, and commitment needed to
heal the world's ills. His conclusion was that surface reforms in the organization and financing of universities, though important, were no substitute
for what he called *metaphysical reconstruction*. He warned: "Education which
fails to clarify our central convictions is mere training or indulgence. For
it is our central convictions that are in disorder" (p. 83). As argued in

chapter 2, purposeful education requires more than the mere transmission of information and know-how. It should also provide *know-why* and *how-to*.

Educational commentators today often lament the lost soul of higher education (Glanzer, Alleman, & Ream, 2017; Schrecker, 2010; Smith, 1997). By this they mean the replacement of central convictions by an almost exclusive focus on business-related remedies, whether it be adopting digital learning technologies or promoting workforce-ready skill training. One of the problems with market-driven schooling is that it tends to shape market-driven students. Not long ago I paused midway through an anthropology lesson to query the 20 students: "How many of you are in college for the sheer love of learning?" Two hands went up. One was an honors student who routinely followed me out of class to further discuss ideas that captivated his hungry mind. Students like this are anomalies, as most professors can attest. Most collegians move from class to class, "jumping through the hoops," as one student put it, hoping to earn high grades with a minimum of work. Too many settle for being what William Deresiewicz (2014) calls *excellent sheep*—polite, compliant, striving, praise-addicted, grade-grubbing, and status-focused, with little intellectual curiosity and a stunted sense of purpose. Students are not entirely to blame. They are products of a *system* preoccupied with its own survival and bereft of a substantive vision of the good, the true, and the beautiful that inspires ways of thinking, learning, and acting adapted to the complexities of our eco-socio-techno-sphere. No wonder that the individual and institutional attitude toward promoting the broader social good is largely indifference.

This chapter argues that there is an inescapable connection between unity of purpose and pedagogy. Questions of meaning shape virtually all decisions related to higher learning generally, and global learning in particular. Suppose that you agree with me that the central goal of education is to equip and energize our students for a certain way of being in the world, and not just for a way of thinking. Suppose further that you agree with me that this way of being can be described as living and learning and working toward the common good as a thoughtful, honest, compassionate, and justice-seeking family and community member. How do we foster that way of being? *What teaching/learning process might help to shape the kind of person we need for the kind of world we want?*

Global educators have yet to develop or debate a unified response to this question. By and large, pedagogy has been an orphan child, deprived of adequate attention and care. Lacking a conceptually coherent theory—even with a small "t"—discussions and initiatives go around in circles. The merits of competing learning systems are poorly understood and rarely assessed. Discussions of cutting-edge practices tend to highlight technological opportunities: creating interactive digital platforms, e-books, video clips, Zoom calls, Facebook groups, and Google docs. In the future, we're told, most of the push and pull of academic exchange will take place in interactive virtual spaces, unbounded by geography or even time zones.

What we rarely consider is whether our thinking about learning is evolving in the right way. How do we best prepare the next generation for major global risks that threaten the well-being, if not the survival, of humanity and the biosphere as we know it? Will practices that focus on the transfer of static information via wires and cyberspace keep up with a context of constant flux?

Automated (online) learning, under certain conditions, has distinct and well-reported educational advantages over the cloistered classroom. For centuries the latter has distanced students from social and environmental phenomena within walled-and-gated academic compounds. But when it comes to learning environments, are we left with only two options: either financially unsustainable but physically proximate (face-to-face) classroom learning safely sequestered from the outside world, or a physically distanced, online "University of Everywhere" (Carey, 2015) that asks students to sit, transfixed, before flickering pixels for hours on end? Is it possible to imagine a third way?

These are the questions that concern us in this chapter. Our exploratory response is offered in two parts. Part one explores the soul-shaping power of our epistemology or ways of knowing, teaching, and learning. Then, in part two, we introduce six features of a pedagogy that is worldly enough to engender a fair share of responsibility for the common good.

Part One: Rival Ways of Knowing

The central mission of every educational program is the generation and transmission of knowledge. But that mission presumes that we know *how* we know and *why* (for what ends). What is the role of experience and reason in generating knowledge? And what good does that knowledge contribute to?

Philosophers use a specialized term to describe the nature, source, and purpose of knowledge: *epistemology*. It is here, in the *way of knowing*, that knowledge is shaped. "The way we teach," says Parker Palmer (1993), "depends on the way we think people know." It follows, then, that "we cannot amend our pedagogy until our epistemology is transformed" (p. xvii). In other words, every way of knowing tends to become a way of learning, and ultimately a way of living. It has a moral trajectory and its own ethical outcomes; there is no ahistorical or acultural position. Where we organize world learning programs, what we expect of learners, and how we position them in relation to phenomena all say something about what we value and how we see the world.

Randy and Rachel

Consider for a moment two students represented by Randy and Rachel. Randy, a fictitious communications major from a public university in Illinois, leaves his suburban campus for a semester in Spain. During his sojourn abroad, he is housed, fed, schooled, transported, and entertained with other compatriots. In fact, Randy rarely, if ever, breaks out of the bubble.

Days are spent in foreigner-only classes that expect—and get—minimal academic effort. Then, at night, program mates gather at Western-styled clubs or binge-watch reruns of American TV shows. Somehow Randy finds time each day to upload photos to Facebook and connect via Zoom with his parents and girlfriend back home.[1] But what he dispatches is from a field that he is largely isolated from, and to a home that he never really left. Spain is a little more than a pleasant backdrop for purely individualistic experiences.

Then there is Rachel (last name Corrie), an actual 23-year-old student from Olympia, Washington. In her journal writings published as *Let Me Stand Alone* (2009), Rachel describes her middle-class family ("average American") and her turbulent teenage and young adult years. Emerging from this period a cause-thirsty humanitarian, she obtains a license to fight forest fires and teaches elementary kids organic gardening. Amid full-time studies at The Evergreen State College, she finds time to join a local living-wage campaign and befriend mentally ill people ("Don't we all hear voices?" (p. 168) she asks in her journal). Campus study introduces Rachel to the social change methods of Gandhi and King, and eventually to the "Palestinian Question." What she learns about the confiscation and occupation of lands precipitates a radical awakening. She puts aside her work with various causes in the Pacific Northwest in order to take up Palestinian human rights as a committed peace activist. Come senior year, she proposes an independent-study project that transports her to Gaza in the Palestinian territories. Before leaving Rachel inscribes in her journal: "I am hungry for one thing I can do" (p. 23).

Arriving at the border town of Rafah, Rachel opts to spend most nights with families whose houses are being threatened with demolition. Other times she sleeps outside, at wells, to protect her hosts from bulldozers. Her way of knowing is through deep solidarity and direct immersion in others' social reality. "No amount of reading, attendance at conferences, documentary viewing and word of mouth could have prepared me for the reality of the situation here," she writes (p. 243). "You just can't imagine it unless you see it." The deprivation Rachel witnesses firsthand has the effect of shrinking her world to that of a refugee. In effect, Rachel becomes a Gazan: "Sometimes I sit down to dinner with people and I realize there is a massive military machine surrounding us, trying to kill the people I'm having dinner with."

On March 16, 2003, wearing a bright orange fluorescent jacket and using a megaphone, Rachel stood in the path of an Israeli Army bulldozer to protect the house of the pharmacist's family who she had befriended. After trying to physically block the demolition, the bulldozer pushed her to the ground, crushing her arms, legs, and skull.

Following Rachel's death, people debated whether she was a selfless martyr who gave her life fighting for the tyrannized, or a reckless young idealist who was overwhelmed by political realities she poorly understood. Completely lost in the discourse was the manner in which Rachel oriented herself to the wider world.

Randy could content himself with absorbing fleeting sensations and bits of subject matter without any real emotional investment or authentic local involvement. Rachel, on the other hand, made herself totally available to understanding and addressing a global predicament. She believed that real knowledge had to be grounded in a vital relationship between the knower and the known. Comprehending Palestinian realities, she reasoned, would require dialogue with group members and studied analysis of the historical, cultural, and social context. The real difference between Randy and Rachel had little to do with family background or intelligence level. Where they parted company was in their personal motivations, their unconscious assumptions, and the daily decisions that marked their respective journeys.

Mental Models

We all carry an epistemology around in our heads, although most of us would be hard-pressed to articulate it. As an aid for bringing what is typically unconscious and implicit to a conscious, explicit level, Table 4.1 contrasts, side by side, various core assumptions that orient teaching and learning. Divergent ideas are organized under the headings "conventional" and "worldly." While labels risk reducing highly nuanced ideas to stereotypes and caricatures, they can also be useful shorthand for naming differences. As Randy's and Rachel's field experiences illustrate, the background beliefs we hold about society, knowledge, and the purpose of education can profoundly influence pedagogical practices and learning outcomes.

After reading each of the two statements, you may wish to mark an "x" on the line following each row to indicate your *strongest tendency*.

Now, look at your "x" marks. Toward what side of the table—the conventional or the worldly—did you find yourself leaning? Perhaps neither pole represents your total perspective. The real world of learning, like all richly human activities, is a complex social process that no abstract model can fully define.

The main point of the exercise is to show how different pedagogical approaches position learners in relation to the world in different ways. An exclusive reliance on indoor classes, for example, will likely lead students to believe that learning is a segregated activity that is conducted for certain hours, in certain places, at a certain time of life. By design, the four walls of a classroom are *meant* to effectively shut students out from the "real world." Abstract knowledge *about* the world pre-empts direct experience *of* the world, and becomes an end in itself. Ivan Illich (1971), the iconoclastic priest and philosopher, once aptly described this time-regimented, teacher-fronted, and classroom-bounded system as a situation where pupils are "schooled to confuse teaching with learning, grade advancement with education, a diploma with competence, and fluency with the ability to say something new" (p. 1).

What Illich failed to say is that, under traditional methods, students *do* become more rational, more critical, and more adept at manipulating

TABLE 4.1. Contrasting Pedagogies

	Conventional Pedagogy	Worldly Pedagogy
View of society	Society is fundamentally fair, orderly, and knowable by the human mind. Social relations regress toward equilibrium, stability, and harmony.	Society is essentially power-based as a site of struggle between groups with opposing aims. Social relations tend toward conflict and disequilibrium.
Core values	Most important in society are order, authority, efficiency, "progress," assimilation, and quantitative growth.	Most important in society are freedom, autonomy, change, equity, reflective action, and qualitative growth.
The mind	The mind is a storehouse to be filled with knowledge and skills.	The mind is human potential to be developed through its own activity.
Human knowledge	Knowledge exists "out there," expressed through abstract generalizations. It comes in chunks and bits through an apolitical system of learning.	Knowledge exists in each person's mind and is constructed through personal experience. It is woven from things felt and intuited rather than things defined.
Purpose of higher education	Higher education exists to provide job training for upward mobility: graduates fitted for managerial roles in a knowledge-based, transnational economy (career).	Higher education exists to stimulate discovery, reflection, and informed judgment: graduates acting to continuously improve the context of human and natural life (vocation).
Curriculum content	Curriculum reinforces mainstream cultural values, transmitted to students through texts and "teacher talk," largely divorced from one's personal life and real-world problems.	Curriculum forwards an alternative model of interconnected life that draws upon historical events, the world of nature, relevant ideas, and spiritual truths to address world concerns.

Learning	The transfer of information from subject matter experts (teachers) and other authoritative sources (books, lectures, websites, video, etc.) to students.	The transformation of knowledge from immediate environment (community encounters), voice (lecture, discussion), text (articles, books), and video.
Location	Learning takes place best in physical classrooms, libraries, or in front of computer screens in virtual spaces.	Learning is best conducted in the world, through everyday encounters that inform relevant learning.
Educational processes	Teachers control the learning environment in terms of content, outcomes, and validation (sage on the stage). Learning is organized by academic calendar. Student groups focus on covering material and testing products ("right answer").	Teachers facilitate learning processes that require learner discovery and problem solving (guide on the side). Learning is organized by student goals. Individual students focus on self-paced learning productivity, with assessment of holistic competence.
Role of emotions	Feelings are discussed but rarely acted upon. Questions of reason and fact are paramount.	Perceptions and feelings are often more relevant than facts. Problems are considered value– and emotion-laden.
Products	Credential or degree symbolizes completion of a regimen of learning. Graduates seek self-advancement without questioning the assumptions or structures related to their careers.	Competencies certify learning. Graduates strive to promote what is good or worthy or humane in local communities through their chosen vocation.

words and abstract concepts. Whether conducted online or face-to-face, the linear, decontextualized, information-assimilation model *does* effectively organize and systematically convey large amounts of information. The big question is whether this educational process promotes deep change in learners or enduring value for the world. "It is a matter of no small consequence," writes environmental educator David Orr (1991), "that the only people who have lived sustainably on the planet for any length of time could not read, or, like the Amish, do not make a fetish of reading" (p. 52). Information that is memorized from texts or lectures, then regurgitated in reports or on Scantron test sheets, may not actually be understood through firsthand experience. Knowledge remains inert—known as fact, expressed in words, but unused in real-world situations.

The assumption underlying the conventional learning model is that loads of good content (learning about) will eventually lead to good practice (learning to be and do). In fact, research by Donald Bligh (2000) found just the opposite to be true: Instead of inspiring students to take intellectual risks, facts and theories delivered in lectures actually reinforce the ideas and habits students have already accepted.

That doesn't mean that conventional designs are, categorically, noneducative. Classrooms can be student-centric, just as virtual spaces can be devilishly teacher-centric. What makes any learning process educative is its ability to deeply connect the inner world of the learner with the outer world of lived reality. This usually requires the kind of experience that is immersed and embodied, igniting students' creativity, curiosity, and passion. Some forms of engaged or experiential learning meet these criteria, but certainly not all. Most of us can recall field trips or service projects that were prepackaged, socially confined, and hyper-managed. Spontaneity, authenticity, and complexity were almost completely filtered out. Outcomes were standardized and experience was commodified as experiential—a technical solution to the unwelcome side of classroom-only instruction.

Transforming Experience

Educators have long sought for ways to bring fresh energy and relevance to learning. In ancient Greece, Socrates sat outdoors on one end of a log and compelled students seated on the other end to think through complex problems. Centuries later, modern colleges are still experimenting with more interactive approaches to classroom learning, ones that require more than just listening to the teacher. Catherine Uvarov, a chemistry instructor at the University of California, Davis,

> peppers students with questions and presses them to explain and expand on their answers. Every few minutes, she has them solve problems in small groups. Running up and down the aisles, she sticks a microphone in front of a startled face, looking for an answer. Students dare not nod off or show up without doing the reading. (Pérez-Peña, 2014)

Less theatrical but highly regarded by global educators are high-impact practices (or HIPs) (Kuh & Schneider, 2008). They include study-away trips, collaborative research projects, fieldwork, service-learning, supervised teaching, global internships, and e-portfolios. What distinguishes HIPs is their commitment to bring real-world relevance to the curriculum, often through creative "gown and town" linkages and multidisciplinary project work. Learners invest significant time and effort in purposeful tasks that apply key theoretical insights to pressing community concerns.

There are two other things that are striking about HIPs. One is their *location*. With the exception of highly interactive, classroom-based courses (like first year seminars and capstones), the most impactful learning experiences are expected to take place *off-campus* and in *nonclassroom* settings. The other is the extent to which these pedagogies are garnished with transformational promise. Much of the discourse of global service-learning, for example, projects an expectation that student consciousness *and* institutional cultures can be fundamentally altered through community outreach initiatives.

Many of these "new pedagogies" are not particularly new; people have been learning by doing for centuries. Given that reforms and fads are a constant fixture in the academic world, it is common for some "disruptive" pedagogy to make claims of suddenly transforming the traditional system. Most have proven to be just that—claims. They generally underplay how resistant core educational assumptions and institutional interests are to fundamental change. New York University president John Sexton (2006) once quipped: "Of the 85 institutions in the world today that exist today as they did 500 years ago, 70 of them are universities."

In an effort to restore real-world relevance and soul to the college experience, educators throughout the world are championing new kinds of active, engaged, community-based, and student-centered learning. They

are bridging disciplines, connecting college and community, and applying critical and creative thinking to complex world problems. They are
harbingers of what Cathy Davidson (2017), the director of the Futures
Initiative at the City University of New York Graduate Center, calls a *new
education*:

> [A] redesign of higher education systemically and systematically, from the
> classroom to the board of trustees, from the fundamentals of how we teach
> and learn to how we measure results, award credentials, and accredit in this
> hyper-connected, precarious time.

Twenty-five years ago, Robert Barr and John Tagg (1995) predicted that a
fundamental shift of this kind would take place in higher education, from
a butts-in-seats model of teaching and learning to what they called a learning paradigm of practice. Similarly, Ernest Boyer (1996) called educators to
move from a one-way "spectator" theory of knowledge to what he called a
"scholarship of engagement." Boyer believed that the transformative potential of scholarly work could only be realized by involving students in real
problems besetting human and natural communities. The classroom had a
key role to play in the learning process, but ultimately learners had to step
out of the ivory tower (home campuses), venture off the island (in overseas
settings), log out (from smart devices), and enter the warp and woof of the
world.

Say learners wanted to better grasp drug overdose deaths in the United
States (which rose from 8,200 annually in 1999 to 77,000 in 2017). How
might they start? They could read *Dreamland*, Sam Quinones's (2015) disturbingly illuminating account of the opiate epidemic, or view any number
of YouTube videos on the subject. But ultimately they would need to visit
treatment centers and talk to the addicts themselves. Only then could they
hope to appreciate the full range of causes, the painful cravings and with-
drawals that addicts experience on a daily basis, and the rippling effects on
families and neighborhoods.

Transformative learning is something of a buzzword in higher education
today, but it essentially describes something quite difficult to achieve—a
fundamental shift in one's way of thinking about and being in the world
(Mezirow, 2000). That sets a pretty high bar. After all, how many people
actually enjoy rigorous self-examination and the questioning of cherished
assumptions? Don't most of us prefer emotional security and ideological agreement over contrary situations and intellectual complexity? Our

natural predilection toward social conformity partially explains why most of what we experience in life leaves us unchanged in any fundamental way.

Transformative learning is different. By pushing us out of our physical, intellectual, and cultural comfort zones, it induces a shift in three dimensions of our lives: *psychological* (changes in our sense of self), *convictional* (changes in our basic belief systems), and *behavioral* (changes in our personal lifestyle). This is a far cry from mere head knowledge or being trained in a narrow set of technical skills.

Yet, that still begs the question: What does it mean to have a truly transformative educational experience? What kind of learning process induces consciousness-change? Over the years, I've tried to answer this question by soliciting personal narratives from good friends and graduated students. I ask them to recall a particular incident or event that caused them to look at themselves, or the world, in a radically different way. Once the episode comes to mind, I invite them to unpack it: When and where did it take place? Who was involved? How did the incident unfold? Then, with these details registered, I ask them to explain how the event impacted them. What specific shifts took place in their basic life assumptions and personal lifestyle?

You may wish to pause here and complete this exercise for yourself.
In the process of deconstructing dozens of stories, a number of elements have repeatedly surfaced. The evidence suggests that, in the majority of cases, transformative-type experiences

- are impelled by a desire to improve oneself and the world (vision, passion);
- are stimulated by the unknown (curiosity, playfulness);
- occur in unfamiliar and often difficult settings (complexity, adversity);
- demand an investment of time and energy (intentionality);
- feature direct encounters with the "Other" (contrasting frames of reference);
- require new roles, relationships, or actions (exploration, experimentation);
- expose personal limitations—physical, emotional, and intellectual capacity (inadequacy, vulnerability);
- produce discomfort and disequilibrium (disorientation);

- unsettle "old ways" of thinking or behaving (dissonance);
- require adaptability and improvisation (creativity);
- present opportunities to act on new or revised perspectives (application); and
- are supported by companions or caring strangers (dialogue).

Two things stand out as I consider these qualities of transformative experience. The first is their dramatic effect: Transformative learning permanently revises one's mind-set and way of being. Mezirow (1978) describes this as "a structural change in the way [learners] see themselves and their relationships" (p. 100). But the second is something equally remarkable. In only one or two reported cases did truly life-changing episodes occur in anything resembling a classroom, either virtual or campus-based. In fact, almost uniformly they took place in settings not designed for learning at all: the homes of strangers, city streets, service organizations, wilderness areas, rickety buses, jailhouses, and so on. Transformative experience was embedded in community contexts, activities, and relations. And in almost all cases, no professional teachers were present.

True, not all students seek transformative experience; nor do all fields of study equally invite them. But I can think of no enterprise more oriented to challenge and change than community-engaged global learning. It is distinctively hands-on and socially meaningful. It engages the whole person—body, emotions, intellect, and moral imagination. To the extent that it also requires the negotiation of sociocultural differences, it can also help cultivate a mode of being and acting that supports human flourishing.

The range of firsthand accounts of transformative experience has forced five judgments upon me:

1. Deep learning that significantly influences behavior is usually not the result of teaching (programmed instruction); it is self-discovered and self-appropriated.
2. We learn best not by taking in abstract ideas through our minds, but by doing new things with our *bodies*—things that require risk-taking and carry emotional force.
3. Learning the new involves unlearning the old, which entails an optimal level of uncertainty, uncomfortable questioning, and contained adversity.

4. Knowledge about the world is not the same as wisdom for the world. For responsible action to follow experience, our minds must be gripped by a vision of the possible. Our hearts then respond by engaging, embodying, and engendering that vision.

5. Thinking cannot change while behavior remains largely unaffected. We don't think our way into right acting; we act our way into new thinking.

The implications of these premises are profound, to say the least. In a talk at Harvard University in 1952, Carl Rogers, the founder of client-centered psychology, reflected on his therapeutic experience and the lessons it might hold for a truly learning-centered educational process:

(a) Such experience would imply that we would do away with teaching. People would get together if they wished to learn. (b) We would do away with examinations. They measure the inconsequential type of learning. (c) We would do away with grades and credits for the same reason. (d) We would do away with degrees as a measure of competence partly for the same reason. Another reason is that a degree marks an end or a conclusion of something, and a learner is only interested in the continuing process of learning. (Rogers, 1969/1994, p. 303)

Rogers's unorthodox musings will surely sound fantastic to the modern mind. I can already hear the push-back: "There's no way that do-it-yourself learning can qualify one to become a dentist, nurse, high school teacher, computer systems analyst, lawyer, or dietician. Professional certification is an absolute requirement." In modern society, this may indeed be true, although I would argue that a degree and an education are not the same thing. Credentialing conflates the two, convincing young adults that education is a commodity to be exchanged for status and wealth in the theoretical future. The desired end, in other words, is a good job. Even so, research by Randall Collins (1979) reveals that most job skills are acquired while on the job, and not through formal training. Credentials primarily act as gatekeepers: They restrict entry into highly competitive fields and squeeze out of the job market those who have acquired their knowledge and skills through other means. They are even less a guarantee that college has actually changed the way a person thinks and lives.

Part Two: A Rough Guide to Worldly Learning

Having sketched the general contours of a worldly pedagogy, our attention now turns to the optimal conditions for facilitating transformative global learning. For several decades, an edge of global-education programs has innovated pedagogical models aimed at promoting transformative effects in students and host communities.[2] Of course, no single set of conditions or methods can *guarantee* transformative experience. Like farming, developing human capability is an organic, not a mechanical, process. All that educators can do is properly prepare the soil in which persons will grow, and then plant the seed; they can't control or predict the yield. Similarly, sailors do their best to adjust the sails, knowing full well that they can't direct the wind and sea conditions.

The rough guide that follows suggests a scheme for tilling the soil and trimming the sails for high-impact, community-engaged global learning. It presents six overarching principles, each one distilling insights from a wide range of educational theories and practices (see Figure 4.1). Together

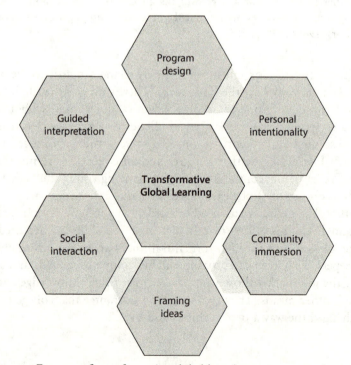

Figure 4.1.   Features of transformative global learning.

they seek to illumine how global learning might be ordered in ways that promote the qualities of transformative experience.

Program Design

Every global-learning program is built around a basic architecture or schema that supports the goals of the sponsoring institution and guides student development in a particular direction. Program designs are artful products. They represent conscious decisions made on everything from where students will learn and for how long to how they'll be housed, taught, and positioned in relation to community residents. Designers and instructors thus exercise significant control over the depth and complexity of student and community learning. This is a good thing according to the editors of *Student Learning Abroad* (Vande Berg, Paige, & Lou, 2012):

> Most students do not meaningfully develop either through simple exposure to the environment or through having educators take steps to increase the amount of exposure through "immersing" them. Instead, students learn and develop effectively and appropriately when educators intervene more intentionally through well-designed training programs that continue throughout the study abroad experience. (p. 21)

The field of education abroad encompasses literally thousands of different programs. We'd expect fundamental differences to exist, for example, between

- a *two-week art history tour* in Europe that requires no second language proficiency, conducts instruction in English, and houses the student group together; and
- a *four-month study-service term* in a nontraditional setting that places students in local families and focuses on independent language and culture learning under the tutelage of host nationals.

No right program exists for all types of schools or students. But nor are all programs equal in their academic, intercultural, and community-development potential. Design decisions invariably carry a certain educational trajectory: they lean toward forming one type of student and away from another. Decisions are further complicated by the fact that every student is at a different level of development. Motivations, life experiences, learning styles, and intellectual abilities vary. Good programs seek to meet learners where they're at and take them to the next level of growth.

It is also true that no aspirational developmental goal—be it intercultural competence or global citizenship—is the result of a single grand journey. Persons evolve through a lengthy, often lifelong, learning process that encompasses times of progress and stagnation, and sometimes even regression. One is always in the process of becoming, never completely arrived. This is why many theorists place intercultural development on a continuum of different stages, phases, and levels of program intensity.[3] Doing so encourages designers to think about global learning *sequentially*— that is, to consider what experiences, in what settings, are developmentally appropriate for different types of students at different points in their lives. A development arc also provides an alternative to the single "significant cross-cultural experience" approach that has become something of a quick fix in efforts to internationalize campuses.

Table 4.2 lists 20 features of program infrastructure, plus three intensity levels. (The features are more fully elaborated in Appendix B.) The model builds upon a classification scheme introduced, and later refined, by Lilli and John Engle (2003, 2012) of the American University Center of Provence, France.

The value that program planners give to each feature (ranging from essential to extraneous) largely depends, as we've said, on institutional mission and student learning goals. A Midwestern university might decide to engage a group of 15 fine arts students in a project that documents the music and dance of Roma/Gypsies in Istanbul's Sulukule neighborhood. In thinking through program infrastructure, a number of questions would immediately arise: At what level—exposure, encounter, or integrative—will the dual purpose of benefiting both students and local residents be met? How will a particular housing choice affect student and resident learning? If students aspire to sing in Turkish, what proficiency level will they need to achieve? Attending to these and other design elements allows us to scaffold the learning potential of different global-learning experiences across students' college experience.

Personal Intentionality

While factors *external* to students (like sociocultural context and program design) profoundly influence student learning, field experiences are

TABLE 4.2. Global-Learning Program Infrastructure

Program Features	Level I: Exposure	Level II: Encounter	Level III: Integration
1. Dual purpose			
2. Destination			
3. Community voice			
4. Duration			
5. Size of group			
6. Diversity of group			
7. Student selection			
8. Student preparation			
9. Housing			
10. Language learning and use			
11. Community immersion			
12. Environmental sustainability			
13. Economic sustainability			
14. Social sustainability			
15. Cultural sustainability			
16. Self-direction			
17. Pedagogy			
18. Organization building			
19. Instruction and mentoring			
20. Sociocultural and disciplinary analysis			

perhaps affected even more by certain *intrinsic* qualities, like motivation, intentionality, and determined effort. Like a theatrical stage, community context and program structure may demarcate the space and circumstances wherein a sequence of action will take place. But what occurs during each scene depends on the actors themselves—how they actually perform.

Student-actors are not blank slates. Each one brings to their learning "stage" a one-of-a-kind amalgam of character qualities, academic abilities, psychological traits, and personal agendas. Some evidence fervent curiosity and initiative, while others struggle to muster sufficient self-confidence and persistence to accomplish tasks without the continuous aid of schedules, classrooms, and staff interventions.

All to say, the chief impediments to transformative global learning are typically more affective than cognitive in nature. Progress toward global competence, as articulated in Appendix A, has much to do with what we desire or long for. Intentionality thus speaks to our inward capacity to pursue certain activities wholeheartedly, and to thereby understand and define ourselves. Educational travel, in Europe and North America as much as in Asia and Africa, involves certain risks. The intentional global learner finds ways to embrace vulnerability and surmount fear.

An oft-repeated truism in learning theory is that novices in any field benefit from the well-timed facilitation of capable mentors (more on that in following sections). And yet children in many traditional societies come to assume adult responsibilities without extensive adult intervention. They imitate and participate. They use trial and error—much of it in the form of play—to learn about their bodies, their immediate environment, and the boundaries of the permissible. As natural explorers, children allow novel experience to be their best teacher. Western societies, in stark contrast, expect young learners to reproduce what the teacher says or the book propounds. School days are filled with alien tasks and unpleasant admonitions. Unsurprisingly, by the time children are adults most of their holy curiosity and natural playfulness has evaporated.

Global educators have long recognized the limitations of learning within the walls of convention. A defining belief has been that the best classrooms are not those surrounded by four walls, fronted by teachers and whiteboards, and linked by corridors. Rather, they are natural, real-world social settings that encourage learners to exercise considerable control over what, when, where, and how they learn. As architects of their own educational process, learners emerge from their improvisation more self-confident and autonomous human beings (Stephens, 2013). Over the years, a remarkable number of returning global learners have declared to me, triumphantly, "I finally became an adult."

Intentionality and directedness have a further educational benefit. The exponential growth in knowledge means that much of what is important today may be irrelevant tomorrow. Teaching today's facts is far less

important than learning how to unlearn, to learn, and to relearn throughout one's life. Rosemary Caffarella (1993) sharpens the point:

> The ability to be self-directed in one's learning, that is, to be primarily
> responsible and in control of what, where, and how one learns is critical to
> survival and prosperity in a world of continuous personal, community, and
> societal changes. (p. 32)

Here it's important not to confuse self-directed global learning with
rootless and aimless wandering. Purposeful learners don't journey through
unstructured space, and their learning projects are neither haphazard nor
solitary. Most want and need flexible structures and intelligent direction,
especially as they wean themselves from more conventional modes of
learning. Comparing bus riding with bike riding has helped me to appreciate the essential difference in learning style. Traditional education is much
like boarding a bus: The head sign indicates where the vehicle is going, the
passengers get on, and the driver controls speed and routing. By contrast,
self-directed learning is more like riding a bike: Riders choose the destination, select the right equipment, set their own goals, and use area knowledge and riding skill to navigate the streets, all at a speed to their liking.

Whether or not students feel ready to fully adopt a cyclo-pedagogy, they
can't avoid making consequential choices before, during, and following
a global-learning term. Will it be a short burst or an extended stay? Will
the primary goal be self-enrichment or civic engagement? Will I hive with
other foreigners or aim to befriend residents? Will I choose experiences
within or outside my comfort zone? These are all questions of purpose and
intentionality. Imprudent learners can sabotage the most brilliant program
design by their everyday choices. But the opposite also holds true: Those
who set clear goals, formulate plans, and refuse to play it safe will find
a way to squeeze high-quality learning from even the most conventional
structures. The clear lesson for global educators is this: If we want people to
become purposeful and empathetic lifelong learners, they must be allowed
to follow their curiosities and passions, shape their own curriculum, and
be responsible for attracting the necessary resources to achieve their learning goals.

Community Immersion

Between the two world wars, cosmopolitan humanists like Polish-born
Bronislaw Malinowski innovated a style of world learning that emphasized

direct participation in, and observation of, the phenomenon under study. Eschewing the leather armchairs and colonial verandahs of an earlier era, fieldworkers designated *community immersion* as the indispensable method for acquiring cultural insight. To deeply understand another social world, they were compelled to leave their native soil and to root in unfamiliar, often unsettling places. There, for an extended period of time (typically one year or more), they would carefully observe and selectively participate in the host community—its organizations and rituals, foods and language, manners and music. Only by "camping right in their villages," wrote Malinowski (1922), could outsiders ever hope to "evoke the real spirit of the natives, the true picture of tribal life." By subjecting themselves to the conditions and constraints under which residents organized their daily lives, world learners could hope to "grasp the native's point of view, his relation to life, to realise *his* vision of *his* world" (p. 25).

Most world-learning programs do a brilliant job of organizing academic *content* on global topics into a coherent curriculum. Where too many flounder, however, is in providing the optimal *process* and *context* for investigating those issues firsthand. Formal lectures within indoor classrooms tend to induce passivity rather than inspire the needed passion and commitment to apply knowledge in real-world contexts. John Dewey (1938/1997), America's most influential thinker on education, warned of a standing danger: "that the material of formal instruction will be merely the subject matter of the schools, isolated from the subject matter of life-experience. The permanent social interests are likely to be lost from view" (p. 8). For Dewey, learning and living, the personal and the social, were indivisibly connected to the social good.

Transformative global learning is fundamentally *embodied* learning, an induction of the whole self into a world full of surprises, novelty, ambiguity, and often distress. Learners *re-situate their bodies* in order to *engage their minds* with the experiences and perspectives of others. Erving Goffman (1989), a leading American sociologist, captured this critical link between immersion and insight:

> It's a matter of getting data . . . by subjecting yourself, your own body and your own personality, and your own social situation, to the set of contingencies that play upon a set of individuals, so that you can physically and ecologically penetrate their circle of response to their social situation, or their work situation, or their ethnic situation, or whatever. (p. 125)

In other words, perspective transformation begins not with taking new ideas into our mind, but by doing new things with our bodies. Denis Goulet (2006), a Notre Dame development ethicist, described this indispensable condition among change agents as "existential insertion in a mode of structural vulnerability" (p. xxxi).

Perhaps Dorothy Day, cofounder of the Catholic Worker movement, best exemplifies the community immersion principle in world learning. As a teenager, she stumbled upon Upton Sinclair's *The Jungle* (1906/ 1985), which described with brutal realism the life of those working in the filth-ridden stockyards of Chicago. Deeply affected by what she read, Day began to take long walks amid the urban desolation of Chicago's South Side. "I walked for miles, exploring interminable gray streets, fascinating in their dreary sameness, past tavern after tavern" (p. 40), she later wrote in her autobiography, *The Long Loneliness* (1952/1996). What she witnessed—the degradation of the city's stockyards and slaughterhouses, the racial segregation, the grim economic realities—stirred an awareness of injustice and led to a reordering of her life values. Thus began her deep, lifelong immersion in the neighborhoods of the down-and-out. Day was a first-rate student, and books were both her constant companions and lifelong mentors. But she understood all too well that the key to solving seemingly insolvable social problems was not to be found in study alone. Day believed that we change our life not by taking in abstract concepts and moral principles, and then hoping that, somehow, we will make ethical application in our life. Instead, we change our lives by changing the way we process experience. And to change the way we process experience, as Franciscan theologian Richard Rohr (2003) points out, we don't *think* our way into new ways of living; instead, we *live* our way to new ways of thinking.

Cultural immersion, especially among society's outcasts, has gotten something of a bad rap in global-learning circles. Some educators are rightly concerned about commodifying poverty and turning strangers into objects of voyeurism. Others associate it, wrongly, with "going native," a derogatory phrase that signifies over-rapport with a given social situation and the loss of critical distance. Although it is certainly possible for someone to become so involved with a community that they lose objectivity, this is hardly a hazard for the average collegian.

As a pedagogical principle, immersion finds its counterpoint in the wisdom surrounding expert intervention in the learning process (Vande Berg et al., 2012). Years ago, anthropologist Erik Cohen (1972) made the case for a right balance of challenge and support in global learning. Cultural outsiders, he maintained, are "able to enjoy the experience of change and novelty only from a strong base of familiarity, which enables them to feel secure enough to enjoy the strangeness of what they are experiencing" (p. 166). According to Cohen, too much disequilibrium and learners would be apt to socially withdraw, often within the protective walls of a foreigner bubble. But the reverse also held true: too much stability and learners would lack what psychologist Nevitt Sanford (1967) specified as "the internal or external stimuli needed to upset the existing equilibrium, make new responses, and expand their personality" (p. 51). Rich, productive learning requires healthy doses of challenging experience with the support of a community of practice.

Framing Ideas

The foregoing should not suggest that conceptual knowledge is in any way dispensable, a trifling adjunct to direct experience. Shifts in consciousness require the *interaction* of the experiential and the cognitive. The quaking and shaking that results from physical displacement may push students out of their cultural headspace. But that doesn't mean they will automatically understand what is happening to them. Action and reflection are interdependent: Individuals can't set aside their cultural prejudices, for example, until they understand *why* other people do things the way they do.

The stakes of acting in ignorance are especially high when it comes to community interventions in the form of homestays, clinicals, practica, internships, or research projects. In such cases, appeals to the Golden Rule—to do unto others as one would wish done to oneself—may not provide sufficient guidance for making ethical decisions. Just because I might wish something done to me does not mean that someone else would want the same for themselves. Ethical action begins not with *what* we can do to aid others, but with understanding *why* there is a problem.

I'm old enough to recall the media coverage of the devastating Ethiopian famine during the years 1983-1985. News reports projected images of the emaciated bodies and plaintive wails of starving children and despairing parents onto television screens worldwide. Tens of thousands of people were understandably aroused to do something to relieve the suffering.

Masses of people gave generously. Tragically, that money did little to transform the on-the-ground political realities that fueled the crisis in the first place. What the reporters failed to adequately present was the crucial social and political *context* of the famine. Because the public was unable to answer *how* and *why* the children were dying, they were prevented from intervening on the basis of an accurate understanding of a complex situation.

Consider another illustrative, albeit fictitious, case featuring two groups of global learners. The first group consists of eight microbiology students from Iowa, studying abroad through a local university in Nairobi, Kenya. Through their studies, they learn of a mutation that protects some Black people from malaria. Because their learning is restricted to the classroom, the empirical information they acquire lacks any vital connection to actual mosquito-infestations in the city's informal settlements.

A second group is comprised of adventuresome British backpackers. They follow their footloose curiosity through the lanes of Kibera, the largest of Nairobi's slums, observing the rhythms of everyday life and informally speaking with mothers about family health burdens. Although they succeed in acquiring an experiential awareness of the major communicable diseases, they are hard-pressed to explain the root causes in biological and environmental terms.

In this scenario, both groups will have gained valuable forms of knowledge: one of the head (conceptual) and the other of the heart (experiential). However, if the purpose of learning is to transform fragments of information into an intelligent response, both are likely to come up short. The microbiology students will have obtained formal knowledge but absent experiential understanding; the backpackers will be able to boast of eye-opening experiences but without conceptual hooks to hang them on. Responsible action in the world requires intuitions *and* cognitions, direct experience *and* intellectual analysis. When the natural partnership of intellect, emotion, and body is dismantled, the potential for transformative learning is lost. Goulet (1995) states the matter bluntly: "Love without disciplined intelligence is inefficient, naïve, and in its bungling good intentions, catastrophic. And intelligence without love breeds a brutalizing technocracy that crushes people" (pp. 193-194).

If we accept *affective intelligence* as a covetable learning outcome, the question then becomes: Where might students find the necessary framing ideas? Informative lectures, e-books, and visual media are, of course, staple sources. Literature by authors from other cultures and countries is especially good at stimulating what Martha Nussbaum (1997) terms a *narrative imagination*. The ability to contemplate lives different from our own is key to developing a complex understanding of the world and its peoples. Consider how Ta-Nehisi Coates and the late Toni Morrison have helped Americans understand African American realities; how Jhumpa Lahiri has illuminated South Asian immigrant psychology and behavior; and how Khaled Hosseini's powerful storytelling has opened windows on Afghanistan. Literature offers lessons in the broader human experience that help us decode the world around us.

Needless to say, a near infinitude of information, on virtually any subject, is available over the Internet through mobile devices. And yet it is precisely this glut of data that presents global learners with real hazards. For all its wonder, searching the Web is like trying to take a drink from a fire hydrant: The overwhelming volume gets us wet but it doesn't allow us to drink deeply. Transformative learning is not simply about the transfer of data, information, or perhaps even "knowledge." The brain is more than a blank hard drive waiting to be filled with data. This is why Mark Bauerlein (2009), editor of *First Things*, is largely dismissive of the educational benefits of online study. Citing multiple studies to make his case, he judges that very little reading goes on with the Internet at all. For the most part, what takes place is superficial skimming that utterly undermines the reader's ability to meaningfully engage the text and to develop the capacity for critical reading and thinking. Philosopher Hannah Arendt warned of a generation becoming "atomized," sucked alone into systems of nonstop electronic information and mindless entertainment that make it impossible to build relationships and structures that are vital for civic engagement.

Social Interaction

Suppose a group of learners succeed in physically embedding themselves in a challenging fieldsite to explore one of the big issues of our time. Let's further assume that literary study has stretched their emotional and mental awareness of those issues with little or no formal instruction. Will immersion, intentionality, and scholarly study inevitably produce deep empathy for and understanding of characters *outside* the text? How important are *direct relationship* and *embodied interaction* in shaping how a person feels, thinks, and ultimately acts in the world?

Bus riding may offer some clues to answering these questions. As narrated in this book's Introduction, buses in major multicultural centers like Los Angeles are literally a world-on-wheels. Fifty or 60 riders from assorted racial, ethnic, linguistic, social class, and religious backgrounds are confined to a 250-square-foot area. Opportunities to engage strangers in conversation are immediate and abundant. And yet most bus commuters choose to sit in silence, utterly absorbed in their smartphone or simply staring out the window. With everyone in a personal bubble, almost no direct eye contact or pleasant conversation is made. The same unspoken rule of noninterference seems to apply to other public spaces, from subways and trains to public parks. In each case, mere physical presence provides no guarantee that members in the setting will meaningfully interact with the strangeness that surrounds them.

After a lifetime of research on human development, Soviet psychologist Lev Vygotsky (1978) concluded that, when it comes to altering consciousness, it's not what happens *around* us that matters, but how we *interact* with and think about those happenings. Knowing and learning, it turns out, are communal acts. Growth in mental and social capacity depends on the frequency, variety, quality, and intensity of interaction with others, and especially with those who know and do things that we do not.

Vygotsky represented this learning edge as the *zone of proximal development*: "the distance between the actual developmental level as determined by independent problem solving and the level of potential development as determined through problem solving under adult guidance or in collaboration with more capable peers" (p. 86). In other words, it is through *relationship* with more capable others—natives, mentors, or facilitators—that we learn more than what is possible in isolation or left to our own devises.

In a similar vein, Kwame Appiah commends "making conversation" (2013) as the first and most important step in world learning. Conversation helps us get used to each other—our respective stories, outlooks, hopes, and fears—without feeling the need to force our beliefs on the other. In cross-cultural contexts, outsiders learn to evaluate other people's ideas and behavior from within a native frame of reference. Beliefs on controversial issues like human sexuality and the death penalty can be seen as responsive to reasons. This is what breaks down prejudice and exclusion. In an interview for National Public Radio, Appiah (2013) notes that:

One of the most powerful reasons why America is less homophobic than it was when I came to it nearly 30 years ago is because lots of gay people came out and started talking to people who weren't very comfortable around gay people, and suddenly those people discovered that you could be comfortable around gay people. Then they got angry that other people were not being nice to them.

The give-and-take involved in honest conversation requires genuine interest and vulnerability. Instead of setting out to "win," there is a willingness to grasp and affirm another's truth. Of course, this is much easier advocated than achieved. Humans have a natural tendency to favor information that confirms their beliefs and to disfavor information that counters them. They do reason, but their arguments aim to support their own economic and cultural interests.

This point was driven home to me years ago on a trip through southern Ethiopia with one of the nation's leading adult educators. Although Ethiopian by birth, he had lived for over 20 years in the United States where he earned a doctorate and founded a successful leadership training organization. As we rolled through the countryside in his late-model Land Rover, he pointed to a cluster of small thatched huts surrounded by cultivated fields. "Can you believe it, Richard?" he announced in a condescending tone. "These farmers have all this land but they still choose to live in huts. Their mental poverty is pathetic." Caught off guard, my immediate impulse was to react with a defensive counter-attack. Instead, I managed to keep my cool enough to calmly respond: "Maybe they don't care for a big house," followed by, "Why don't we stop and ask them?" My host replied with a dismissive chuckle. I turned to silently gaze out the window.

Contrast this case of aloof detachment with the empathetic interaction described by Grecia, an undergraduate global studies major, after a week-long village stay in India:

During my time in the village, I was never with one specific family but often roamed around the village from house to house trying to make a connection with those that invited me in, whether it was with the elders, children, young girls, or women in the community. Language often became a barrier when asking questions or listening to stories. There were moments, however, where the barrier actually served as a form of empowerment. We found new ways to transfer our thoughts and feelings through simple words and lots of observation. Afternoon conversations invariably ended up with lots of laughter, some understanding, and a clear sense of mutual caring, despite our real differences.

Accounts like these are becoming increasingly rare. In the brave new world of instant information flows and electronic connectivity, we have learned to expect more from technology and less from each other. Within our lifetimes the full immersive power of virtual reality and artificial intelligence could make it possible for millions of people to experience distant strangers in ways akin to inhabiting their body. Peoples and places will be experienced—*really* experienced—with all the actual sights, smells, touch, and interaction. With full cultural immersion available through virtual body technology, it's not difficult to imagine masses of educational travelers opting to stay home in order to learn abroad, courtesy of the nearest virtual reality delivery location.

Immersive digital experiences that mimic reality have the potential to give people empathetic insight into other ways of life, along with the environmental challenges they face. The question is whether any virtual medium can ever hope to approximate the interactional struggle and the full range of sensory inputs—the tiny signals from the eyes and voice tone, the warm laughter and hugs, the assorted awkwardness—that made Grecia's encounter with the villagers so impactful. Harvard psychiatrist Edward Hallowell (1999) doesn't think so. What virtual learning lacks, says Hallowell, are "human moments" that require people to do two things: *share the same physical space* and *capture each other's emotional and intellectual attention*. Without emotional investment and visceral connections, people lack the commitment to learn as much as they can. We need only imagine conducting our most cherished relationships—like marriage—via Zoom or Facebook. Although we might achieve a certain level of communication, emotional and social progress would likely stall.

Guided Interpretation

Thus far, we've argued that transformative global learning involves a continuous movement between a quality program design, learner intentionality, immersive experience, framing ideas, and undiluted interaction. A final condition is the ability to appraise reality in ways that lead to informed action.

I can still recall when Haley (a pseudonym), a bright and adventurous undergraduate, reported to me how eye-opening and life-changing it was to spend a month dispensing material comfort and company to dying destitutes at Kalighat, the hospice Mother Teresa founded in Kolkata. At one point in our conversation, Haley began to well up with tears as she described a workplace of hollow-eyed patients on plank beds, and a surrounding area dominated by grim slums and gridlocked traffic. Leaning forward, I gently probed: "How do you explain the deprivation and desperation that you witnessed? What root causes did you uncover?" After an elongated pause, she replied, "I have no idea."

Haley's exposure to Kalighat was intensely personal, even revelatory. What it lacked was a reflective process capable of mining the deeper *whys* and *hows* behind the confounding *whats*. Without a mechanism for making sense out of what we are seeing or doing, opportunities for transformative learning readily devolve into highly personalized, one-off, been-there-done-that episodes, with little educational value. Psychologist George Kelly (1963) famously underscores the point:

> A person can be a witness to the tremendous parade of episodes and yet, if he fails to keep making something of them, he gains little in the way of experience from having been around them when they happened. It's not what happens around him that makes a man experienced; it is the success of construing and reconsidering of what happened, as it happens that enriches the experience of his life. (p. 73)

Sensational experiences in cross-cultural settings often leave learners with aroused emotions but a vacant mind and imagination. The pedagogical puzzle is not how to get people stirred up or even informed (we are absolutely suffused with information); it's how to get people to *think*—to interpret that information in its broader context. David Kolb (1984), following Dewey, emphasized this imperative in the two interpretative operations of his four-stage experiential learning cycle (Figure 4.2).

For experiential educators like Kolb, what matters most is not head knowledge, or even unforgettable experiences. It is the ability to mull over knowledge and experience until it changes the way we perceive and act on the world. Reflective observation and abstract conceptualization signal the process of transforming knowledge *of* the world into wisdom *for* the world. Far from automatic, data fragments and lived experience must be

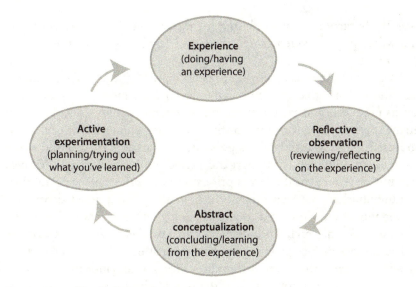

FIGURE 4.2.   The Kolb learning cycle.

methodically recaptured and pondered in order to explain *why*, exactly, things are the way they are.

A team of students might decide to investigate mass murder in the United States, one of our most vexing domestic problems. Over 345 mass shootings took place in the United States in 2017, killing 14,000 and wounding 29,000. This was many times the gun homicide rate in Canada, Sweden, and Germany combined. What explains these gross disparities? Is the problem too many guns in the hands of too many people? Poorly managed mental illness? Violence-saturated Hollywood films and video games? An expansive war culture? Assuming there is no single cause of the violence, the researchers would be challenged to sort out a tangle of factors.

Their first step would be to establish a base of concrete sense experience. They would need to interact, as directly as possible, with facets of their home culture where violence manifests. Unfortunately, there are all too many entry points: the 40-billion-dollar arms industry; the three-million-strong National Rifle Association; the vast network of federal and state prisons; political attack ads and war rooms; desperate gangsters in over-crowded and segregated urban pockets; the so-called "intimate terrorism" of domestic violence; blockbusters like *American Sniper* and *Fifty Shades of*

Grey; the burgeoning porn industry; the rape culture on college campuses; and wildly popular video games like *Grand Theft Auto*, *Mortal Combat*, and *Until Dawn*.

All of these American institutions and cultural forms offer a window into the violence that is deeply ingrained in the American psyche. Each has its producers and members, its consumers and victims. Global learners might select any one (or more) of the institutions, interact with its forms and participants as intimately as possible, and carefully register and weigh the range of opinions. To support this period of *reflective observation*, learners carefully review the most relevant prior studies on mass violence. Published and unpublished materials present the key concepts and policy debates on a given topic. With enhanced conceptual sensitivity, students are better prepared to make interpretative judgments based on their personal experience.

The exercise of interpretative imagination naturally leads to *abstract conceptualization*. Here the research team looks for key conclusions and public policy prospects that could reduce the risk of similar events of rampage violence. At root is the question of whether or not mass shooting events can be predicted and prevented. If they can, what individual and institutional factors can be controlled? What measures to reduce the risk factors are politically feasible?

The abstract conceptualization dimension of transformative global learning also involves an inward journey of self-appraisal: How does violence manifest in my own life? In what ways does my own intolerance, unfair judgments, and aggression connect with violence-infused social structures? What do I need to do or refrain from doing to wage peace? Mature thinkers are able to take ill-defined social problems, connect them cognitively to the reality of human corruption, and finally compare their self-observed behavior against some standard. Self-generated judgments of this kind might seem to require high levels of cognitive and moral development. But they play an indispensable part in helping global learners regard change in personal behavior within their relational radius as a proximate solution to seemingly insoluble social ills.

Finally, the quality and potential impact of learning is deepened as individuals encounter examples of the ideas under study, and then engage in the processes of interpreting, applying, and evaluating those ideas. As previously noted, reflective practitioners and teachers play crucial roles as models, networkers, encouragers, and dispensers of timely advice and cultural knowledge. Mentor-teachers promote transformative experience not only by helping protégés craft project plans but also through a process of reflective dialogue where they help mentees evaluate evidence and arguments as they search for a common understanding of the relationship between theory and data. Without the aid of able integrators of in-field and online learning experiences, most young adults find it exceedingly difficult to generate fresh insight about social life. Effective mentoring is a critical determinant of success, whether dispensed by program directors and faculty leaders or by nonprofessionals like host family members and community activists.

Conclusion

The Great Work of advancing a more just, beautiful, and prosperous world calls for a learning process that equips persons to do that relative good which is possible now. In this chapter we began to envision a dynamic and flexible educational ecosystem that is *learner-centered* and *community-driven*. At the heart of that system are learners in relationship with an open and evolving community of coeducators, each with shareable skills and knowledge. They include national campuses, local families, grassroots organizations, online learning platforms, skilled mentor-teachers, hyper-texts, and a variety of mobile apps. Each hosting space supports diverse learner interests that connect to real-world problems in local communities.

Traditional schools and universities perpetually struggle with the question of how to create learning spaces that shape wise, empathetic, self-directed, and artful persons. History will likely reveal that education was most enlightened when it was most "worldly," when it intimately connected the inner world of self- and conceptual understanding with the broader world of other living beings, learning with and from each other.

Transformative global learning, it turns out, shares much in common with good farming. To be gainful, both must employ local immersion, intimate involvement, careful observation, accurate information, deep caring, extended commitment, patient deliberation, and hopeful practice. These are the qualities that enrich the human experience, whether acted out on a domestic or an international stage.

Notes

1. "A University of California-Santa Barbara researcher found one group of students averaging 4.5 hours per day online, and 83% of their contacts were with other Americans, either at home or in the country they were visiting" (Pope, 2011).

2. Among the vanguard of these programs are the University of Minnesota's Studies in International Development (MSID), World Learning's School for International Training (SIT), and the International Partnership for Service Learning (IPSL). Each one stands on the shoulders of experiments made during the 1960s and 1970s, including the field study programs at Michigan State University and Cornell University.

3. David Hoopes (1981) proposes "Stages in Developing an Intercultural Perspective"; Theodore Gochenour and Anne Janeway (1993) "Seven Concepts in Cross-Cultural Interaction"; Alvino Fantini (2006) four "developmental levels"; and Milton Bennett (1993) "Six Stages from Ethnocentrism to Ethnorelativism."

FROM DOORSTEP TO PLANET

Redrawing the "Field"

I must attempt to care as much for the world as for my household.
Those are the poles between which a competent morality would balance and mediate:
the doorstep and the planet.
— WENDELL BERRY, *The Long-Legged House*, 1969

AMONG THE MEMORABLE characters in Charles Dickens's novel *Bleak House* is the formidable Mrs. Jellybe. Of aristocratic birth, and intent on solidifying her status through charity, she resolutely devotes every waking hour to projects designed to relieve suffering in distant Africa. All the while she ignores the plight of the ill-fed, poorly clothed, and untended members of her own household, and at her own doorstep.

Like Mrs. Jellybe, global educators have dedicated themselves to expanding their knowledge of distant peoples and places. For over 100 years, they have employed geographically marked language—like *distant* lands, *overseas* study, education *abroad, offshore* and *international* education—to define their

109

work. World learning was expected to mainly take place across a body of water or geopolitical border. The pattern persists today. Techno-economic and sociocultural integration may be the chief drivers of our age, transcending all national boundaries, but global education continues to be largely organized around the opposition between the faraway and the nearby. *Global*, almost exclusively, is identified with *international*—that is, with places geographically, rather than socioculturally, distant from home. We might call it the "Mrs. Jellybe syndrome."

This condition has produced notable achievements. Education abroad professionals have created a stunning array of overseas study and service opportunities. Many have earnestly synthesized literature from allied fields—like anthropology, sociology, political economy, literature, and applied linguistics—to explore global issues with a transdisciplinary bent. Global learners can now pursue their personal and professional interests almost anywhere on the planet.

At the same time, the actual mapping of global learning is undergoing critical re-evaluation. Much of the scrutiny surrounds the question of "field" or place:

If global learning is to help mend the world, where—in what settings or locations— should we expect students to best learn how?

What follows ventures a tentative response. It proposes a basic geographic redrawing of world learning to include vital engagement with ideas, identities, human organizations, and ecologies within multicultural *domestic* settings. Perhaps more controversially, it makes the case for a *tactical progression* of worldly experience from the nearby (doorstep) to the faraway (planet). The effort to reposition the local/regional as priority field is not meant to force an either/or choice between education at home and education abroad. The aim is much more sublime: to bring the domestic and the international into a dynamic, both/and dialogue that rebalances the territorial locus of global learning.

The chapter unfolds in three parts. Part one explores the disciplinary borderlands of home and field, complicating both. Part two analyzes two impediments to constructing a more inclusive model of global learning: the first, an undomesticated cosmopolitanism, and the second, the stubborn partitioning of internationalism and multiculturalism. Finally, part three proposes two pedagogical repairs for the institutional rift. The first, presented through a four-fold rationale, is to begin global learning at home. The second urges students to connect domestic learning to projects in international settings, allowing for rigorous comparison and selective borrowing of lifeways critical to constructing vital responses to the challenges of the twenty-first century.

Part One: Disciplinary Borderlands

There is nothing mere to the local.

— ARJUN APPADURAI, *Modernity at Large*, 1996

Today, nearly every academic field is preoccupied with the interface between the national and the international. Anthropology provides an especially salient example. As mentioned in chapter 4, since the time of Bronislaw Malinowski anthropology has been distinguished by the practice of fieldwork. The *field* was understood as a rather fixed entity—typically, a semi-isolated, technologically simple, small-scale tribe or village that was inhabited by exotic others and located in distant lands. Sites of exploration and discovery were almost always *there*, rather than *here*.

The opposition between home and field in early (eighteenth century) anthropology and sociology was grounded in a number of familiar dichotomies: modern/primitive, first world/third world, West/Rest, North/South, center/periphery, familiars/strangers, nearby/faraway. These oppositions reflected the fact that most of fieldwork during this time was undertaken in outposts of Western colonial empires. This imperial network included Native Americans in the United States, recognized by the federal government as *domestic dependent nations*.

French anthropologist Claude Lévi-Strauss, in *Tristes Tropiques* (1955), explained these binaries as cultural products spawned through Euro-American capitalist expansion into the purported New World. In time, the totalizing and differentiating logic that supported colonial rule could no longer hold up to empirical and political scrutiny. But not before dichotomous language became naturalized, whether along the lines of gender (male travel versus female domesticity), social class (bourgeois traveler versus soulful poor), race/culture (White moderns versus dark-skinned primitives), or place (Europe and North America versus Asia, Latin America, and Africa).

It took fieldwork in Western domestic settings to gradually break down the binaries. Beginning with the Chicago School in the 1920s and 1930s, the attention of nonanthropologist scholars—urban sociologists, social historians, geographers, and cultural studies specialists, among others—turned to burgeoning U.S. cities. Their studies of groups and communities featured complex articulations of race, social class, ethnicity, gender, and sexuality. Like the faraway-focused anthropologists, the nearby scholars sought to make the familiar strange and the strange familiar. But unlike the anthropologists, domestic researchers were unburdened by geography. Gradually a perspectival shift took place. Robert Park (1925), the famed University of Chicago sociologist, was among the first to recommend the ethnographic method for investigating domestic realities:

> The same patient methods of observation which anthropologists like Boas and Lowie have expended on the study of the life and manners of the North American Indian [i.e., non-Western cultures] might be even more fruitfully employed in the investigation of the customs, beliefs, social practices, and general conceptions of life prevalent in Little Italy on the lower North Side in Chicago, or in recording the more sophisticated folkways of the inhabitants of Greenwich Village and the neighborhoods of Washington Square, New York. (p. 2)

Park's declaration predated by decades the dramatic demographic shifts set in motion during the second half of twentieth century. Extensive migrations would radically redraw the map of home and field, especially in metropolitan areas. The shorthand term—*globalization*—indicates a world no longer confined to sovereign borders. Goods, capital, and people are all on the move, nothing staying in their places. Today, world cities like New York, Los Angeles, and London are not only command centers for transnational corporations but also extraverted centers of meeting and mixing for the world's cultures, classes, and creeds. The result is innumerable "contact zones" where peoples once geographically and historically separated now "meet, clash and grapple" (Pratt, 1991, p. 501).

All to say, the Other now meets us at our regional doorsteps. Mark a 25-mile radius line from my residence in Los Angeles County, and you will have what is perhaps the greatest diversity of language, cultural tradition, religion, food, and music found anywhere in the world. The population boasts a 10-million-strong minority majority that includes a dazzling kaleidoscope of groups—Latinos and Blacks, Chinese and Thai, Filipinos and Arabs, Koreans and Indians, Iranians and Samoans, to name just a few. The poor and working class, those who can't afford to travel the world, now find the world traveling around them. The educational implications, as travel writer Pico Iyer (2000) notes, are defining: "There is the sense that learning about home and learning about a foreign world can be one and the same thing."

Los Angeles may be an extreme case. But in 78 counties in 19 states (including California) minorities now outnumber Whites. In the fast-approaching future, what geopolitical analyst Robert Kaplan (1998) experienced during an evening dinner in Santa Monica is becoming the norm:

> I sat down at an outdoor Thai-Chinese restaurant for an early dinner. The manager was Japanese, the hostess Iranian, and the other help Mexican . . . On the sidewalk beside my table a large crowd watched a Black youth tap dance to Brazilian music. (p. 2)

Home, as experience teaches us, is not simply territorial; there are also social and psychological dimensions. A White, suburban-bred American thirty-something may actually have more in common with her upwardly mobile counterpart in New Delhi or Barcelona than with immigrant service workers in her own hometown. Geography has no special claim on diversity. Nor on marginality. Multiethnic cities tend to be unequal cities. The same place that *includes* high-value people into its "network society" also excludes low-value people within its depressed neighborhoods and expendable jobs. No doubt there are corners of North America and Europe that are still predominantly monocultural, monoclass, and monolingual, but they are harder and harder to find. In most places, the traditional boundaries of home and field have been permanently transgressed.

This presents global educators with one of those precious "aha!" moments. Since its modest beginnings in the year 1190, when Emo of Friesland traveled from northern Holland to study at Oxford University, the international-education narrative has drawn a clear boundary line between *civic engagement* at home and *education abroad* in geographically distant locations. The *global* in global learning has largely been situated in the international, even as its *learning* has been defined by the alleged strangeness of faraway peoples and places.

Acknowledging this reality doesn't erase the special distinctions of domestic and international locations. International sojourns often reveal life-and-death issues that we seldom face at home. Human and ecological degradation is obviously far greater in Dacca and Freetown than in

London or San Francisco. At the same time, we need to ask whether a semester in Oaxaca, Mexico, will *inevitably* prove more broadening for middle-class non-Latinos than a semester in East Los Angeles or Hialeah, Florida, both of which are over 95% Latino and poor. The precise lines that separate doorstep and planet are often difficult to draw. Even so, this isn't an argument for collapsing the international into the domestic (or vice versa). Our interest is simply to *enlarge the canvas* on which the art of world learning is performed.

Global educators labor in a field between fields, allowing them to be highly fluid and synthetic. So it is somewhat surprising that we have yet to settle on language that adequately fits contemporary reality. Today, "one no longer leaves home confident of finding something radically new, another time or space," explains James Clifford (1998). "Difference is encountered in the adjoining neighborhood, and the familiar turns up at the ends of the earth" (p. 14). We may not have fully come to terms with this social fact, although we do recognize that the global is uncannily close, no longer somewhere only out there; it is here *and* there, nearby *and* faraway.

Grant Cornwell and Eve Stoddard brought this reconfigured social landscape to the attention of global educators through their smart monograph *Globalizing Knowledge: Connecting International and Intercultural Studies* (1999). Their discussion spotlighted the complementarity and potential synergy between two historically disconnected movements: multicultural education and international education. Building on this work, the American Council on Education's *At Home in the World* initiative (2007) advocated for a more inclusive and integrated curricular approach to global learning. More recently, the various programs profiled in *Putting the Local in Global Education* (Sobania, 2015) reveal how diverse domestic communities can fully support a set of essential global-learning outcomes (see AAC&U, 2011; also Olson & Peacock, 2012). The authors in the Sobania volume helpfully employ the term *study away* to indicate the broad range of global-learning experiences available to students in domestic off-campus settings.

Part Two: Stumbling Blocks

The task of enlarging the spaces of global learning confronts two major stumbling blocks. One is ideological in nature; the other is institutional.

Undomesticated Cosmopolitanism

As economic and social relations continue to spill over national boundaries, the language of *global citizenship* or *cosmopolitanism* has gained new currency in colleges and universities. As mentioned in chapter 2, the concepts signify an attainable educational goal: the broadening of our "ways of thinking and living within multiple cross-cutting communities—cities, regions, states, nations, and international collectives" (Schattle 2007, p. 9).

Cosmopolitanism rests on two key principles. The first is that *we have much to learn from our differences*. The planet hosts a wild array of human societies, each with its own languages and literatures, ceremonies and songs, traditions and tastes. *Our* way of doing things is just one of many ways of doing things—one necessarily constrained by chance and upbringing. The second principle is that *one should act with an impartial concern for all*. Human beings—*all* human beings—are irreducibly precious. As such, they are entitled to equal worth and consideration irrespective of morally arbitrary traits resulting from the lottery of birth, including nationality, race, gender, natural endowments, and socioeconomic circumstances. Each of these may mediate a person's relation to the world, but they don't define it. And they don't take priority over the interests of the world community of human beings.

The metaphor long used to stretch thinking and living outward is that of an *expanding circle*. Ralph Waldo Emerson, in an 1841 essay titled "Circles," describes human life as "a self-evolving circle that, from a ring imperceptibly small, rushes on all sides outwards to new and larger circles and that without end" (see Figure 5.1). Following Emerson, Anglo-Irish historian and philosopher William Lecky (1955) considered an ever-expanding circle of obligation to be the mark of a truly developed—that is to say, cosmopolitan—person. "At one time the benevolent affections embrace merely the family," notes Lecky. "Soon the circle expands to include first a class, then a nation, then a coalition of nations, then *all humanity*, and finally, its influence is felt in the dealings of man with the animal world" (p. 285).

For cosmopolitans like Emerson and Lecky, the world's true frontiers are not geopolitical, but moral: they have to do with boundaries of human sympathy rooted in reason. It follows that no temporal authority—not family, not friends, not the state—deserves first allegiance. Moreover, no natural differences should be allowed to erect barriers between ourselves

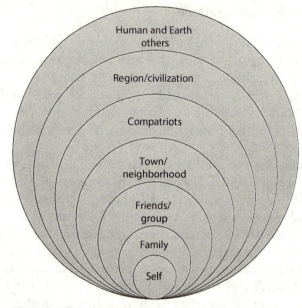

FIGURE 5.1.   The expanding circle.

and other members of the Earth community. With an outlook staunchly universalist, the cosmopolitan ambition is to overcome parochialism and to bring distant others closer into our intimate sphere of concern.

Well-designed global-learning programs can potentially support this grand enterprise. Far too often, however, the cosmopolitan ideal is undermined by discordant program features. The once dominant models of year- and semester-long study abroad programs have largely been replaced by program durations of eight weeks or less. With these time constraints, only minimal community immersion and sustained interaction with local residents is possible. Friend-making is largely restricted to other program participants, resulting in an individualistic, what's-in-it-for-me experience.

Another impediment is the over-identification of cosmopolitanism with the far away. The appeal is understandable. Hypermobility gives us a rush. Cruising down the highway at 75 miles per hour, or flying at 35,000 feet, can feel liberating and empowering. The downside is that it conditions us to be blissfully oblivious to the human and natural communities that we pass through or over. We learn to think *beyond* roots, *beyond* relationships, and *beyond* responsibilities. Like the lawless buccaneers featured in *Pirates of the Caribbean* blockbusters, we become accustomed to traversing places and peoples without being obligated to any.

To *domesticate* cosmopolitanism is to reverse our flight from those realities and responsibilities we might prefer to ignore. It's about rebuilding the social architecture of global learning in ways that bring geographically near but socially distant peoples into what Marc Dunkelman, in *The Vanishing Neighbor* (2014), describes as our *middle ring*. According to Dunkelman, people naturally tend to inner-ring relationships with family members and close friends. They also give effortless attention to a vast online outer-ring network of social media contacts. But they are less and less likely to be involved in the middle-ring world of strangers, causes, and organizations at their community doorstep.

Proximate peoples offer abundant opportunities to cultivate a more cosmopolitan consciousness. Pulitzer-prize-winning journalist Chris Hedges (2012) narrates his own transformation that began in the back regions of Boston:

> I am not sure when I severed myself irrevocably from the myth of America. It began when I was a seminarian, living for more than two years in Boston's inner city on a street that had more homicides than any other in the city. . . . I was sickened and repulsed. My loyalty shifted from the state, from any state, to the powerless, to the landless peasants in Latin America, the Palestinians in Gaza or the terrified families in Iraq and Afghanistan. Those who suffer on the outer reaches of empire, as well as in our internal colonies and sacrifice zones, constitute my country. . . . For a poor family in Camden, N.J., impoverished residents in the abandoned coal camps in southern West Virginia, the undocumented workers that toil in our nation's produce fields, Native Americans trapped on reservations, Palestinians, Iraqis, Afghans, those killed by drones in Pakistan, Yemen or Somalia, or those in the squalid urban slums in Africa, it makes no difference if Mitt Romney or Obama is president. And since it makes no difference to them, it makes no difference to me. I seek only to defy the powers that orchestrate and profit from their misery.

Structural Separation

The next obstacle to enlarging the canvas of world learning has to do with the historic and institutionalized separation between international education and multicultural education. Most colleges and universities can boast of an impressive list of *on-campus* structures and activities with an international or multicultural essence: international student services, foreign language instruction, multiethnic student associations, globally oriented courses, ethnic and women's studies programs, and diversity training. Although these initiatives may share a campus compound, when it comes to program activities, office space, staff, and budgets, they typically operate in silos.

The rift only widens when we look at study, service, and research activities in *off-campus* settings. A primary and fateful distinction is made between the following:

- *Domestic off-campus programs:* Educational activities that occur away from the student's home institution but within the same country (e.g., service-learning, field study, border study)
- *Education abroad programs:* Educational activities that occur outside the student's home country (e.g., Fulbright scholars, cultural exchanges, study abroad, international research) (The Forum on Education Abroad, n.d.).

Two things stand out as one surveys the landscape of on- and off-campus global-learning programs and practices. The first is the sheer *diversity* of activities; the second is their fortified *disconnection* from each other.

With rare exception, ethnic, international, intercultural, and global courses and programs have grown on U.S. campuses like individual flowers in a largely unkempt garden. Foreign language training is rarely paired with country- or region-specific coursework in, let's say, political science or international business. Area studies programs dealing with East and South Asia, Africa, or Latin America tend to exclude American Studies. Noncredit volunteer events seldom interface with academic service-learning. The divide doesn't stop there. On almost all campuses, one can expect to find "diversity" offices in one place and "internationalization" offices elsewhere. Minority student concerns are treated largely independent of services for both international students and study away participants. International programs also tend to operate in isolation from community/urban studies and other civic engagement programs. And this doesn't begin to touch the structural separation maintained between *undergraduate* programs and those offered at the *graduate* level.

The fateful divergence of international/cross-cultural initiatives from those with a domestic/multicultural focus is traceable, at least in part, to their respective histories and motivations (see Table 5.1). Internationalism

Table 5.1. Internationalism-Multiculturalism Divergences

Internationalism *International Education*	Third Space *Global Learning*	Multiculturalism *Civic Engagement*
Top Down: Spearheaded by mainstream academics, government administrators, and private foundations in the post–World War II and Cold War eras		*Bottom Up:* Spearheaded by marginalized groups as a response to a legacy of racism, social subordination, and restricted educational and economic opportunity
Eurocentric: Identified with privileged White people traveling to European destinations and studying European languages and cultures		*Multicentric:* Identified with progressive social movements representing the realities and interests of marginalized women and people of color
Strategies: 1. Foreign language study 2. Study/service abroad 3. International students 4. Internationalization initiatives		*Strategies:* 1. Ethnic studies 2. Women's/gender studies 3. Urban studies/service-learning 4. Diversity initiatives
Goal: To promote international understanding and U.S. strategic interests within overseas settings		*Goal:* To right historical wrongs and strengthen group identity for U.S. minorities in domestic settings
Support structures: Academic affairs: curricular programs (e.g., global studies, modern languages)		*Support structures:* Student affairs: multiethnic clubs, cultural celebrations, diversity training

grew up in the aftermath of World War II and during the Cold War. These two events reshaped the once distant relationship between the federal government and the university into a close partnership (Chomsky & Nader, 1997). University programs that facilitated the exchange of ideas, information, and other aspects of culture were now expected to help the United States achieve its diplomatic goals.

To more fully institutionalize the nation's soft power, area studies programs were installed in major U.S. universities starting around 1946. Initially they were funded by private foundations, and then covertly by the Central Intelligence Agency. The academic goal of acquiring knowledge about foreign territories merged explicitly with U.S.-state interests to control or combat its foreign enemies.

During this same period, various international educational exchange and service programs were either founded or expanded: the Institute of International Education (1920s), its Fulbright Scholar Program (1946), the Council on International Educational Exchange (1947), and the Peace Corps (1961). Young adults had the opportunity, not just to gain a fuller understanding of their own and another society, but also to serve as cultural ambassadors for their nation. Politically volatile "third world" countries, in particular, received tens of thousands of adventurous, college-educated development workers over the succeeding decades. In short, the public diplomacy mission has been woven into the fabric of international education and exchange for nearly seven decades.

Implicit in internationalism's historical trajectory is an easily over-looked but hardly trivial fact: International education programs were founded and led almost exclusively by middle-aged or older White men embedded within dominant institutions (governmental, military, and business). This is significant not just because they all came from a common origin of privilege. More importantly, they shared a common world-view—a community of interests—that predisposed them to make decisions that would strengthen and extend, rather than challenge, the structural status quo that had created them and in which they wielded power (see Piff, Stancato, Côté, Mendoza-Denton, & Keltner, 2012).

C. Wright Mills, one of the most tough-minded sociologists of this era, analyzed the complex intersections of race, class, gender, profession, and politics with laser-like precision. The central insight in his books *White Collar* (1951) and *The Power Elite* (1956) was that occupations define social class, social class shapes political interests, and political interests powerfully influence policies and programs. By and large, the early architects of international education policy and practice lived in social worlds with little direct contact with disadvantaged persons of color, or their problems. They reasoned from within a worldview that effectively disregarded minority communities as sites for shaping student consciousness toward the common good.

The roots of multiculturalism were quite different. The idea arose not within elite institutions but through social protest movements in the 1950s and 1960s (civil rights, Chicano, antiwar, women's, etc.). Economic deprivation and social dislocation, not the extension of soft power, were primary catalysts of activism. Whereas the vast majority of internationalists were White, male, and affluent, the early multiculturalists were mostly working-class persons of color. Multiculturalism was seen as a way to reduce domestic (race/ethnic/class/gender) divides, and the cultural mis-/underrepresentation that resulted. Toward that end, interdisciplinary ethnic studies and women's studies programs were founded across the country. The new language and the new consciousness they offered would, in time, get translated into critical pedagogies and what we know today as the civic engagement movement. The latter expresses multiculturalism's unfinished project: to transform U.S. colleges and universities into democratic centers of critical thought and social responsibility.

Thus, a deep *cultural* divide underlies the structural separation of internationalism from multiculturalism. As a consequence, they tend to define themselves competitively. Professionals in both fields claim different professional turf, consecrate different traditions, advocate for different causes, and populate different conferences. Moreover, they tend to view each other with suspicion. Multiculturalists generally perceive internationalists as white-bread elitists whose sense of racial or ethnic superiority prevents them from forming all but functional or patronizing relationships with people of color. Internationalists can be equally derisive in their judgments of minorities as professional victims obsessed with inequality and identity politics. In their mind, there are enormous environmental, economic, financial, and social problems needing to be solved, and identity politics only distracts from the hard work needed to build a more universalistic and less "ethnic" global consciousness.

Clearly, stubborn cultural and structural issues prevent internationalists and multiculturalists from turning inherent tensions into a richer, more comprehensive model of global engagement.

Part Three: Repairing the Rift

Are we left, then, with a rootless internationalism and an immobile multiculturalism? How might the two factions be reconciled and the internationalism-multiculturalism rift repaired? In his confessional essay "The

Crack Up," F. Scott Fitzgerald (1945/1993) challenged the human propen-
sity toward binary, either-or thinking. "The test of a first-rate intelligence,"
he observed, "is the ability to hold two opposed ideas in mind at the same
time and still retain the ability to function" (p. 69). The present polariza-
tion need not handicap the quest for an integrated model of global learning. In fact, concealed in the tension may be an important educational
opportunity *if* it can lead us to consider a "third space" that transcends
and transforms the historical divides.

Toward that end, a growing number of campus offices have rebranded
themselves—from *study abroad* and *international education* to *study away, off-
campus,* and *global engagement.* In doing so, they highlight sociocultural difference, rather than geographic distance, as the distinguishing marker of an
internationalized education.

A groundbreaking example is Pitzer College's Institute for Global/
Local Action & Study (IGLAS). Intentionally established to build pedagogical linkages between the school's community engagement and international education missions, the IGLAS infuses global/local themes
throughout a sequential, experience-based curriculum. The old *home* and
field categories are transcended without abandoning the interests and
insights that continue to give them meaning. Nigel Boyle, the institute's
founding director, explains the critical synthesis: "Restoring the civic
[via domestic engagement] and embracing the global [through education abroad] are neither discrete nor merely complementary educational
objectives. . . . Their combination opens up exciting opportunities for
transformative learning" (Pitzer College, 2014, p. 70).

Finding common ground is the necessary basis for pursuing common
cause for the common good (see Table 5.2). White internationalists have
much to learn from minority sisters and brothers about how power circu-
lates in multiethnic communities. Likewise, multiculturalists of color are
challenged to extend their vision beyond the domestic arena to appreciate the global forces of history, politics, and economics that are always
enmeshed in local realities.

Although global education is a well-established, worldwide movement,
AAC&U has helped inject *global learning* into the professional lexicon of
American educational discourse. The idea tactfully weaves together global
studies, intercultural education, multicultural relations, and social/eco-
logical responsibility.[1] A set of essential learning outcomes guides students in making connections across disciplines *and* spatial contexts. As
a bridging construct, global learning attempts to repair the rift between

TABLE 5.2. Finding Common Ground

Common subject	Real-world problems, disproportionately affecting vulnerable populations, in nearby and faraway settings
Common context	Diverse communities with complex histories, institutional realities, languages, values systems, and group practices
Common values	Respecting differences (national, cultural, racial, class, gender) and righting wrongs
Common concerns	Promoting global flourishing, including economic opportunity, human rights protection, and climate stability
Common pedagogies	Interdisciplinary, experiential, community-based learning (study, service, research) processes
Common aversion	To a single, monocultural "melting pot" social ideal that homogenizes and assimilates global diversity
Common outcomes	Essential cognitive, attitudinal, communication, and collaboration knowledge and skills

the local and the global, civic engagement and education abroad (see Figure 5.2). It invites us to imagine a twenty-first-century global education where students attend both to the welfare of nearby communities and to the matters that affect and afflict the wider world. The result is a competent pedagogy and morality that alternates between doorstep and planet.

Making the Familiar Strange: The Doorstep

Democracy must begin at home, and its home is the neighborly community.

— JOHN DEWEY, *The Public and Its Problems*, 1954

At this point, we might readily embrace a model of global learning that combines doorstep (domestic) and planet (international) experiences. But what if we were to propose that students move *from* doorstep *to* planet? In other words, global learning would begin not in international settings, but in multiethnic domestic communities, whether *local* or *regional*. The

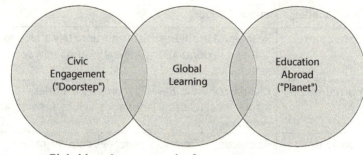

FIGURE 5.2.   Global learning as a nearby-faraway nexus

following sections discuss the four reasons that compel us to privilege a
model of global education that starts at home.

Doorstep-to-planet learning checks exoticism

During the colonial era, people of power and wealth traveled to subjugated
lands to revel in peculiar peoples and customs. The colonial system constructed not only the West/Rest binary but also an intimate tie between
Whiteness and wealth. Citizens from developed countries possessed both
the financial means and the legal documents to travel most anywhere; those
in developing countries had access to neither. Edward Said famously used
the term *Orientalism* to describe the way Westerners Other-ized so-called
nontraditional places and ways of life by portraying them as primitive,
authentic, and enchanting.

Exoticism, the charm of the unfamiliar and distant, continues to be
an occupational hazard in world-learning programs, especially those
operating in the Global South. Quaint and colorful cultures are often
valued as intriguing exceptions to modernity: like museum pieces, they
are best admired and visually consumed before they fade away. The
irony is that such cultures no longer exist. Few places on Earth have
not been mapped and commercialized as hyper-managed objects of the
tourist gaze.[2]

In more "traditional" destinations, the exotic is often packaged as unen-
cumbered fun. Berlin, Madrid, Florence, London, and Tel Aviv are all
renown as travel fantasylands, serving up everything from historic districts
and natural monuments to booze cruises and all-night pub-crawls. I mention this, not to throw a wet blanket over good times abroad, but to spot-
light how the paths of pleasure and of public diplomacy clearly diverge.
Regrettably, the proverbial "ugly American" still remains a standard fixture

abroad, especially in places with a low drinking age and a thriving party scene.

Doorstep global learning has the tendency to interrupt the charm-seeking that roughly correlates with the physical distance of destinations from home. Learners need not travel far to undertake significant self-exploration. In fact, most home campuses offer abundant opportunities for students to interact with racial, religious, and political groups whose views are substantially different from, if not opposed to, their own.

Then, sometimes right outside the campus gate, are heterogeneous spaces of splendid unpredictability. In contrast to popular foreign destinations abroad where virtually everything has been carefully ordered for tourist consumption, domestic sites are largely freed from the burden of performance. The everyday worlds of West Philadelphia and South Chicago, for example, are neither themed nor simulated. They have no corporate sponsors or staged productions. Social relations are unrehearsed and struggles unscripted. Authenticity is found in the raw, unmediated life of city streets, households, buses, restaurants, storefront churches, hospitals, and jails. True, these are not venues that are likely to attract rootless travelers or endless fun-seekers. But that's precisely the point. Domestic global learning offers a practical self-sorting and screening mechanism that effectively weeds out party animals from serious world learners.

Doorstep-to-planet learning frames the world in local-personal terms
The next problem consistently arises when learners go straight from their native place to faraway lands: Global concerns that require sustained focus to fully grasp are left "over there" in their consciousness. Touristic enthusiasms encourage learners to bracket social realities encountered across the globe from those same realities that they might encounter at their doorstep. Many program designs unwittingly reinforce the disconnection. Participants are expected to *occupy* and *consume* site locations, but rarely to *inhabit* them on the basis of intimate knowledge and affection. Unsurprisingly, when returnees arrive home, few give a second thought to how their experiences abroad might practically influence their lives at home. An abstract "world love" substitutes for tangible duties toward next-door nations. The sociological dictum would seem to hold true: Those closest to us are always the ones furthest away.

One antidote to the urge to compartmentalize the *far away* and the *close by* is to begin with where we are and with what we see before us. Travel into any major U.S. city with eyes wide open, and we soon discover that the world's most vexing social problems know no geographic boundaries. What we typically associate with a distant "developing" world—sprawl, transportation gridlock, wealth inequality, organized crime, depression, biodiversity loss, and water depletion—are pervasive features of every American and European city. The divide is primarily social and economic, not geographic, as Manuel Castells (1998) reminds us:

> Every "First World" city has in it a "Third World" city of infant mortality, malnutrition, unemployment, communicable diseases and homelessness. Similarly, every "Third World" city has in it a "First World" city with high finance, fashion, and technology. The conventional distinctions between North and South are misleading diplomatic artifacts. Instead, the global divide runs through each society between the globalized rich and the localized poor. The First and Third worlds now live around the corner from each other, mutually dependent everywhere.

In 1962 Michael Harrington chronicled America's hidden "third world" underbelly in *The Other America*. Six decades later, Chris Hedges and Joe Sacco reported on the same internal colonies of invisible and forgotten have-nots in *Days of Destruction, Days of Revolt* (2012). They describe vast swaths of America that have been reduced to "sacrifice zones" by economic disinvestment or environmental damage. I have personally witnessed many of the places that Hedges and Sacco detail: the coalfields of Kentucky and West Virginia, the Pine Ridge Reservation in South Dakota, and the produce fields of San Joaquin Valley and South Florida. A few weeks or months spent in any one of these locales will reveal a complex picture of hardship mixed with hope. In Immokalee, Florida, female migrant farm workers toil in virtual slavery, enduring long working hours and routine sexual exploitation. On the Pine Ridge Reservation, in South Dakota, drug abuse, alcoholism, and teen suicide are so rampant that a boy's average lifespan is shorter than in any country in the world, except for some African states and Afghanistan. Mind you, this is in the center of the world's wealthiest nation.

A firsthand experience of the irreversible social and environmental decay resulting from failed policies and egregious corporate practices within one's own country profoundly relocalizes, and personalizes, world learning. Several years ago, the debut of the HBO series *The Newsroom* (2012) featured a scene that has garnered over nine million Internet hits. The protagonist anchorman, played by Jeff Daniels, is asked by an earnest young woman what makes America the greatest country on Earth. In response, Daniels delivers a biting diatribe that synthesizes statistical data on a broad range of quality-of-life issues. Despite being the world's largest economy and most powerful nation, Daniels reminds the audience that, among industrialized nations, the United States has the highest homicide rate, the highest incarceration rate, the highest prevalence of mental-health problems, the highest obesity rate, the second-highest high school dropout rate (behind Spain), the greatest wealth inequality, the highest military spending as a portion of GDP, and the highest carbon dioxide emissions per capita.

This unpleasant picture of "home" tends to get lost in the rush to witness a fragile humanity elsewhere. Learners are often denied the opportunity to critically question the systems that entangle their everyday lives. Why has the American Dream turned nightmarish for so many? Why are tens of millions either chronically poor or part of the new working poor? Why have many of our most important institutions failed? Why does the marketplace now rule without constraints? Why have loneliness, depression, and drug overdoses reached epidemic proportions across America's small towns and cities? A semester in Melbourne or Barcelona is not likely to illumine such questions. Every global community has its own quality-of-life questions, but without a body of insight formed at home, global learners will tend to reflexively interpret realities abroad using unquestioned assumptions (what they *think* they know) to answer them.

Doorstep-to-planet learning brings social privilege and disadvantage to light
When conducting antiracism training with law enforcement officers, Tim Wise (2008) asks, "What's the first thing you think when you see a young Black or Latino male driving a nice car in your neighborhood?" Without exception, the officers respond, "Drug dealer." Wise then asks, "What's the first thing you think when you see a young White male driving the same type of car in the same community?" Again, without exception, they say, "Spoiled little rich kid."

Race may have no biological validity, but White America continues to use a racial lens to view social acts, and then to deny that one's own response to them has anything to do with race. The problem is highlighted in education abroad, an enterprise that has overwhelmingly enrolled students whose identities have been formed within normative White culture. Majority groups have the privilege of knowing little or nothing about minority groups—their history, their everyday experiences, their hopes and fears. They can afford to remain blissfully ignorant of how social identity confers advantages and disadvantages, with both economic and social consequences. The 400-year-old grand narrative of America is about epic journeys in a promised land as a single, united people. Largely obscured in this story are the grim and pain-filled ways that racial prejudice, xenophobia, sexism, and greed derailed the nation's founding ideals.

One of the things that differentiates subordinate from dominant group members is that the latter are able to "forget" the systematic state violence against native peoples; the enslavement of Africans; the Chinese Exclusion Act; the internment of Japanese Americans; the denial of equal pay for women; and, more recently, the scapegoating of Muslims, undocumented workers, and gay persons.

Boarding a plane for a far-off land rarely corrects this collective amnesia. In fact, it often widens it. Whiteness and wealth, and to a lesser extent being American, act as passports to privilege that are rarely checked in overseas settings. Foreigners enjoy a kind of diplomatic immunity from being chastised for behaviors that would instantly be called out as bigoted or bourgeois back home. This positive discrimination allows them, as temporary guests, to remain safely suspended above the fray of economic disparity and intergroup conflict.

In domestic settings, that courtesy is largely withdrawn. Near-neighbors are much more likely to relate to students in terms of the perceived power relationships inscribed in skin color, language, dress style, and personal manners. Little prevents them from telling outsiders what they really feel and think. This became strikingly clear the day I escorted three very White, well-groomed students to Skid Row, a predominantly Black colony of the destitute and mentally ill in Los Angeles. As we stood on a corner preparing to cross a street lined with tents and cardboard encampments, two Black women on the other side stood up, faced us, and shouted out, "Whassup white bread. Y'all come down here to pet the mice?"

We all froze, uncertain of what to say or do. Days after the incident, we were still rehashing the experience, questioning ourselves and the larger context. Were our reactions biased more by liberal racial pity or by conservative racial contempt? Why, as Martin Luther King Jr. (1968b) once asked, do so many White Americans "experience the opportunity of life, liberty, and the pursuit of happiness in all its dimensions," while so many Black Americans face a "daily ugliness" that leaves only "the fatigue of despair"? Although the doorstep experience didn't yield settled answers, it pressed us to ask better questions by exposing our homegrown prides and prejudices. Iyer (2005) writes in *Sun After Dark*:

> The modern, shifting world has brought disorientation home to us, and mystery and strangeness; even in the most familiar places we may come upon something unsettling, just through the alien presence at our side . . . all the spirits we like to keep, locked up—suspicion, defensiveness, fear—suddenly rear their heads. A stranger is always at our door, nowadays, with an offer, an inquiry, and we don't know what to make of him. (p. 10)

The stranger at our doorstep invites us on an inward journey where we confront our locked up spirits and unspoken judgments. It might be the idea that Blacks, simply because of their skin color, mark a neighborhood or school as bad; that Muslims are bearded terrorists or repressed women in *burqas*; that immigrants are a drain on the American economy; or that gay persons, however sensitive and intelligent, are promiscuous, lonely, and likely to be child molesters. Coming out of denial means admitting that one has a perception problem and needs to get help. For most of us, it is a lifelong process that requires us to continuously negotiate our self-definitions *relationally*. This inevitably involves difficult questions related to power and privilege at our doorstep. Starting the transformative journey with strangers nearby guards against the impulse to travel afar in order to meet the kinds of people we consciously avoid at home.

Doorstep-to-planet learning supports a more accessible, diverse, and sustainable global education

The conventional model of education abroad faces three formidable challenges. The first entails *accessibility* for those representing the new majority of American higher education—low-income, first-generation students of color. The second concerns the *under-representation* of racial minorities participating in overseas programs. And the third is the long-term *sustainability* of the current, fossil-fuel-dependent education abroad paradigm.

Since the 1870s, overseas study has attracted a fairly uniform student-participant: financially secure White females, typically in their early 20s. Coming from privileged families, a normal part of growing up was travel vacations, mission trips, and table conversations on international topics. Study abroad during the college years simply extended and broadened prior travel experiences.

This traditional profile looks largely the same today. What has taken a distinctly *nontraditional* turn, though, is the typical college student. According to the National Center for Educational Statistics (U.S. Department of Education, 2018), a quarter of undergraduates are older than 25, and about the same number are single parents. The new normal is for the typical college student to be lower-income and minority, with a high percentage having to earn while they learn (a startling 40% of students work at least 30 hours a week). Trends project a 25% increase in Black students and a whopping 42% increase in Latinos by 2021, with only a 4% increase in Whites.

In short, colleges and universities are challenged to meet the global-learning needs of students of color, first-generation students, international immigrant students, undocumented (non-U.S. passport holding) students, students from less advantaged families, and students who are working full time and attending part time. How will they do this? The ranks of the new majority include people who possess a wealth of cultural experience and perspective, yet their presence is largely absent within conventional study abroad, despite the mushrooming of programs in non-European locations. Most new majority students simply cannot afford to quit work, pay thousands of dollars in program fees, and take off for a semester in Bolivia or Ghana.

Under-representation in study abroad is also shaped along color lines. Only about 5% of Americans who participate in overseas study programs are Black. Program administrators may presume, falsely, that "All Blacks are poor, that they lack the necessary educational requirements, or that study abroad is not relevant to their lives" (Simon & Ainsworth, 2012). Often a subtle racism is at play. But it is also true that few minorities, Blacks in particular, see themselves reflected in either the leaders or the participants of international programs. Racial minorities naturally wonder whether anyone understands the stereotype threats that students of color often face abroad. Then there is the question of whether program outcomes justify the price tag. What value does education abroad add to those who have *already* learned to see themselves, and the world around them, through foreign (dominant White) eyes (Lugones, 2003)?

Finally, we need to ask whether a fossil-fuel-dependent model of global education can be sustained as the climate system continues to warm. Transporting tens of thousands of students from their homes to destinations abroad requires large amounts of jet fuel that emit harmful

greenhouse gases in the sensitive upper troposphere and lower strato-
sphere. In fact, hour for hour, the quickest way for a private citizen to
worsen climate change is to fly someplace far away. A round trip from Los
Angeles to Kolkata, or from Boston to Quito, produces about three tons
(6,000 lbs.) of CO_2 per passenger. That's roughly equivalent to driving a
Honda Accord 8,000 miles (333 gallons of gasoline).[3] Two climatologists,
reporting in the prestigious journal *Science*, estimate that a single passenger's share of emissions on a 2,500-mile flight melts 32 square feet of
Arctic summer sea ice cover (Notz & Stroeve, 2016). Once we recognize
the act of flying as an exercise of privilege (globally, only about 20% of
humans have ever flown), how do we reconcile the impacts of carbon-
intensive study abroad with the negative effects of climate disruption on
the very peoples and places that a global education seeks to illuminate?
The tacit assumption seems to be that the educational and personal value
of education abroad, seemingly regardless of program quality, outweighs
the ecological impacts. Does it?

I have no crystal ball to predict the future. Nevertheless, it's a fairly
safe bet that the combined effect of nontraditional students and global
climate breakdown will increasingly challenge the legitimacy of high-cost,
high-polluting models of global learning. Rather than seeing a dramatic
expansion of education abroad participation, we could witness its steady
contraction for all but a tiny mobile elite.

For at least these four reasons, local or regional communities provide the
indispensable starting gate for world learning. Educationally, study away in
diverse domestic communities can include almost all of the same processes
as an overseas program, including the study of a language, family stays,
meaningful internships, and community research. All without a passport,
a customs line, or a major climate impact. Then there are the many ways
local, community-engaged global learning at home might serve the public good. Ira Harkavy (2015), a national expert in university-community
engagement, highlights some of them:

> Ongoing, continuous interaction is facilitated through work in an easily
> accessible location. Relationships of trust, so essential for effective part-
> nerships and effective learning, are also built through day-to-day work on
> problems and issues of mutual concern. In addition, the local commu-
> nity provides a convenient setting in which a number of service-learning
> courses, community-based research courses, and related courses in different

disciplines can work together on a complex problem to produce substantive results. . . . And finally, the local community is a democratic real-world learning site in which community members and academics can pragmatically determine whether the work is making a real difference, and whether both the neighborhood and the higher education institution are better as a result of common efforts.

A number of domestic global-learning programs are worthy of emulation. Some of the most sophisticated are semester-long, full-immersion models that have operated for decades in domestic milieus of rich human or ecological diversity, including Chicago, Philadelphia, New York, the Pacific Northwest, Minneapolis, Los Angeles, and the U.S./Mexico frontier.[4]

Making the Strange Familiar: The Planet

> It is indispensable to be perpetually comparing their own notions and customs with the experience and example of persons in different circumstances from themselves: and there is no nation which does not need to borrow from others, not merely particular arts or practices, but essential points of character in which its own type is inferior.
>
> — JOHN STUART MILL, Principles of Political Economy, 1848

Thus far we have argued in favor of prioritizing the doorstep in a socially and ecologically responsible global education. Having made that argument as forcefully as I can, I want to be careful not to equate starting at home with staying at home. To become intimate *with* a particular place—its landscape and peoples and culture—is not to sever ties *across* other places. Global learning entails roots *and* shoots, as Scott Russell Sanders (1993) explains:

> To become intimate with your home region, to know the territory as well as you can, to understand your life as woven into local life does not prevent you from recognizing and honoring the diversity of other places, cultures, and ways. On the contrary, how can you value other places, if you do not have one of your own? If you are not yourself placed, then you wander the world like a sightseer, a collector of sensations, with no gauge for measuring what you see. Local knowledge is the grounding for global knowledge. (p. 114)

Ghanaian philosopher Kwame Appiah (2004) captures a similar ordering of doorstep-then-planet with his idea of *rooted cosmopolitanism*. As individuals move cognitively and physically outside their spatial origins, their primary ties continue to be domestic, even as the circle of relationships and responsibilities expands into other societies. Rooted cosmopolitans imagine a world where persons are "attached to a home of one's own, with its own cultural particularities, but take pleasure from the presence of other, different places who are home to other, different people" (Appiah, 1997, p. 618).

Among the many "aha!" moments during a high-impact term abroad is realizing our basic connectedness and interdependence with distant places and peoples. Few places on Earth are not permeated with ideas and people and products from elsewhere. Of course, interconnectedness can be either beneficial or damaging for local communities. Economic integration has consistently raised local wages and work standards within low-income countries. But it has also encouraged environmental degradation and cultural homogenization. Communities stretching from Peru to Cambodia feel the almost irresistible force of American fast food chains and pop culture. What is more, there is probably no place on Earth untouched by the global financial and military architecture, dominated by megabanks, transnational corporations, special interest lobbies, and the Pentagon. Each and every one of the planet's places is inexorably enmeshed in cultural, economic, and political relationships.

Planet learning builds on the social sensibilities and practical wisdom spawned in communities at our doorstep. Through what some anthropologists call *multi-sited field study* (Marcus, 1995), students venture outside the borders of their homeland to investigate how those in *other* national cultures define and address our shared challenges.

Cultural comparison and borrowing

Cultural exchange is itself an art form. It involves the creative engagement of another way of life by informed, respectful, and humble guests. While every human society is cut from the same genetic cloth, it is a unique manifestation of reality, endowed with its own raw genius and timeless virtue. Japanese loyalty and discipline. Indian mysticism. Latino graciousness. American dynamism. African rhythm/informality. French generosity. Vietnamese love of learning. German industriousness. Cultural borrowing enables the world's customs and mores, objects and insights to flow across social and political boundaries, thereby enriching the entire human community and supplying it with resources for dealing with its shared challenges.

The planet pole encourages global learners to take their personal passion and follow it across world societies, both traditional and modern. A student's special interest may be in a particular *population* (migrant workers, refugees, trafficked persons); a certain *branch of knowledge* (media, politics, religion); a thorny *controversy* (immigration policy, gender identity); or a pressing *predicament* (the new poverty, climate disruption, arms trade). With competence acquired at home, they establish residence in other places that have special relevance to their issue of interest. They then use native wisdom to trace the local shades of global concerns.

Multi-sited global learning aspires to something more than merely fostering an intellectual appreciation for cultural variation, as alluring as that might be. It is finally to construct deep and complex understandings that might potentially inform broader public action. Applications might extend from education and land reform to legal protections for children. Even a seemingly apolitical topic like art is illuminated through cultural comparison. "The question is not whether art (or anything else) is universal," notes anthropologist Clifford Geertz (1983). "It is whether one can talk about West African carving, New Guinea palm-leaf painting, quattrocento picture making, and Moroccan versifying in such a way as to cause them to *shed some sort of light on one another*" (p. 11, emphasis added).

It might be tempting for some to view one art form shedding light on another in negative terms, as a form of *cultural appropriation*. In fact, virtually all the cultural practices and objects around us, including yoga, rap, dreadlocks, haircutting, bindi, and drums—are products of intermixture. Paper was invented in China. Our symbols representing numbers were invented in India. The endless process of cultural borrowing and revision is a kind of constructive "contamination" (Appiah, 2006), embellishing the human experience. Most cultural appropriations tend to be personal, superficial, and morally benign: two Euro-Americans in California go out for sushi or Vietnamese *pho*, or a Chinese tourist buys several pieces of indigenous art in Santa Fe, New Mexico and carries them back home. What we're most interested in is *deep borrowing*, the kind that becomes a public good. Almost all religions, for example, incorporate teachings or practices from other faiths, and have thereby raised the moral and ethical character of millions. The essential idea is that someone from one society finds something in another society good and important and useful. They then decide to allow those cultural features to alter their way of living in the world.

Transformative potential is often found in unlikely places. For global learners reared under and enamored by modernity, an unexpected source of cultural wisdom might be found within certain place-based economies. Rural villages, informal urban settlements, indigenous societies, Amish communities, transition towns, eco-villages—these living experiments, tens of thousands of them, reveal alternative ways of knowing and being. Like any good teacher, they challenge us to radically rethink how we live in relation to the divine, to material things, to other people, and even to ourselves. In so doing, they impart tangible lessons on how to shape a more human-scaled, low-impact, and convivial mode of life.

On the surface, the Los Angeles Eco-village and a remote village in Rajasthan may appear to be wildly different places—and they are. But experiential journeys into both communities would reveal a number of surprising features that they share:

- People are intimately connected to each other, to the land, and to local knowledge.
- People rely on their wits to satisfy their daily needs with locally supplied resources.
- Little is wasted and much is shared.
- The ruling ideas elevate neighborliness and contentment over competition and consumption.
- The residents haven't "progressed" from a foot, pedal, or horse economy to a fossil fuel economy.
- More time is spent outdoors than sitting indoors in front of screens.
- Basic knowledge—of husbandry, horticulture, carpentry, and basic mechanics—is highly valued by members and passed down from generation to generation.

Alternative communities hold up a great mirror to the modern world, compelling us to think hard about the pros and cons of the industrialized way of life we've inherited. Why, asks Jared Diamond in *The World Until Yesterday* (2012), are children in small-scale societies rarely lonely, overweight, morally confused, monolingual, or insecure in their identity? How did these cultures develop arguably superior ways of training children, caring for the elderly, and settling disputes? Diamond doesn't idealize traditional peoples, whose lives are often poor, nasty, brutish, and short. What he hopes his readers recognize is that every society is not debt-saddled and largely unhappy, working endlessly and consuming gluttonously. Some of them, by virtue of being cut off from globalized cities, offer learners the rare opportunity to gradually *unlearn* a way of life based on expansion, extraction, and consumption, and to *relearn* new patterns of desire, diet, resource use, technology dependence, and energy consumption. The key is to actually *live the alternative* long enough to create a "new normal."

If small-scale societies model some of the *individual* (lifestyle) changes needed to help repair the world, some of the broader, more *systemic* solutions are showcased within some of the world's great urban centers. Most of humanity is now irreversibly urbanized. It follows that there can be no healthy planet without healthy cities, and there can be no healthy cities without social innovations that scale up into new policies and institutions. Valuable lessons in building durable urban societies are to be found, as Ireland President Michael Higgins (2012) rightly noted in his remarks to The Forum on Education Abroad, in "the interaction of inherited tradition with a technologically driven modernity."

Take, for example, the rising rates of traffic congestion and obesity in North American cities. How might the combined wisdom of cultural tradition and technical innovation suggest a way forward? In search of an answer, a group of students from a car-centric American city—say, Houston or Atlanta—might explore transportation policy and planning in Copenhagen, Denmark. Despite frigid conditions (it's spring semester), the students immediately notice that the people of Copenhagen are as comfortable on bicycles as North Americans are in cars. In fact, 50% of the residents pedal to work, school, or college every day, even in the dead of winter. How can this be? The students talk to bicycle commuters and city officials, hoping to uncover potential "borrowings"—distinct values and ideas and policies that, if successfully transplanted to communities back home, could help achieve a fundamental shift in mind-set and commuting behavior.

Good ideas and policies are strewn across the planet. In his 2016 documentary *Where to Invade Next*, Michael Moore discovers that many countries do certain things significantly better than America. Instead of industrial slop washed down with sugary soft drinks, France serves nutritional food to its elementary school children, including several kinds of cheeses. In Finland school children have no homework or standardized testing, but still rank among the world's best educated. Across Italy, mothers have five months of paid maternity leave, and in the Islamic nation of Tunisia women enjoy free healthcare. When Moore visits Norway, he discovers a criminal justice system that actually works: Murder sentences are capped at 21 years and no one is locked in solitary confinement, yet the crime rate is low, as is recidivism.

The future of the planet depends on cracking global-scale problems with the best ideas the world can offer. Global learning supports this project as a vehicle to educationally plunder groundbreaking innovations as they emerge across the planet. It often seems that nations and peoples have received different assignments, as it were, with reference to creating human and ecological systems that support global flourishing. Global learners practice the art of arbitrage every time they take up residence elsewhere, reach down deep into native soils, and draw out traits, ideas, and practices that nourish a new consciousness. Changes in collective consciousness create the basis for public solutions to seemingly incurable problems. Is it really so far-fetched to imagine a model city—one that integrates Singaporean and Colombian urban transportation, Cuban food sovereignty, German clean energy, Canadian healthcare, Spanish worker-owned cooperatives, American scientific ingenuity, Finnish and South Korean public education, Swedish welfare policies, Norwegian criminal justice, and Bhutanese happiness?

Conclusion

In the early 1950s the distinguished urban intellectual Lewis Mumford (1951) laid out a global-learning strategy that would begin at one's doorstep and extend to localities strewn across the planet. Scores of women and men, journeying nearby and faraway, would receive a boon of wisdom to improve life back home. In Mumford's words:

> The result of such transmigrations would be to enrich every homeland with mature young men and women, who knew the ways and farings of other men, who would bring back treasures with them, songs and dances, technical processes and civic customs, not least, ethical precepts and religious insights, knowledge not taken at third hand from books, but through direct contact and living experience: thus, the young would bring back into every village and city *a touch of the universal society* of which they form an active part. (pp. 278–279; emphasis added)

That such an ideal may never be attained or, if achieved, would require eternal vigilance to maintain is no reason to not pursue it. Doorstep-to-planet learning is ultimately a pedagogy of hope through which we re-imagine our collective selves through encounters with places and peoples that do things far better than what most of us think we do best. As chapter 6 suggests, the benefits to both learners and host communities can be recip-rocal and far-reaching.

Notes

1. As defined by the AAC&U, *global learning* is "a critical analysis of and an engagement with complex, interdependent global systems and legacies (e.g., natu-ral, physical, social, cultural, economic, and political) and their implications for people's lives and the earth's sustainability. Through global learning, students should (1) become informed, open-minded, and responsible people who are atten-tive to diversity across the spectrum of differences, (2) seek to understand how their actions affect *both local and global communities*, and (3) address the world's most press-ing and enduring issues collaboratively and equitably" (Hovland, 2009; emphasis added). Other constructs that link the particularities of the local to the transna-tional forces that shape them have been proposed: global citizenship (Schattle, 2009), study away (Sobania & Braskamp, 2009), interculturalism (Deardorff & Jones, 2012), and grounded globalism (Olson and Peacock, 2012).

2. Examples abound: Polynesian hula dance shows in Hawai'i; guided slum tours in Mumbai; and indigenous performances at luxury lodges by the Maasai in Kenya, the hill tribes of northern Thailand, and the Mayans in Central America. Most moderns know that the promise of authenticity is mostly hype. Nevertheless, they are content to revel in the carnavalesque simulacra of tourist traps, without letting superficial associations with native style detract from their enjoyment (see Urry, 1995).

3. These figures don't account for the huge plumes of exhaust released by jets during taxiing, idling, takeoffs, and landings. Nor the energy used in the airport buildings, facilities, baggage systems, airport service vehicles, concession facilities, aircraft fueling, airport construction, air navigation, and safety operations.

4. See the Chicago Program offered through the Associated Colleges of the Midwest (ACM); the Philadelphia Center program founded by the Great Lakes Colleges Association; the New York Arts program of Ohio Wesleyan University; Whitman College's Semester in the West program; the Metro Urban Studies program sponsored by the Higher Education Consortium for Urban Affairs (HECUA); Azusa Pacific University's Los Angeles Term program, and the Earlham College Border Studies program. A number of these programs are profiled in Neal Sobania (2015).

BALANCING THE BENEFIT

The Art of Intervention

The transaction by which I seek to bring about change in the direction of justice for another is one in which I come to be as much in the others' debt as they are in mine.
— ROWAN WILLIAMS, former Archbishop of Canterbury, New Perspectives on Faith and Development closing keynote lecture, 2009

SOME TIME AGO, in Addis Ababa, Ethiopia, I found myself sitting with the director of an Ethiopian organization that serves as an umbrella for over 300 national and international NGOs. The agency's four-story office complex was elegant by any standard, North or South. As we shared the customary macchiato, I began to explain the purpose of my visit. My university, in partnership with respected higher education institutions in the city, was preparing to launch a new master's degree program focused on urban-poor leadership development. Because the program featured a total of five internships (one in each of five different development sectors), we needed his help in identifying the most respectable organizations for potential placements.

The director listened attentively as I explained how community-based global learning powerfully grounds academic study in the lived experience of marginalized groups, enabling students to put a human face to social theory. I carried on for two or three minutes, and wanted to pontificate further, but paused for him to respond. After taking a long sip on his macchiato, he set the cup down, leaned forward, and simply asked:

So, how do our member NGOs stand to benefit from your students' involvement?

There was no rebuff in the question. Having supervisory responsibility over hundreds of Ethiopian organizations, the director needed, reasonably, to collect as much information as possible before deciding whether or not to lend his support. For him the query was innocent enough. But for me it exposed what is often the elephant in the room in discussions of engaged global learning: *community benefit*.

I did manage to piece together a response to the director's question, although I knew it painted an incomplete and idealized picture. Foreign volunteers, I said, bring fresh energy and empathic concern. They offer contrasting perspectives and certain technical skills. Some are even able to leverage financial resources and social networks to strengthen organizational capacity.

My host nodded approvingly. He then reached across his desk, graciously shook my hand, and announced, "We would be happy to facilitate service placements for you." With that our conversation ended, but like a pebble in a shoe I couldn't shake his friendly pushback. Over the next few months, it produced something of a limp in my professional gait, compelling me to confront an essential question:

How might community-engaged forms of global learning create just relationships and reciprocal benefits for both guests and hosts?

What follows can be considered a tentative resolution. Borrowing from theatrical performance, the "act" of balancing the benefits of world learning unfolds in three "scenes." Scene one opens with a discussion of reciprocity as an ethical imperative in working with communities that host world learners. Scene two then offers an analysis of the benefit *im*balance, attempting to explain why the community perspective receives such scant attention. Finally, in scene three, we put four interlocking factors—ethical vision, student selection, program design, and organization placement—in dialogue with each other. In the process, we can begin to imagine optimal conditions for mutually beneficial world learning.

Scene 1: Who Benefits?

Global education has a long and rich tradition of rooting students' intellectual and intercultural development in the resources of human and natural communities. *Global engagement* speaks to purposeful and well-structured efforts to bring real-world relevance to student development by deliberately inserting learners into the life of foreign communities. There they learn to bridge differences, deepen their intellectual inquiry, and create something of public value (Paige, 1993; Lempert & Briggs, 1996; Lutterman-Aguilar & Gingerich, 2002).

And yet the question of *focus* remains: Is global learning exclusively about students' own development—serving their interests, their needs, their desires—or does it also have a public purpose? In other words, who is expected to profit from community-based learning? Who is really providing a service to whom, and who are the primary recipients of those services? Whose reality and knowledge counts? Whose voice matters? Who assesses outcomes and determines "success"? (Chambers, 1997; Holland & Blackburn, 1998). In short, who benefits?

Questions like these are validated, at least rhetorically, within the global service-learning literature. Nevertheless, the broader field of international education has yet to advance a systematic model that balances the benefits between participating students and host community members. By and large, the "for whom" question is answered in terms of the reality and agendas of uppers (privileged outsiders), while the interests of lowers (more vulnerable community residents) are largely ignored. Universities and third-party organizations may see themselves as being *in* the community, and even providing valuable services *to* the community, but rarely are they *of* and *for* the community in ways that intentionally seek to improve the local quality of life. In fact, the *for whom* question is regularly dismissed as futile moralizing. "Don't get too caught up in ethical considerations," a senior professional once counseled me. "Just do your travel study or service, try to be respectful, and enjoy yourself. In today's world, everyone's a tourist!"

For several decades now, the civic/global engagement movement has sought to recenter the community "as a resource to empower and be empowered by" (Musil, 2003). A central conviction has been that educational institutions operating in domestic or international contexts have an ethical responsibility to use their considerable resources in ways that contribute to the commonweal through their teaching, research, and service missions

(Boyer, 1996; Carnegie Foundation, 2008; Kezar et al., 2005). Respect and reciprocity are elevated as cardinal virtues in socially responsive learning.[1]

Almost all of the big questions bearing upon a survivable future are fundamentally ethical questions. Community-engaged global learning thus becomes, inescapably, an ethical endeavor. As high-status moral agents, world learners typically enter the communities of others with an external set of assumptions, agendas, and social habits. They unwittingly intervene in the lives of lower-status residents and institutions with divergent values and affinities. Certain effects, whether positive or negative, are inevitable. Privileged outsiders can either strengthen or weaken family ties; increase or deplete the supply of basic material goods; overcome or reinforce patterns of discrimination; create or reduce jobs for the unemployed; protect or imperil cultural traditions and identities; and either help repair or further despoil the natural world. Power dynamics saturate all intercultural relationships. Community-engaged global learning is always, inevitably, entangled in particular historical, cultural, geographic, and political contexts. Living and learning "above the fray" and shorn of consequences is an impossibility.

Family homestays provide a salient example. Foreign guests have the potential to ease financial hardship within select households through direct room and board payments. But they might also introduce behaviors—like substance abuse, sexual promiscuity, and excessive energy use—that disturb customary cultural and environmental norms. The risk of harm only increases when guests of relatively greater economic and social power are inserted into human and nonhuman communities that are resource-poor, unstable, and fragile. The very nature of the stay changes the home.

World learners are rational beings, able to choose to behave in ways that "give back" to the communities that support their learning. Recognizing this fact, global educators have entered new language into their lexicon—terms like *public purpose, sustained partnership, community voice, local ownership, gender inclusion, mutual respect,* and *reciprocal benefit.* This is fundamentally the language of justice. When incorporated in ethical codes and standards of practice, it calls attention to the question of how power might be used to minimize harm and maximize good.[2] One example is The Forum on Education Abroad's *Code of Ethics for Education Abroad* (2011). It urges "institutions and provider organizations [to] be aware of and sensitive to host community cultural norms and expectations in program planning and execution, including . . . reciprocal opportunities that benefit both the sending and receiving country's educational institutions, students and broader communities" (p. 8). Precisely *how* program benefits might be balanced between student-guests and hosts is left up to each sending organization. Nevertheless, the reciprocity principle holds: Global learners, and the organizations that facilitate them, have a moral obligation to exercise their financial and cultural power in ways that are fair and beneficial to all parties.

World Learning as Capacity Building

To speak of a public purpose for world learning is to call up a development term of art: *capacity building* (Ubels, Acquaye-Baddoo, & Fowler, 2010). All positive learning (development) is ultimately about expanding human potential and enlarging human freedoms. It is about individuals, groups, and organizations developing the capabilities that empower them to make choices that allow them to lead lives that they value.

Consider a group of Canadian nursing students setting out to improve lives at an under-resourced health clinic in Sumatra, Indonesia. The demands of the situation, both physical and intercultural, will no doubt test the limits of each volunteer's capability. Almost immediately they will need to understand the local context; manage emotional responses; communicate, however haltingly, in the local language; and patiently learn what forms of healthcare are culturally appropriate. Lacking such capacity development, their interactions with residents will likely *not* add much value, to either themselves or others. In fact, the service project could prove detrimental to both.

Global educators have succeeded in developing fairly sophisticated models of *student* capacity development, typically using the language of outcomes or competencies (Deardorff, 2012; Hovland, 2009). And yet two dimensions of competence are generally left undefined. The first has to do with the particular moral, social, and ethical responsibilities of global learners. The second is how student capability relates, developmentally, to the strengthening of community capacity.

Capacity development at the community level invariably revolves around skilled and dedicated individuals within families, businesses, government agencies, religious congregations, and other community institutions. Small-scale, grassroots organizations are often the primary vehicles for organizing local residents and providing essential goods and services where governments fail to do so. During the state of emergency in Chile under military general Augusto Pinochet, for example, women in the slums of Santiago formed public kitchens to feed families and give local women a public forum to meet and discuss problems. Illustrative cases are present in virtually all human communities.

Although internal divisions and special interest groups can riddle unified action at the grassroots level, the greatest challenge to community capacity-building is actually located *outside* engaged organizations and local communities. Resident mobility, lack of economic opportunity, entrenched political interests, and mal-distribution of resources are all factors that exert tremendous influence and can prove highly resistant to change, whether from the inside or the outside.

Since this chapter focuses on the potential role of the foreign volunteer in community capacity-building, it's important to point out that the duty of outsiders is generally not to do anything directly *for* local residents. They can lend extra hands to projects already in place, and otherwise facilitate and support. But ultimately the development process must be controlled and led by the people themselves in the areas of health, sanitation, education, business enterprise, water supply, agriculture, public works, security, and social welfare.

Generally speaking, short-term foreign workers are unversed in the country's intricate history and culture. Additionally, high program turnover rates and steep learning curves make gaining local acceptance difficult at best. Hosting organization, can justify engrafting outsiders into their operational work to the extent those outsiders bring proper intentions and practical competence in areas like grant writing, field research, and program evaluation. The local group hosting the Canadian nursing students, for instance, would expect the foreign volunteers to patiently listen and learn from the people they are trying to help; to assume supportive, noncommanding roles alongside national staff; and to employ whatever technical knowledge and skills they had to assist in delivering vital services. In so doing, they could hope to become a valued asset to the community organization (Burkey, 1993; Kaplan, 2002).

Capacity building is an art that grows in degrees as a result of trust relationships; expertise; and hard, sustained work. World learners must learn to manage their own field presence while negotiating as many as six other stakeholder groups: their sponsoring school, college, or congregation; faculty leaders; a brokering (third-party) organization; a particular group of people in the foreign community (e.g., a grassroots NGO or local congregation); the broader residential community; and public officials. Each group has its own particular stake or interest in program activities.

Sometimes those stakes converge; at other times they diverge. If the foreign nursing students were to prioritize skillful helping, and the resident beneficiaries prioritized physical and mental wellness, there would be a potential win–win. But what if these same students were to enter the host community with few technical abilities and little cultural understanding? And what if the primary motivation of the partner organization was to secure ongoing project funding from a Northern partner? The two entities would likely find themselves at cross-purposes, unwittingly creating conditions that potentially introduce real harm to community members.

Obviously, the extent to which world learners actually interact with community members and organizations will vary from program to program. Students enrolled in a two-week, faculty-led art history trip to Florence will rarely be expected to develop deep empathies toward and alliances with resident Italians. On the other hand, students enrolled in a semester-long program addressing human rights and migrant labor in Immokalee, Florida, the epicenter of America's $600 million winter tomato-growing industry, might be urged to actively probe the experiences and perspectives of the industry's growers, harvesters, packers, organizers, and enforcers. To do so, they would likely need to hone their Spanish language skills and obtain permission to labor in the fields alongside farmworkers, sharing their low wages, physical strain, and health vulnerabilities. By choosing to *live from the inside* rather than merely *look from the outside*, engaged global learners could hope to acquire a firsthand, in-depth understanding of the official (institutional and financial) powers, as well as the under-studied and easily dismissed power of the grassroots campaigns conducted over the last two decades by tenacious groups of tomato workers.

Scene 2: The Benefit Imbalance

Given how pervasive the norm of reciprocity is in human development, it's rather surprising that foreign student-volunteers remain the chief, if not exclusive, beneficiaries of most global-learning programs. Educators might genuinely hope that local residents will be enriched by the presence of these students. But common practice is for study-service programs to locate *in* communities without feeling any particular responsibility *to* them. The tacit assumption seems to be that groups of earnest 20-somethings have an unqualified right to enter the habitat of others, and will produce few, if any, negative effects.

A handful of studies do allege positive outcomes for foreign *students* serving in certain types of community service projects (see Birdsall, 2005; Crabtree, 2013; Eyler, Giles, Gray, & Stenson, 2001; Frumkin & Jastrzab, 2010; Irie, Daniel, Cheplick, & Philips, 2010; Jameson, Clayton, & Jaeger, 2011; Lasker, 2016; Lough & Sherraden 2012; Lough et al., 2014; McBride, A.M.; Reardon & Forester, 2015; Stoeker, Beckman, & Boo Hi Minn, 2010; Stoeker & Tryon, 2009; Worrall, 2007). And yet the preponderance of research provides little concrete evidence for long-term *community* benefits as a result of global-learning programs. Dan Butin (2010), after a thorough review of studies on the subject, comes to this doubtful conclusion: "There is little empirical evidence that service-learning provides substantive, meaningful, and long-term solutions for the communities it is supposedly helping" (p. 12).

Global educators have treated the subject of *student* learning through education abroad programs with commendable breadth and clarity (see Vande Berg et al., 2012). What we lack is an equally serious effort to demonstrate positive, sustained benefits to community stakeholders. Although global educators might hope to select and equip first-rate *capacity builders*—learners who are self-regulating, insatiably curious, and endowed with abilities that field partners value—this is a high-water mark that few institutions achieve. The reasons, as we will see, have much to do with a confused bottom line. Success in service-learning or community research programs is routinely assessed by the rewards volunteers receive from their work, rather than the benefits received by the served. The result is that community stakeholders endure a chronic imbalance of benefits vis-à-vis participating students (Figure 6.1).

Acknowledging this reality, we might then ask: *What accounts for the overwhelming bias within global-education programs toward serving and developing students rather than the communities that host them?*

Five main issues help frame a response. The first is associated with a functional disciplinary division that shapes global education. The other four are firmly entrenched in cultural, conceptual, institutional, and behavioral patterns.

Functional Divide

Global educators juggle a complex and often contradictory mix of mandates. They are called upon to generate revenue, organize fruitful educational experiences, and prepare graduates for the workforce, not to

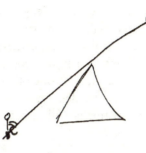

STUDENT BENEFITS	COMMUNITY BENEFITS
Real-world experience	
Self-and cultural awareness	
Second language skills	
Disciplinary deepening	
Challenged assumptions/values	
Problem-solving & leadership skills	
Intercultural development	
Independence & adaptability	Low-cost assistance
Opportunity to "do good"	Cross-cultural awareness
Exchange of perspectives	English language acquisition
Résumé building	Fresh energy and ideas
Desire for further involvement	External power connections

FIGURE 6.1. Benefit imbalance.

mention help students apply their learning to their life. In an era of academic capitalism (Altbach, Berdahl, & Gumport, 2011), educators no longer have the luxury of choosing freely between mission and market imperatives. At the same time, we risk becoming educationally rudderless without some collective verdict on what is perhaps our most fundamental question: *global education for what, and for whom?* (Bhandari, 2013; Deardorff, 2013).

The absence of a clear and compelling answer to this question is traceable to the functional separation of two fields of practice: international education and community development. On the one hand, international educators have traditionally concerned themselves with *student* learning in modernized Western societies. On the other hand, the energies of development practitioners focus on moving materially poor and marginalized people from deprivation to sufficiency. Geographically and functionally the two fields diverge. Professionally, each group inhabits its own disciplinary silo: They read different books, attend different conferences, research different issues, design different types of programs, articulate different kinds of outcomes . . . and rarely talk to one other.

Humphrey Tonkin (2010), president emeritus of the University of Hartford, clarifies the cause of this fateful disconnect as it relates to international service-learning (ISL):

> American models of ISL stress impact on students rather than on the community—sometimes to an unsettling degree. . . . One reason for the relative neglect of community impact is the fact that, historically, ISL emerged as an expansion of study abroad in the direction of community service, rather than an expansion of community service in the direction of study abroad. This perception is reinforced by . . . the damaging notion that the larger world exists as a kind of classroom where the American student can learn values or skills that can be transferred to the United States and that student's adult life. To see the world in this way is to lose all sense of reciprocity, an issue central to service learning. . . . At best, study abroad programs are expected to do no harm to the communities in which they are located: rarely is the question raised as to how they can actually do good. (p. 193)

The notion of contributing a "good" through educational and service-oriented travel is not new. Most notably in the nineteenth-century missionary movement, and in the U.S. Peace Corps today, foreign workers have consciously intervened within global communities with developmental intent. What is remarkable is not that education-to-make-a-difference takes place; it is that global educators have yet to engage development practice in any significant way (Crabtree, 2008).

This is especially regrettable given the strong ideological and pedagogical intersections that exist between experiential education, global service-learning, and community development. True, mainstream development schemes do have a notorious dark side, and many Peace Corps volunteers report being sorely ineffective. But global development practice isn't what it used to be. Many new-generation activists are dedicated to the ideals of empowerment, collective action, and self-reliance. In some of the most difficult places on Earth, they join local leaders and groups in efforts to solve local problems with local resources (see McKinnon, 2011). This should only encourage us to bring the wisdom of people-centered ideas and practices into strategic conversation with the learning structures and resources of study abroad and global service-learning (Figure 6.2).

Consumer Mind-Set

Another cause of the benefit imbalance has to do with the central role of the market in human relationships. Marketplace relations tend to transform everything (including educational processes) from intrinsic worth to use value, and thence to exchange value. The dynamics of commodification and commercialization symbolically convert ordinary places, peoples, and cultural practices into consumer products through the tourist gaze. While every gaze is different, they all tend to be constructed, endlessly, by a constant stream of media images and the creative marketing of otherness.

Even programs with a genuine commitment to community benefit find it hard to resist commercial pressures. Upwardly mobile parents expect sponsors (sending institutions, program administrators, and placement organizations), along with partners (field organizations), to satisfy their offspring's need for extraordinary and life-changing experiences. Providers then compete with one another to deliver those experiences, knowing full well that student-consumers will invest themselves only as long as they receive more than they are required to give. The nonbinding nature of an essentially consumerist relationship means that program sites (communities) readily transform into a global classroom or laboratory for encounters that are transitory, nonrepetitive, and often unequal in power. Any

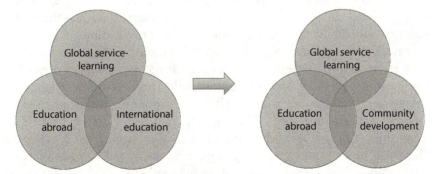

FIGURE 6.2. Theoretical progression.

negative effects at the program site are accepted as a reasonable cost for facilitating student development.

Grassroots organizations can also be infected with a mind-set that draws their attention away from the interests of community members. It's not unusual for cash-strapped organizations in resource-poor settings to seek out Western educational partners, and not because they actually *need* foreign volunteers; able and willing local residents abound, many of them un- and underemployed. A North–South partnership promises to elevate the organization's local stature and perhaps guarantee its financial survival. Over time, something like a codependent relationship develops: Upwardly mobile outsiders find volunteering organizations to channel their sense of obligation to intervene on behalf of others; the volunteering organizations recruit local agencies to provide challenging on-the-ground learning experiences for paying students; and the grassroots agencies pick up the desperately needed cash and connections that a Western partner brings. The resulting patron-client power imbalance acts to compromise the self-determination of host communities, even as it tempts nonpoor outsiders to play God in the lives of the poor.

Conceptual Confusion

The next reason for the lopsided effects of global-learning programs lies in imprecise and even conflicting conceptions of *community*. What or who is the "community" in community engagement? Is it geographic or social, face-to-face or virtual? Does it include the nonhuman communities of soils, plants, and animals? If community equals a particular community organization—a hosting clinic, a school, a church—do we assume that it stands in for the broader network of private, public, and civic agencies in a bounded area? What about those community residents—the vast majority—who are neither staff nor clients of the organization?

In reality, most hosting organizations, and those served by them, are not, properly speaking, communities. They are distinctive subsets of a much larger collectivity. Like Russian nesting dolls, they sit within neighborhoods, towns, and municipalities. Although community residents might look and act alike to the eyes of foreigners, they will invariably be differentiated by ethnicity, age, tribal affiliation, religion, and economic status. There will be in-groups and out-groups, hierarchies and exclusions. No single, unified identity and set of relationships will exist. The differentiated nature of their society makes it exceedingly difficult to specify the parameters of community work or community impact, since we are always dealing with a surrogate entity.

Practical Constraints

Even with the conceptual issues settled, two practical concerns remain. The first surrounds questions of impact assessment. How should we try to gauge community effects, and at what intervals? Who should drive the evaluation process and analyze the data it generates? And what is the appropriate unit for measuring change? Is it the partnering organization? The lives of individual service recipients? Some larger social group or geographically bounded settlement? Practicality would seem to dictate that impact assessments be limited to one or two beneficiary groups associated with one or more grassroots organizations.

A second functional obstacle in the path of rebalancing student and community benefits has to do with the culture of post-secondary academic life. Community-based pedagogies present a unique set of challenges that keep learners and educators focused on a limited set of student learning goals. Development-oriented global-learning programs, in particular, are a hard sell for students who are more concerned about making friends and building a résumé than on repairing the world. Faculty may also shy away from community engagement, but not because they prefer the Ivory Tower over the wider world. Heavy teaching loads and onerous promotion and tenure requirements keep them tethered to conventional programs with a narrow focus on content instruction.

Charity Orientation

These four pressure sets combine to create a general orientation toward host communities best conveyed by a single word: *charity*. A charity ethic, explains Keith Morton (1995), a pioneer in the civic engagement movement, "involves individual acts of caring that transcend time and space . . . with no expectation that any lasting impact will be made" (p. 20). In most cases, relatively well-off persons dispense "help" on behalf of less-advantaged persons. Depending on program goals and local needs, volunteers might teach English, build homes, or care for AIDS orphans.

There is a definite upside to charitable action. Learners have the opportunity to break out of indifference, make empathetic person-to-person connections, and better understand perplexing realities. But helping also carries certain hazards. Altruistic behavior is often bound up with self-interest, as when one of our nursing students dispenses medicines in the Sumatran health clinic to assuage guilt and gain professional status. Charitable service risks helping givers feel good about actions that actually do very little good. Peter Buffett (2013), son of grand philanthropist Warren Buffett, calls this "conscience laundering." Rich people, says Buffett, can "feel better about accumulating more than any one person could possibly need to live on by sprinkling a little around as an act of charity, [all the while] keeping the existing structure of inequality in place." To be sure, houses get built, wells get dug, and kids get tutored. But the short-term and one-off nature of most volunteer programs pretty well ensures that interventions will be "a mile wide and an inch deep," with little attention paid to the broader issues that make helping necessary in the first place.

Beyond Charity

In contrast to the dominant charity model, let's try to imagine global-learning programs being organized according to widely-accepted capacity-building principles and practices (Ellerman, 2005; Mayer, 1994). The energy for deep, reciprocal learning is the result of strong, respectful relationships formed between ready and willing grassroots organizations and well-qualified outsiders. Hungry to learn formally and informally, the outsiders embed themselves in local households and citizen groups. They seek to take onto themselves some of the life-constraints of those radically different from themselves, as discussed in chapter 4. They listen as residents narrate their life experiences and priority concerns. They engage in activities that create a bridge between treating symptoms and working for institutional change. A fair trade of inputs and benefits is secured through respectful, reciprocal, and sustained relationships.

Table 6.1 attempts to delineate some key philosophical and operational differences between charity and a more capacity building approach to global learning. The distinctions are not absolute and may be slight caricatures or idealizations. Nevertheless, they serve to highlight the lines along which any rebalancing work might take place.

TABLE 6.1. Charity-Development Contrasts

Charity *Service Providing*	Development *Capacity Building*
Focus on *server growth*	Focus on *healthy communities*
Change from *top down or outside in*	Change from *bottom up*
Understanding from *formal teaching*	Understanding from *direct immersion*
Power from *credentials*	Power from *relationships*
Community as *needs and deficiencies*	Community as *assets and abilities*
Focus on *individuals or families*	Focus on *organizations or communities*
Students as *service providers*	Students as *community members*
Residents as *clients, beneficiaries* (paternal)	Residents as *citizens, partners* (reciprocal)
Problems rooted in flawed *persons, cultures*	Problems rooted in broken *systems*
Servers respond to *symptoms*	Servers respond to *root issues*
Bias toward *outside ("expert") knowledge*	Bias toward *local wisdom*
Mind-set of *blueprinting, doing for*	Mind-set of *participating, doing with*
Interventions emphasize *projects*	Interventions emphasize *people*
Services relieve *immediate conditions*	Services strengthen *community capacity*
Assessment based on *outputs*	Assessment based on *outcomes and impacts*
Entry point	Ending point

There's an old cliché in grassroots development: "Give a man a fish, you feed him for a day; teach him how to fish and you feed him for a lifetime." On the surface, it sounds self-evidently true. But hearing it also makes me somewhat uncomfortable. Do poor people not know how to fish? Aren't women—even more than men—the ones who need fish? And what good is it to be taught how to fish if the rights to the fish are owned by powerful landlords? Or if fisherfolk must sell their catch to monopoly companies who command unfair prices? Or if fish stocks have already been emptied by commercial fleets, despoiled through mining or timber operations, or dried up because of extensive water use upstream? These circumstances have nothing to do with the people's actual knowledge of fishing. They involve tenacious differentials of power that prevent their access to fish. A campaign of fish distribution, however well-meaning, would do nothing to alter these structural conditions.

Even so, a strict separation between charity and development as two types of community engagement obscures the fact that they are more complementary than contradictory. The ancient Judaic principle of *tzedakah* merges the two approaches:

> Suppose, for example, that I give someone £100. Either he is entitled to it, or he is not. If he is, then my act is a form of justice. If he is not, it is an act of charity. In English (as with the Latin terms *caritas* and *justitia*) a gesture of charity cannot be an act of justice, nor can an act of justice be described as charity. *Tzedakah* is therefore an unusual term, because it means both. (Sacks, 2013)

The respective instincts of charity and justice thus intersect at the point of affirming the inherent dignity and irreducible value of persons. Individual acts of charity, when carried out with a high degree of social solidarity, can result in enduring positive effects. Doing good can also lead to doing what is best, acting as a sort of "home base" for longer-term actions oriented toward institutional reform. Thus, charitable service and justice-seeking activism are best understood not in juxtaposition to one another, but rather in the ways each deepens our involvement in the other.

Where does this leave us as learners and educators? How might world learning become more deliberate, more responsive, and ultimately more "radical" (from *radix*, going to the root) in its ability to facilitate a two-way flow of benefit between world learners and host communities?

Scene 3: The Art of Intervention

Intervention is always tricky business, especially when carried out by cultural outsiders. Development means change, and change is always mysterious, context-dependent, and unpredictable. Which is why well-intentioned interventions often lead to unintended consequences, many of them far from beneficial.

- Breakthrough technologies like laptop computers and smartphones can facilitate income generation for poor farmers in the Congo; however, they can also incite armed conflict and human rights abuses over the mining of minerals (like coltan) that are used in their production.
- Subsidized corn in the United States is used to make ethanol, a fossil fuel alternative, but it ends up causing dramatic increases in global food prices and food rioting in at least 30 countries.
- The Gates Foundation and the World Health Organization administer billions of vaccinations in developing countries, but when single-use plastic syringes are burned in small furnaces, a mixture of carcinogens and other toxic gases is released.
- Foreign volunteers mobilize to help build schools, train teachers, and buy textbooks so that young Afghan girls can learn how to read and write (as detailed in Greg Mortensen's *Three Cups of Tea*). But because of strict patriarchal codes, chronic teacher absenteeism (due to low wages), and the need for children to labor for their families, little educational development results.

When philosopher Appiah (2010) is asked to explain his life philosophy, he typically replies, "My philosophy is that everything is more complicated than you thought" (p. 198). Working out the real-world implications of doing good is far knottier than we first imagine. External resources—labor, knowledge, money, and technology—when infused into resource-poor communities, may, under certain conditions, help empower previously excluded or marginalized groups. But just as easily those same resources can end up reinforcing community deficiencies and creating crippling dependencies. Our challenge is to do everything in our power to minimize the harm and maximize the good to the receiving society.

When this is done, intervention becomes an act of art making. Artistry can be as thin as connecting with geographically dispersed others using social media or as thick as participating in a multi-stakeholder action research process cutting across an entire sector within a community. The truest character of outsider handiwork, whether in the role of e-pal, house-guest, volunteer, or investigator, primarily depends on the *qualities of self* they bring to it. Of course, individuals don't act in a vacuum. Character

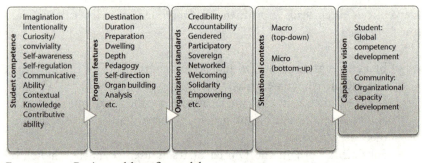

FIGURE 6.3. Reciprocal benefit model.

and behavior interact with various *external factors*—program designs, partner organizations, and dynamic field contexts. When considered together, all of these factors create an intervention ecology that can either expand or restrict reciprocal and transformative benefits (Figure 6.3).

The precise relationship between learners, organizations, contexts, and impacts is extremely difficult to sort out or make generalizations about. The modern world is simply too complex to predict, much less control, all that is happening or can happen. At best, good theory can reduce the number of unwelcome surprises. What follows, then, is not a detailed blueprint designed to forecast the exact direction of learner and community change. It is simply a tree to climb, a vantage point from which to see more of the forest and consider connections between parts of the landscape. From that position we can better plot the path toward answering our central query:

Under what conditions might community-engaged global learning be sufficiently transformative, both for learner-participants and for host organizations, to make a modest contribution to the common good?

Capabilities Vision

To answer this question, we necessarily start with the end in mind. When artists set out to create, they begin with some mental picture, to which they add forms and lights and colors and shadows. The initial image orients their choices and guides their hands. Likewise, if we are to balance the benefits of world learning, we begin with some *vision* of an ultimate collective good. From that internal compass pointed to True North we work backward, considering how certain types of learners, in conjunction with certain types of program designs and field partners, intervening in particular ways, might produce the kind of on-the-ground experience that generates positive learner and community outcomes.

If someone were to ask you to describe the kind of world you would wish to leave to your children's children, what would you tell them? However speculative, what we picture as good and valuable and possible in human society subtly directs our work in the world. Carl Jung, the groundbreaking Swiss psychiatrist, believed that transformation only takes place in the presence of images, not concepts. Until we first reimagine the world and ourselves in it, nothing happens. In Jung's words, "The dream drives the action."

Every way of life is energized by a defining set of collectively held aspirations and ambitions—a zeitgeist. The cultural dream of most moderns is easily recognizable, what we might call *The World as It Is*. It can be summarized as follows: The world is an arena in which nations, nongovernmental groups, and businesses compete for advantage. The progress or development of peoples within this theatre of activity is best understood in terms of the aspirations, organizational structures, and technical procedures of industrial culture. Rural peoples advance from underdeveloped to developed status by forsaking their natal lands, moving to major cities, taking up residence in high-rise apartments, and laboring away in factories to produce goods and services that moderns no longer provide for themselves. Sometime in the future, the system can be expected to generate enough wealth to "lift all boats" to Western economic standards. Languages and cultures may be lost. Scores of people may be made redundant. The planet's natural systems may suffer desolation. Industrial pollution may trigger runaway climate change. And property and capital may continue to concentrate in the hands of the few. But the basic logic and operations of the system are immutable and, in any case, unproblematic.

Within this storyline, engaged forms of global learning set out to fulfill their public mission by equipping entrepreneurial types with the world knowledge necessary for launching ventures of "purposeful profit" that can improve the fortunes of others. With a critical mass of altruistic cosmopolitans, the benefits of the present system can hope to be extended worldwide (Friedman, 2005; Norberg, 2017; Prahalad, 2009).

Now, let's consider an alternative narrative—*The World as It Might Be*. This story exists as a creative response to worsening social, psychospiritual, environmental, and economic conditions associated with the modern way of life. Humanity finally realizes a manner of life that is inclusive, peaceful, healthy, productive, and biologically and culturally diverse. Progress is no longer primarily identified with short-term profits or material consumption. Quality of life replaces standard of living as the central indicator of the wealth of persons and communities. "More" is still a primary value, but not necessarily more money or more of what money can buy. The desire is for more qualitative fulfillment and fewer conspicuous consumption; more creative expression and less impersonal bureaucracy; more clean energy production and less toxic pollution; more locally-owned shops and fewer superstores; more public places and fewer privatized spaces; more cycle lanes and train tracks and fewer highways; more reused materials and fewer landfills; more mutual aid and less individualistic competition; more self-acceptance and less social status-seeking (Gibson-Graham et al., 2013; Korten, 2007; McKibben, 2010; Heinberg & Lerch, 2010; Wheatley & Frieze, 2011). In the vision of *The World as It Might Be*, student and community outcomes are referenced to the Great Work of reinventing a viable human situation on a survivable planet. Table 6.2 summarizes the contrasts between the two stories.

Rural and urban poor populations, like their more privileged counterparts, also carry a vision of a preferred future. For them, "development" primarily and ultimately entails the realization of a basic set of freedoms and capabilities, which is to say, a fully human life (Nussbaum, 2011; Sen, 1999). Adequate nutrition, meaningful work and leisure opportunities, decent healthcare and education, self-respecting relationships, political freedoms, and property rights—these are the basic building blocks for wellbeing for an individual, a household, community, a city, or a nation.

What might a fully realized capabilities vision look like at the local level? Appendix C presents one possible model in terms of a five-fold "bottom line": material security, psycho-cultural vitality, sociopolitical equity, moral-spiritual integrity, and Earth community. Under each goal nests a set of measurable indicators of community health or capability. These standards were originally defined by poor people in over 23 countries when asked what their development priorities were (see Narayan et al., 2000a; Narayan et al., 2000b). The list of indicators suggests some measurable thresholds for judging the long-term effects of community interventions.

Student Competence

With characteristic playfulness, Henry David Thoreau (1854/1919), in *Walden*, calls attention to the unsavory side of meddling in other people's business: "If I knew for certain that a man was coming to my house with

TABLE 6.2. Alternative World-Stories

The World as It Is	The World as It Might Be
Global markets (bigger is better)	Community/regional economies
Profit maximization (make a buck)	Contributive work
Growth imperative (more is better)	Ethic of enough
Standard of living (consume)	Quality of life (plenitude)
Organized/controlled by few (power over)	Self-organized and self-governed
Hierarchy, power-based (follow orders)	Complementarity, task-based
Competition (compete or die)	Cooperation
Exploitation (race to the bottom)	Conservation
Dehumanization (technological control)	Connection
Quantification (show me the numbers)	Quality of person and product
Wasteful (use up, discard, pollute)	Waste nothing
Uniformity (join the crowd)	Cultural and biodiversity
Mobility (indifference to place)	Embedded in place
Earth as "raw materials" (neutralize nature)	Earth as gift, stewardship
Global cultures as attractions (tourist gaze)	Global cultures as repositories of wisdom
Private benefit (normative inequality)	Public good
Vulnerable and unsustainable	Resilient and sustainable

the conscious design of doing me good, I should run for my life . . . for fear that I should get some of his good done to me" (p. 82). Thoreau would probably not run if he found himself in desperate straits and made a personal appeal for help. The hazards of service are most apparent when volunteers attempt to do good without being asked or without the requisite competence. Legitimate criticism is leveled at aid workers, service-learners, voluntourists, and missionaries for development work that features noble intentions but negligible long-term benefits. The persistent pattern of "virtuous failure" raises some searching questions:

Is it even possible for well-heeled outsiders to enter communities in a nonpaternalistic mode, and to make positive contributions, without fostering dependency and other unintended consequences? If so, what type of person holds the greatest potential for contributing to community betterment?

Americans like to think of themselves as tenderhearted and tough-minded individuals. Our almost obsessive celebration of hero-types serves to confirm a certain self-image of ones who ramble through remote and dangerous places in order to bring light and learning to others. Madonna in Malawi, Oprah in South Africa, Jason Russell in Uganda, Paul Mortenson in Pakistan and Afghanistan . . . the list goes on and on. Even when they are mocked as "Whites in Shining Armor" (Cole, 2012), they continue to be held up as emissaries of American optimism and generosity. Rarely do they learn from their mistakes.

Global educators can find themselves caught between two extreme forms of idealism. One is the idealism of development specialists who contend that the dignity of poor people is demeaned by having foreign amateurs initiate *any* change. The other is the idealism of do-gooders who seek to fulfill a sense of *noblesse oblige* by loading up depressed communities with subsidies and services. In truth, neither ignoring unfortunate communities nor turning them into collective clients of outside fixes will do much to secure even a minimum level of well-being.

Yes, but do privileged outsiders, whether foreign or national, actually provide any real benefits to less-fortunate communities? Is any measurable difference made beyond providing temporary assistance to a limited number of individuals? If capacity development is largely an "inside job," where does that leave the Good Samaritan volunteer or researcher? Hasn't a half-century of largely unsuccessful top-down and outside-in development "solutions" demonstrated the inability of even the smartest and gutsiest outsiders to make a real difference?

These are uncomfortable but fair questions. Our response carries two somewhat controversial assumptions. The first is this: *Materially poor communities beset with broken systems rarely rebuild themselves exclusively from within—that is, with no help from outside their communities.*

For deteriorated areas to turn around, residents need energy and vision, expertise and material resources, reinvestment and reneighboring. After decades living and working in rural Uganda, development educator Stan Burkey (1993) recognized the indispensable role played by outsiders: "Only rarely do participatory development activities arise from within poor groups without any form of outside stimulus" (p. 75). Some communities find the strengthening they need through public agencies, whether at the municipal, regional, or national level. At other times an external activator is needed, which might take the form of capable foreign volunteers.

A second assumption naturally follows: *Outsiders of a special character and competence can play beneficial roles in helping communities help themselves.*

Our emphasis here is on an often-neglected element of global-learning programs: the screening, selection, and preparation of service-learners and community-based researchers. The neglect of quality assurance is systemic, and responsibility more or less equally shared by learners, educational agencies, and field organizations. Many young adults sincerely want to achieve something positive for others, yet lack the know-how and character development to be cocreators of capacity instead of mere consumers of service or research experiences. Cultural and linguistic neophytes, they can easily monopolize staff time with their daily needs without providing much of value in return. Educational organizations can also be part of the problem. Operating in a fiercely competitive marketplace, they often feel intense pressure to sign up any live body with a minimum grade point average. Then there are the field organizations that host volunteers and researchers. Many agree to host foreign workers without raising some fundamental questions: Do they bring anything of value to the organization or community? Will servicing them—arranging lodging and food, work and research sites, supervision and entertainment—cost us more than we can hope to receive in return? (Lupton, 2007).

Despite their good intentions, the limited time and cultural insight available to most short-termers only heightens the risk of misguided action. Development theorist Paul Collier (2008) highlights the hazard with his warning against *headless hearts*—those who are sincere in their desire to be useful to others but lack the requisite experience, skill training, and contextual knowledge to add real value to a situation.

Headless hearts have an evil twin—the *heartless heads*. These are foreign workers who possess good intellectual grounding, but lack the moral sentiments necessary to build enduring trust relationships. Instead of setting out to form affective ties with residents, they dodge opportunities to learn their names, to eat and drink with them, to listen to their stories and tell their own. In short, they lack genuine concern. Denis Goulet (1995) sums up the detrimental effects of both capacity defects: "Love without disciplined intelligence is inefficient, naïve, and in its bungling good intentions, catastrophic. And intelligence without love breeds a brutalizing technocracy that crushes people" (pp. 193-194). Given the steep learning curves facing outsiders as they gain local knowledge and local acceptance, it is certainly reasonable to question whether relatively brief ventures into community development will accomplish the dual purpose of learner *and* resident benefit.

Kate Stefanko, placement director at People and Places, thinks they can, if done right. "We believe that a carefully placed, thoroughly screened, well-prepared, skilled volunteer can—and does—have a positive impact," says Stefanko (2015). In other words, much depends on whether a passion-driven amalgam of character and competence can be deployed in people-centered community projects (Figure 6.4). One thing is clear: If reciprocity of benefit is to become a normative feature of community-engaged global learning, practitioners can no longer sidestep the question of whether or not participants are actually worthy of export.

Program Features

The assessment of factors *internal* to learners finds its complement in the evaluation of various *external* factors that influence the potential level of practical reciprocity. Student traits are not easy for educators to alter, much less control. What they can manipulate are various features of the programs they create or manage. Which leads us to ask: *What kind of program design holds the greatest potential for achieving an optimal balance of student and community benefit?*

As noted in chapter 4, a stunning variety of global-learning program types exist, ranging from domestic urban field study and short-term faculty-led travel seminars to direct enrollment in universities abroad. Together, they bear witness to the creative genius and endless adaptability of civic

FIGURE 6.4.   Vital capabilities in volunteering.

and global educators. Yet once the 3 Rs—respect, reciprocity, and responsibility—are seen as central values in the educational process, some critical distinctions must be made. Programs differ in terms of location, duration, student housing type, language of instruction, and a host of other factors (see Appendix B). By considering these distinctions, component by component, one thing becomes immediately clear: Program designs are far from equal in their student *and* community development potential. Program leaders can't expect a two-week program that effectively isolates students from the daily life of residents to achieve the same results as a semester-long program that has a continuous presence at the location and fully immerses students in community life. Two weeks is simply too short a period for most outsiders to become a valued part of a local family, comprehend the tangled causes of community problems, and ensure that their work actually serves the best interests of beneficiaries. Without a depth of belonging and cultural understanding, the hope for balancing benefits in any meaningful way dissipates.

Private benefit program designs are still normative in study away. They generally favor the international over the domestic, Western over non-Western, urban over rural, control over vulnerability, short-term over long-term, commonality over contrast, classroom over community, and charity over development. Program participants typically live and learn with other expatriates. Their interactions with the national population are mostly transitory, nonrepetitive, and oriented to satisfying private goals.

By contrast, shared good programs tend to operate from an alternative set of values and principles. They are characteristically small-scale, mission-driven, continuous, and longer term. Participants are vetted for personal character and competence. Pre- or in-field training aims to equip learners to comprehend the big-picture forces that shape the field situation. Students learn how to ask questions and to listen closely. Within their host community, bonds of affection and solidarity develop through common residence (family stays), common communication (language learning), and common cause (collaborative work and research). Sustained partnerships with select community organizations correct the turnover effect, allowing mutual learning to emerge out of authentic relationships instead of narrowly instrumental exchanges. Something of a social covenant begins to emerge, with students *and* residents committing themselves to the welfare of the other.

4. Organization Standards

Positive student and community outcomes depend on not only joining a certain kind of *student* to a certain kind of *program* but also bringing both into relationship with certain kinds of *field organizations*. Independently, cultural outsiders cannot determine the content or direction of community change. Primary responsibility falls to operational or advocacy-focused entities or groups that operate in the trenches for the public interest, day in and day out. They have a primary stake in defining what the problems are, which goals need to be prioritized, and what actions are most appropriate. By standing in for the wider community, they provide a vital relational bridge and developmental doorway for engaged global-learning programs.

Just as host organizations want to be confident in the character and competence of the foreign workers, the converse is also true: Workers deserve to know that the organizations they chose to affiliate with also meet basic quality standards. Purposeful volunteers often have questions that rarely get verbalized: What is the public reputation of this community organization? Has its credibility, local impact, and sustainability ever been vetted? Does it take a Band-Aid approach to issues or does it get at root issues? Can I realistically hope that the organization will be better off because of me than without me?

The task of evaluating prospective field partners requires a specific set of criteria (Cannon, 2013). Toward that end, Appendix D suggests 15 nondefinitive standards deemed to correlate with organizational quality. The standards are based on the practical experience and ethical reflection within movements for sustainable, responsible, pro-poor, and fair trade travel (Cleverdon & Kalisch, 2000; Hartman, Paris, & Blache-Cohen, 2014; Tourism Concern, 2017). Concerned with optimizing a two-way learning process, this diagnostic tool invites global learners to consider the many factors that affect organizational performance.

Collaborating organizations vary wildly in size, structure, focus, membership, and sphere of influence. They range from large corporations and government agencies to small, resident-driven self-help associations. Some work for big-picture reform of public policies and practices, while others focus on microlevel actions among smaller populations. Spend some time in any human community, anywhere in the world, and you'll soon discover that business cooperatives, religious groups, neighborhood councils, issue-oriented NGOs, schools, credit unions, and sports clubs enable struggling members to live healthier and happier lives (see Bornstein, 2007; Hawken, 2008).

Paradoxically, the most attractive community organizations tend to need outside assistance the least. They are *sovereign* in the sense that they stand tall, assured in their own strengths, with no need to approach Northern partners "hat in hand." Ivan Illich (1968), in his provocative speech "To Hell with Good Intentions," goaded a group of volunteers in Mexico: "If you insist on working with the poor, if this is your vocation, then at least work among the poor who can tell you to go to hell." Local organizations that are secure enough to tell outsiders where to go often make the best coeducators. They *expect* much from foreign workers—to be humble, other-centered, and self-starting—but they also *give* much in terms of meaningful support roles and dependable supervision. Not to mention a world-class education in indigenous forms of mutual aid and self-help.

Conversely, when organizational capacity and sovereignty are low, student energies run the risk of being unnecessary and noneducative—in short, a waste of time. This is often the result of organizations becoming dependent on, and beholden to, sources of labor, funding, and expertise from outside the community. When this happens organizational structures and outreach activities gradually conform to the templates of short-term, Western-financed project cycles. This is not an argument against strategic linkages with Northern universities and other provider organizations. But if the collaboration aims for long-term community empowerment, the locus of power and authority must firmly root at the local level.

Situational Contexts

A final component of the reciprocal benefit model concerns the particular contexts—historical, economic, social, and political—in which global-learning programs and community organizations operate. How an organization makes sense of the world around it inevitably shapes the character of its interventions and the level of confidence it has to effect real change.

External realities rarely carry equal importance for all stakeholders. Much depends on their social position and what they are trying to achieve. A foreign graduate student completing a two-month internship with a low-income-housing advocacy organization in California may decide to disregard the larger political situation in favor of her immediate work relationships. However, the sponsoring NGO may have much broader aims (e.g., trying to ease density restrictions near transit hubs) that require diligent, long-term negotiations with private and municipal entities. Positive social change requires power, hence attention on the part of advocacy-oriented organizations to politics and the institutions within which power is exercised.

Development specialists often sort capacity development efforts into two levels or situational contexts: the macro and the micro. The first is the *macro* setting, and it consists of a network of interlocking institutions—cultural, economic, political, legal, educational, medical, ecological, and so on—that operate at the municipal, national, or regional levels. Macrolevel practice typically aims to influence decision-makers to change the policies and practices of these institutions. Advocacy efforts might aim to amend unjust laws, decentralize bloated bureaucracies, expand access to education, reduce substance abuse and homelessness, beautify ugly landscapes, or promote active transportation. These public goods are secured through reforms that are typically top-down, funding-driven, government-sponsored, and expert-dependent. Insider groups are usually the ones to hammer out particular courses of action within particular sociopolitical environments. Outsiders often play a critical supportive role, contributing moral energy, extra hands, novel perspectives, and research skills.

The second context of development consists of *micro* activities within geographically or socially bounded groups. For individuals and families, empowerment is a decidedly small-scale and bottom-up process, drawing on high levels of social solidarity and shared commitment. Capacity development "from below" reminds us that the common good needs to involve *all* levels of society. Macro plans developed at the municipal or national levels require organic, workable solutions led by entrepreneurial searchers at the grassroots (Easterly, 2007).

Community organizations have an intensely personal stake in finding solutions to common problems. At the same time, every local community is inexorably linked to broader institutional structures, along with political and economic activities that stretch across regions and continents. These interconnections and interdependencies render grassroots initiatives exceedingly vulnerable to forces outside their direct control.

Picture a small group of foreign volunteers landing in the Philippines to work with a leading antitrafficking organization. In time they realize that most of the conditions that render women vulnerable to sexual exploitation—such as poverty, patriarchy, and political instability—have roots that can only be addressed *indirectly*. Their personal expressions of kindness and care may help to allay the damaging psychological effects of exploitation and humiliation, but, in themselves, cannot hope to undo the complex web of factors that constrain the women's lives. Similarly, a peasant association in rural India finds itself largely impotent when it comes to building roads to distant markets, rewriting bank-lending rules, or affecting the structure of global agricultural policies. Community-engaged global learning, for all its development potential, must accept the fact that local communities cannot do it all, or do it alone. "Small may be beautiful," notes sustainability guru Alan Durning (1989), "but it can also be insignificant" (p. 5).

The upshot is this: For world learning to empower reciprocal learning (change), the bird's-eye view and the worm's-eye view should be integrated into a bifocal way of seeing and acting in the world. An in-depth understanding of the conditions and needs of folk at the *community* level naturally links to the interests and demands of government and business stakeholders at the *municipal* and *national* levels. Working from the bottom up, the main concern of outsiders and insiders alike is whether projects are producing tangible, material benefits to local groups. A clear grasp of a multilayered situational context provides the necessary basis for maximizing the impact of strategic action.

Conclusion

The Ethiopian director introduced at the opening of this chapter may never know the intellectual journey that was set in motion by his unsettling question: *So, how do our member NGOs stand to benefit from your students' involvement?* Questions related to mutual respect and reciprocity of benefit, given the ever-widening gap between the global haves and the have-nots, have never been more urgent. When global learners are in right relationship with community stakeholders, both parties are positioned to be both givers and receivers. The epigraph by Rowan Williams (2009) at the head of this chapter captures this essential truth.

Over the last two decades, dedicated educators have made a convincing academic case for community-engaged learning by answering the question,

"Where's the *learning* in service-learning?" (Eyler & Giles, 1999). Needed now is an equally rigorous effort to establish the public value of that knowledge by asking, "Where's the *community* in community engagement?" In mounting a confident response to this question, global-learning leaders will not only learn how to strengthen what is distinctively human around the world but also find a path to reclaiming its civic soul.

Notes

1. Ethical theory embeds the norm of reciprocity in discussions of justice and gratitude. The essential moral idea is that we owe a fitting and proportional good to others who do good to us. Benefits are returned for benefits. As a social rule, reciprocity checks the tendency of privileged people to get benefits without returning them, thereby undermining the common good. See Lawrence Becker, *Reciprocity*. Chicago, IL: University of Chicago Press, 1990.

2. See Canadian Council for International Cooperation (CCCIC). (2009). *Code of ethics and operational standards*. Retrieved from https://www.bccic.ca/wp-content/ uploads/2015/09/001_code_ethics_operational_standards_e.pdf; Community-Campus Partnerships for Health. (2010). *Position statement on authentic partnerships*. Retrieved from https://www.ccphealth.org/principles-of-partnership/; Comhlámh (2013). *The Comhlámh code of good practice (CoGP) for volunteer sending agencies*. Retrieved from https://forum-ids.org/wp-content/uploads/2014/05/2014-Comlamh-Code-of-Good-Practice.pdf; and three documents from The Forum on Education Abroad. (2018): *Code of ethics for education abroad*, 2nd ed. Retrieved from https:// forumea.org/resources/standards-of-good-practice/code-of-ethics/; *Guidelines for undergraduate health-related programs abroad*. Retrieved from https://forumea.org/wp-content/uploads/2018/06/Guidelines-for-Undergraduate-Health-P3-edited.pdf; and *Guidelines for community engagement, service-learning, and volunteer experiences abroad*. Retrieved from https://forumea.org/wp-content/uploads/2018/03/Guidelines-for-Community-Engagement-P4.pdf

3. The key is to *narrow* institutional sponsorship to those programs that minimally satisfy student quality standards, while also *broadening* the participation of students. How might this be done? By adopting some kind of *level-based classification system* that distinguishes between program types, and that progressively moves learners toward more sophisticated, development-oriented program types (see Appendix B). Build high-quality programs that spread horizontally, then scale up.

STEWARDING THE TRANSFORMATION

The Art of Becoming Different

People don't resist change. They resist being changed.
— PETER SENGE, *The Fifth Discipline*, 2006

Having just returned from six months in Honduras, Jenna was beginning to settle back into the familiar, comfortable routines of home. But all was not well.

I want to say that I love being home and it is everything I have been waiting for and more, except, that has not been the case. It's strange, but I can't seem to put my finger on it. Yes, I have enjoyed finally being able to sleep in my own bed and eat what I want, when I want. Not to mention taking

169

hot showers and being able to understand everything that is being said to me. But there's something that makes me feel so sad and uncomfortable and confused in my own home. What is it?

Many global learners can relate to Jenna's ambivalence. After extended immersion in another social world, they return to the relative ease, predictability, and security of home. They expect a speedy, smooth transition, only to find themselves struggling to reconcile the person they left home as—formed through years of cultural programming—with the person they are now moving toward, courtesy of a relatively short but intense set of cultural experiences. A story possesses them from within—one that is often untold and unresolved, yet forming them in imperceptible ways.

Community-engaged global learning, whether carried out nearby or abroad, typically removes learners from their everyday world on campus, with family, or at work. Inserted into an unfamiliar environment and imagination, their minds are opened to new, and potentially transformative, experiences. Global learning essentially says, "Try this! Make the effort to move outside your comfort zone. Leave your certainties and usual routines at home. Encounter new people, adopt new roles, and express yourself through a new tongue and a new set of rituals. Learn to value people over projects." The truly fortunate ones return home with altered attitudes, alternative perspectives, and newly formed habits—and then wonder how they could have ever thought or acted with such unquestioned staunchness before.

Journeys into other social worlds teach an essential truth: Persons learn to *think different* when their life experiences press them to *live different*. In chapter 2, we called attention to Plato's allegory of the cave in *The Republic*. The humans in Plato's cave are shackled for the duration of their lives until the day that some of the prisoners manage to break their bonds and confront the immensity, chaos, and confusion of the outside world. At first blinded by the glare, their eyes eventually adjust to the light. After returning to the cave, they are unable to see in the dark as they once did. Those who never left the cave ridicule them, vowing never to go into the light lest they, too, be blinded by the light.

Plato was trying to teach us that people learn freedom as they become aware of their outer and inner chains. Both by nature and by nurture, we are stubborn provincials. We assume that our way, if not the *only* way, is surely the *best* way. Until we have our own reality rendered less invisible, we tend not to question the narrow limits of our native world. "For some," says James "Gus" Speth (2008), "it is a spiritual awakening—a transformation of the human heart. For others it is a more intellectual process of coming to see the world anew" (pp. 199–200).

To see the world anew—this has long been the grand prize of a globalized education. Intrepid souls leave home to encounter alternative modes of life that often cause them to rethink their place in the world. Family stays, volunteer service placements, community-based research projects, and memorable field excursions serve up opportunities to reconsider their unique answer to a fundamental question: "What does it mean to be human and alive?" (Davis, 1998, p. xi). Seeing the world anew thus begins by leaving our inherited "cave" existence and rubbing up against different models of reality. The promise is that, in doing so, we will be led to see the world, and ourselves, with new eyes.

Those who lead or manage global-learning programs know all too well that such outcomes are far from automatic. Educational travel has ambiguous effects: It can either encourage learners to extract personal pleasures *from* the world, or it can support them in constructing a competent and caring response *to* the world. Much depends on the conditions discussed in the preceding chapter. The art of world learning is ultimately the art of world loving. Although accurate knowledge *about* the world is indispensable to right living in it, the building of moral and ethical capacity is not primarily the result of formal knowledge. A different kind of life must be greatly *desired* and *practiced.*

Contrary to popular belief, the homecoming experience of serious travelers does not necessarily include what has customarily been termed *reentry shock.* Many returns are all too smooth and uneventful, apart from a brief recovery from jet lag. The language of reentry and recovery borrows heavily from NASA programs, which use sophisticated guidance and landing systems to usher spacecraft and their crews safely back to Earth. For space travelers, the metaphor points to the critical importance of a controlled descent and reentry, but it may be poorly suited to describe the process of psychological and social change as a result of world-learning experiences. Ben Feinberg (2002) writes:

> Students return from study-abroad programs having seen the world, but the world they return to tell tales about is more often than not the world they already knew, the imaginary world of globalized, postmodern capitalism where everything is already known, everyone speaks the same language, and the outside world keeps its eyes on those of us who come from the center.

This might explain why a group of students returning from a semester in London or Cape Town might struggle to see the personal relevance of a mandatory reentry or re-integration program. Having never really left their native ground, they hardly expect a dramatic splashdown. They may wish to join other returnees in breaking bread together, swaping stories, and sharing photos, but feel little need to connect their experiences abroad with the way they think and live back home. Consumed like any other luxury commodity, travels are ultimately placed in a private been-there-done-that box.

Which raises the central questions of this chapter: *If we return from our sojourns only to resume a former mental state and lifestyle, what's the point? What larger purpose might our new understandings and skills serve? In other words, world learning for what?*

What follows is a cautious response to these defining questions, organized in two parts. Part one profiles three different styles of homecoming following a global-learning term. Part two follows with a reply to the *for what* question in terms of five moves or operations that guide us in rethinking and recreating our presence on Earth.

Part One: Homecoming Styles

Some time ago, I found myself sitting around a conference table with 15 hand-selected study abroad returnees from a prestigious national university. All were well spoken and tastefully dressed. Several minutes into our conversation, the group's self-appointed spokesperson expressed how "life changing" their travel-study experiences had been. Ever eager to appreciate the impacts of transnational civic practice, I asked: "What changed, specifically, in the way you think and live as a result of the experience? In other words, how are you different?" I half-expected them to run over each other in chronicling the changes. Instead, I was met with blank stares and muted voices.

I have no doubt that the claim of having a "life changing" experience was sincere for the majority of these students. Many, I'm sure, had their eyes opened and their hearts moved by the weight of a contrasting reality. But the line of causality between the students' field experiences and personal changes still remained blurred. Unfortunately, scholarly research on the alleged impacts of educational travel on student consciousness offers dubious insight. Small sample sizes and selection bias fail to establish whether self-reported impacts are the result of actual field experiences or the preexisting characteristics of participants. Moreover, the focus on short-term impacts (like those expressed by the student group) tend to obscure any sustained changes in personal lifestyle choices, career direction, and ongoing civic engagement (Murphy, Sahakyan, Young-Yi, & Magnan, 2014; Paige, Fry, Stallman, Josic, & Jon, 2009).

How, then, should we think about student claims of the experience being "life changing"? Some of it is sincere aspiration. A greater part, however, is likely to reflect what psychologists call *social desirability bias*: the tendency for respondents to report on themselves or life experiences in ways that either exaggerate (overreport) positive outcomes or edit out (underreport) what might be viewed negatively by others (Giannetti, 2000). Constructing the experience as life changing does not mean that returnees are being deceitful. Overreporting functions, quite innocently, to help maintain an image or opinion that is favored by significant others, including peers and authority figures.

This only begins to explain why the stories students *tell* about their world-learning experiences tend to disconnect from what they actually *do* with those experiences after returning home. A change of mind or heart without a change in actual practice is ultimately futile—just one more pointless luxury. The trick is to translate educative moments into concrete, sustained change.

Costs of Conformity

One of the central insights of anthropology is that persons rarely deviate from the values, feeling-saturated habits, and lifestyle expectations that have been drilled into them since birth. Our family and social environments etch a web of assumptions—regarding success, progress, beauty, human value, and the like—deep into the psyche. As a result, most people, most of the time, go through life blissfully unaware of the cave that they indwell. Even aspiring global citizens run up against an almost overwhelming pressure to jettison lessons and insights from elsewhere, and to revert to their homegrown consciousness and habit patterns. Some of this is quite natural: We all, to varying degrees, are compelled to adjust ourselves to those around us. Even when we secretly disagree with "the crowd," the thought of deviating from groupthink and risking rejection can seem crazy or terrifying. So we adopt what Richard Kiely (2004) calls a *chameleon complex*, an unconscious inclination to reflect the views and behavior of our peers.

Social conformity is not without its practical benefits. Returnees stay predictable to their family and friends—those who'd shudder to think that their beloved might change in ways that strain the relationship. Being normal also saves us from the experience of feeling fearfully alone and insignificant. Peer pressure, far from being a pernicious influence, helps us to feel connected, accepted, and liked by others. Conformity can also help to secure a bright future. With a little bit of luck, those fortunate enough to study away can hope to graduate college, find Mr. or Mrs. Right, settle down, find a decent-paying job, raise a family, and otherwise live honestly and honorably.

But there are also downsides. Prioritizing personal security and social approval in life invariably cripples the best sides of ourselves. Crowd pressures unconsciously condition our minds and feet to move to the rhythm of the status quo. We are tempted to choose the way of least resistance, becoming settlers instead of searchers. Rather than explore the creative but often unpopular edges of things, we more readily submit to cultural convention and common sense. What we learn in the reflected gaze of others is what others are. "To put it briefly," writes social psychologist Erich Fromm (1945/1994), "the individual ceases to be himself. He adopts entirely the kind of personality offered to him by cultural patterns; and he therefore becomes exactly as all others are and as they expect him to be" (pp. 159-160). This loss of one's true self comes with a high price. It guarantees that everyone likes us but ourselves. That's because, in the act of surrender, we forfeit two essentials of human freedom: conscience and critical thought.

Conscience is an intuitive sense of what is conducive to life and what is destructive of life. Conscience aids us in evaluating our behavior in light of world realities. In contrast to slavish obedience to external social norms and authority, conscience dares to follow the voice of moral reason. "Conscience, by its very nature, is nonconforming," writes Fromm (1955) in *The Sane Society*. "It must be able to say no when everybody else says yes" (p. 173).

With rational conscience neutralized, the ability to think critically also withers. Rather than question things as they are, unthinking agreement is given to the images and opinions projected by high-prestige institutions. We view a Rembrandt in a Berlin or New York gallery and deem it beautiful, not because of any genuine inner response, but because we know we're supposed to find it so. We get drawn into the hype of advertisers, oblivious to the market's drive to maximize profit. Then there's the hugely profitable entertainment complex, perhaps the biggest moral-intellectual capacity killer. Celebrity culture, in particular, creates a kind of permanent collective amnesia. This week it's Jen's new romance or Kim's latest Photoshop scandal. Next week it's Selena's postrehab, super smiley selfie with Taylor. In between we sit, transfixed, before *Parks and Recreation, Dear White People,* and *The Walking Dead.* Style and story substitute for the capacity to look within ourselves and within our society. Questions of right and wrong, reality and illusion dissolve in favor of a constant stream of mind-numbing amusement. The result is a profound moral and intellectual fog that distracts us from facing the world with eyes wide open.

Between Two Worlds

World learning is potentially the great inoculator against cultural programming. Much depends on whether or not it is allowed to stimulate our consciousness with the necessary counter-ideas. From an enlarged perspective on the world, we begin to shed the false selves foisted upon us by mainstream media outlets, commercial culture, politicians, entertainers, and religious ideologues. Public theologian Reinhold Niebuhr (2001) believed that only "a sublime madness in the soul" (pp. 276–277), the radical freedom of individual conscience, was capable of resisting the egoism of human nature and the stubborn inertia of techno-commercial culture. Without it, individuals naturally lived for the approval of the system rather than to save its soul. Martin Luther King Jr. (1963/2010) reached a similar conclusion when, faced with the crises of his day, and knowing the enormous temptation toward social conformity, he called for creative maladjustment and resistance as central modes of civic engagement.

> Our planet teeters on the brink of atomic annihilation; dangerous passions of pride, hatred and selfishness are enthroned in our lives; truth lies prostrate on the rugged hills of nameless calvaries [*sic*]; and men do reverence before false gods of nationalism and materialism. The saving of our world from pending doom will come, not through the complacent adjustment of the conforming majority, but through the *creative maladjustment of a nonconforming minority.* [emphasis added]

Engendering a positive madness of soul requires an equally mad pedagogy—one that whirls us around, turns us upside down, and stands much that we take for granted on its head (Iyer, 2000). As pointed out in chapter 4, disciplinary knowledge needs direct, visceral experience if it is to be more than inert theory.

Of course, the trick with upside-down learning is to get right-side-up again. I recall two students who, like Jenna, found themselves unable to be fully at home after coming home. Nicole arrived back in San Francisco after six tumultuous though deeply affecting months in Dhaka, Bangladesh. This was in 2007, the year of Storm Sidr, a tropical cyclone that resulted in at least 5,000 deaths and sent hundreds of thousands of others searching for clean water and food. Once home, she reported entering a local supermarket and suddenly bursting into tears. It was the 30 kinds of bottled water and 80 kinds of dry cereal that did it. Similarly, Brittany finished a four-month internship with the Fistula Hospital in Addis Ababa, assisting some of the poorest women in the world. Months later she still struggled to reconcile the world's suffering with a caring, all-powerful God.

For both young women, unforgettable images and conversations kept replaying in their minds. They couldn't just "get over it" and "move on." They were caught, inescapably, between two worlds. Who they were and how they should live was no longer obvious. Reinstating the pre-field person was no longer possible. At the same time, they felt impotent to effect the change they desired.

How do I reconcile my knowledge of the world's pain with the fact that I can do very little about it? (Nicole)

Why even try to fix things? Wouldn't my best efforts to change customs and conditions only be based on my own skewed understandings? (Brittany)

At this point, Nicole and Brittany could have easily abandoned hope and succumbed to despair and apathy. Cynicism is always a besetting temptation, one that ultimately justifies inaction. If we assume that no real change is possible, why not retreat from reality and free fall into overdrinking, oversmoking, overshopping, and the like? Ironically, cynical complacence often masquerades as progressive enlightenment. Claiming to have seen through it all, cynics descend into stoic indifference, unable to be moved by what they see and hear. English essayist Dorothy Sayers (1949) described this mental state as "nothingness": "The sin that believes in nothing, cares for nothing, seeks to know nothing, interferes with nothing, enjoys nothing, hates nothing, finds purpose in nothing, lives for nothing, and remains alive because there is nothing for which it will die" (p. 81). Absolved of any personal responsibility, the cynic simply curls into the mental equivalent of the fetal position.

The Way of Transformation

Nicole and Brittany had another option—beyond conforming reversion and world-wearied withdrawal. In an effort to steward their emerging transformation, they could allow the real dissonance they feel to awaken a courageous questioning of things as they are: What accounts for the misfortune and injustice that people suffer? How is my life implicated in those conditions? What is in my power to change? Instead of trying to magically dissolve the incongruity between their foreign experience and home life, they would use the dissonance to open themselves up to larger truths without succumbing to despair or disengagement.

In many world cultures, the generally painful process of finding one's place in the world actually constitutes a rite of passage. Among the Lakota Sioux, young boys and girls often undertake a vision quest upon entering adulthood. Secluded in the wilderness, away from familiar people and creature comforts, they learn to measure themselves against the immutable forces of nature. Personal control is surrendered to providence. The acute disequilibrium they experience acts to radically revise limiting or distorted views of the world. They return to the tribe having "grown up": A childhood sense of self and status is left behind; adult purposes and roles are accepted.

British anthropologist Victor Turner (1969) used *liminality* (from *limen*, meaning threshold) to depict this process of separation, transition, and incorporation. In a liminal state, says Turner, "entities are neither here nor there; they are betwixt and between the positions assigned and arrayed by law, custom, convention, and ceremony" (p. 95). One's life is not as it once was, nor is it what it will become. The deep changes in a person may be gradual or sudden, but they result in a type of hero's journey from the "old self" toward a new, more integral self and way of life (see Table 7.1). William James (1961), in *The Varieties of Religious Experience*, describes this state of positive mental health as being *twice born*.

Liminal journeys are often far from pleasurable. They involve a kind of death to self, the shaking of the personal, natural, and cultural foundations of one's life. Old, ingrained attitudes and habits die hard. Like a river that carves, over time, a canyon into even the hardest rock, doing anything consistently enough cuts a deep gorge into our psyche. Recently I came across a fascinating medical research article that reported on a large sample of people with life-threatening heart problems, all of whom were facing surgery. All were told by their doctors that, irrespective of the surgery, they would have to change certain established behaviors (eating, drinking,

TABLE 7.1   From Old to New

Movement from the Old ...	... to the New
Fear of the "Other"	Other as "brother" and "sister"
Attraction to sheltered, beautiful places	Pull toward forgotten places & peoples
Physical and social separation (bubble)	Embodied; immersion (baptism)
Disconnection and indifference	Engagement and empathy
Independence, control	Accompaniment, vulnerability
Racial and cultural superiority	Intercultural empathy
Nationalism	Cosmopolitanism
Entitlement, personal advancement	Gratefulness, common good
Money values, material excess	Life values, spiritual fulfillment
Passive consumption of experiences	Active experimentation
Helping motivated by pity or guilt	Service as solidarity, mutual liberation
Individualist ethos	Structural thinking
Moral obliviousness	Critical questioning

smoking, and exercise) or they would die. Astonishingly, only 10% of the sample actually changed their behavior. When faced with the choice of changing their behavior or death, 90% of the study participants chose the latter option!

Transformative change (learning) happens ever so slowly, even when empirically convincing arguments and evidence would dictate radical and immediate change. Movement from old attitudes, values, and habits typically requires a willingness to separate ourselves, however temporarily, from our native cultural system and experience a radical difference. As we might expect, young adults are the most likely to do so because of their openness to new experience. "Adolescence and early adulthood," writes Stanford neuroscientist Robert Sapolsky (2017),

are the times when someone is most likely to kill, be killed, leave home forever, invent an art form, help overthrow a dictator, ethnically cleanse a village, devote themselves to the needy, become addicted, marry outside their group, transform physics, have hideous fashion taste, break their neck recreationally, commit your life to God, mug an old lady, and be convinced that all of history has converged to make this moment the most consequential, the most fraught with peril and promise, the most demanding that they get involved and make a difference. (p. 155)

The readiness of teens and 20-somethings to challenge normalcy and experiment with new sides of themselves should give global educators great reassurance. Properly organized, world learning has the potential to open up provincial minds to fresh, previously unimagined human possibilities. The process of internalizing fresh insight follows a somewhat predictable pattern: Learners *step outside* their native pattern of perceiving and behaving long enough to *take in* new information and experiences. By *paying attention* to the world, they allow themselves to be impacted by novel experience. After acknowledging, however reluctantly, that their way is just one way among many (and not necessarily the better way), they *carefully weigh* the relative merits of contrasting ways of life. To this point, Theroux (2014) writes, "There has to be revelation in spending long periods of time in travel. Otherwise it is more waste" (p. 350).

With new revelation, learners then have an inescapable choice. They can continue to perceive and respond to the world in their habitual manner. Or they can allow themselves to change, as they experiment with ways of thinking and living that better fit the kind of world they want. Old mental frames and habits are not so much ousted as *outgrown*.

Part Two: Transformative Moves

The outgrowing that occurs through engaged global learning remains largely a mystery. Learners are, in many ways, like young seedlings. They have the possibility of a tree, but to realize that possibility the initial plant must have water, nutrients, sunshine, and space to grow. Gardeners don't stand in front of a plant and mutter, "Okay, grow. C'mon grow!" Change has its own timetable. The wind that blows a sailboat through the open seas is an uncontrollable force of life. Sailors can't command the direction of the wind; they can only adjust the sails to reach their ultimate destination.

It's one thing for field experience to stimulate personal change. It's quite another to *sustain* that change without slipping back into old ways. A student once asked me: "How do I keep that which is changed in me?" She intuitively realized that behavior change, much like unwanted weight, is much easier to lose than to keep off. I don't recall how I framed a response to her question, but if asked today my reply would highlight five essential moves (Figure 7.1).

Move #1: See the Beauty (Appreciation)

The first move, fundamental to all the others, is a readiness to see beauty in the things around us. Juliette de Bairacli Levy (1979), after years of living with gypsies, farmers, and livestock breeders to learn the ins and outs of animal care and herbal medicine, wrote in *Traveler's Joy*, "There is an expression—walking with beauty. And I believe that this endless search for beauty in surroundings, in people, and in one's personal life, is the headstone to travel" (p. 4). We protect and conserve only what we love and value. The impetus for life-giving change must therefore arise from wonder and affection.

Every culture enriches the planet through its distinctive soul. That soul is reflected in its arts and architecture, foods and customs, family life and community associations. Who is not awed by the splendor of India's Taj Mahal or the New York cityscape? Or by the pure gastronomical delight of Italian and Malaysian cuisines? The Surma and Mursi peoples of southern Ethiopia turn human bodies into living canvases by painting their skin with the pigments of powdered volcanic rock, and then adorning it with flowers and shells. The beauty they express differs from that of an iPhone or a painting by Monet. But it is no less magical in its endlessly inventive use of form and color to express their innate aesthetic sense.

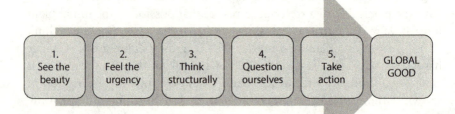

FIGURE 7.1.   Moves in stewarding the transformation.

Beauty and wisdom are like shards of a shattered mirror strewn out across the world's peoples and places. Parts of that shattered mirror are to be found everywhere, but the whole of it nowhere. Seeing the beauty thus begins with the revelation of ignorance—an admission that our fragment of knowledge can never be imagined as universal. This can be especially difficult for those of us who reflexively assume that *our* culture, *our* politics, *our* language, and *our* religiosity (or lack of it) is truer, richer, and more life-enriching than others'.

Seeing the beauty, therefore, is the exercise a proper humility toward a wonder-filled world. Beauty draws us out of ourselves and into others' experience. Like good treasure hunters, we search out and gather up that which is good and true and beautiful in that which surrounds us. Disposed to grasp the creative genius resident in every place, the last thing we want to do is pass immediate judgment on what we see, hear, and, in any case, barely understand.

Soon after we wed, Leslie and I took up residence in a crowded informal settlement on the outskirts of Hyderabad, India. In the public imagination, there may be no place more miserable than the third-world slum. The very phrase conjures up apocalyptic images of grossly substandard housing, extreme overcrowding, and chronic health hazards. These hardships are indeed real. But looking at these chaotic, sprawling neighborhoods from the inside brought a surprising perspective that had far less to do with deprivation and helplessness than with the people's collective intelligence and ingenuity.

All dwellings had been independently built using local knowledge and materials. The streets were vibrant and energetic, filled with playing children and gossiping neighbors (quite unlike the colorless suburbs where we were raised). Clothes were washed by hand and dried on a clothesline. Bathing was done either with a bucket and cup or by turning on and off a showerhead. The few appliances in our host's house were typically unplugged when not in use. Residents walked, biked, or took buses rather than drove. Instead of industrial lawns and domesticated yards, the area was dotted with small organic gardens on family plots. Unbeknownst to residents, the entire settlement exemplified many new urbanist principles: high-density, mixed use, walkability, and low-energy. Here, amid material scarcity (and, for some, wretched poverty), most residents managed to lead socially rewarding lives with virtually no environmental impact.

This is not to romanticize materially poor people or to minimize the hardships that mark their daily life. But reality is as beautiful as it is ugly.

Places of poverty and quiet desperation can also contain stunning levels of resourcefulness and resilience. The ability to recognize beauty amid want enables the will to protect and extend what is loveable and life-affirming in the world—an indispensable impulse in global learning.

Happily, the search for beauty doesn't require a long-haul flight. The Amish communities of North America offer artful models of living well without living ever-larger. Everyday affairs are managed without cars, modern appliances, or computers. Their simple clothes are air-dried, and their hearty meals home-cooked. Emotional attachments are not to stuff but to a place, a people, and a religious practice. The divorce rate is less than 1%, and out-of-wedlock births are nearly nonexistent. No members are impoverished, although high land values and productive businesses have begun to create economic disparities. A tradition of communal sharing and Earth-friendly entrepreneurship has resulted in some of the healthiest farms and highest average happiness levels in the country. The Amish open up beautiful possibilities for how basic material and nonmaterial needs might be met within the limits of a finite planet.

Move #2: Feel the Urgency (Compassion)

The ability to marvel at the world—to be awestruck and radically amazed at its generosity and beneficence—profoundly shapes a person's emotional and ethical acuity. "In a very real sense we have two minds, one that thinks and one that feels," writes Daniel Goleman in *Emotional Intelligence* (2005, p. 8). Sadly, in the modern era, the feeling mind has largely shriveled. Most schooling is an indoor and purely cognitive sport, strictly controlled by the reins of rationality. Our discussion in chapter 4 acknowledged how a thinking (subject-object) mode of knowing has enabled extraordinary scientific and technological achievements. But it has also left the public underdeveloped in their capacity to feel a deep sense of urgency over issues that threaten human and planetary well-being. The predictable outcome is a dispassionate, onlooker angle of vision that privileges rational detachment over active engagement.

It is quite possible for a person to acquire detailed knowledge *about* the world without being personally affected *by* it. Human emotions, in such cases, are too often regarded as a touchy-feely impediment to sound reasoning. Moral philosopher Martha Nussbaum (2001) argues that quite the opposite is true: Strong feeling drives deep thinking. Emotions tell us what to pay attention to and care about. When we experience fear in vulnerable situations, or rage over the others' misfortune, or hope that circumstances can be bettered, we are compelled to make sense out of what has been sensed. Because emotions indicate judgments made about the world, they help us discover what is of value in life. Abstract moral principles are inadequate to provoke the kind of thinking and motivation that leads to collective action. Only as learners enter empathetically into the lives of those in radically different circumstances do they then begin to imagine what it might be like for another's life to be their own.

An unexpected exemplar for the indivisibility between thought and feeling in world learning was the Polish anthropologist Bronislaw Malinowski. In the early twentieth century, Malinowski urged his students to step outside the closed study of the theorist and enter into the thought and feeling of others' experience as if it was their own. During his residence with the Trobriand people of New Guinea, Malinowski (1922) wrote: "To study the institutions, customs, and codes or to study the behaviour and mentality *without the subjective desire of feeling by what these people live, of realising the substance of their happiness*—is, in my opinion, to miss the greatest reward which we can hope to obtain from the study of man" (p. 25, emphasis added).

Empathy draws attention to another world of experience, and then attempts to reconstruct it. When Nicole and Brittany chose to live and learn in Bangladesh and Ethiopia respectively, they consciously moved from the ordinary and protected place of home to an unknown territory. They positioned themselves as receivers in their new places, coming under the cultural direction of local families and organizations. For several months each of them occupied simple rooms in rudimentary homes. There was no air-conditioning, Wi-Fi, or Starbucks. By virtue of their indwelling, a previously alien world was able to penetrate their being, even as they penetrated the being of that world. Indwelling didn't guarantee that empathy and compassion would take root, but it did ensure that both would have the right kind of soil in which to grow.

Once an empathic bond had been formed, the challenge was then for Nicole and Brittany to *sustain* it after returning home. Would their absence from intimates abroad make their hearts grow fonder, or would they soon forget the people and predicaments that were no longer visible or present (the "out of sight, out of mind" dilemma)? Psychologists speak of person/object permanence as the cognitive ability to understand that someone or something *continues* to exist, even if they cannot be seen, heard, or touched. They are out of sight, but still *in mind*. Given the thousands of miles that separated Nicole and Brittany from their distant hosts, it remained to be seen whether they would find some way to steward their transformation by remaining emotionally close to that which was no longer physically near.

The two students faced some immediate tasks at home: to graduate college, to land a decent-paying job, and to become a full-fledged, financially independent adult. And yet, amid all the academic and social demands, their minds continued to replay emotionally charged images and events from prior months. Instead of trying to shake, repress, or otherwise get over the memories, they struggled to know what life lessons might be gleaned from them. Each time they recalled the struggles of others, they were reminded of their own related vulnerability: "What would my life be like if my host family and I were to trade places?" In short, the urgency of others' lives began to irreversibly change the students' relation to the world. What they now had to figure out is precisely how.

Move #3: Think Structurally (Analysis)

At this point, Nicole and Brittany's story overlaps with my own. During my college years, I tended to view the world through a social ethos largely defined by the American Dream. My duty in the land of opportunity was to pull myself up by my bootstraps by working hard and competing well. Eventually I would be rewarded with success and affluence.

Individualism, as a basic life orientation, has been likened to a game of baseball. The world is a playing field, essentially just and fair, and everyone has an equal chance at bat. Some, by reason of greater intelligence, ingenuity, and moral discipline, manage to hit the ball better and run the bases faster than others. They are to be congratulated, whereas those who fail to hit the ball hard enough and run the bases fast enough can only blame themselves.

This story is so ingrained in American consciousness that most of us have a hard time accepting that forces outside individual talent and effort might determine social outcomes (McNamee & Miller, 2009). Prior to his firsthand exposure to human suffering as president of World Vision, Rich Stearns (2010) had uncritically adopted this blame-the-victim mind-set:

> I fell quite easily into the bias that poverty was somehow a choice one made
> . . . In truth, my hard work as a young man produced results largely because
> my circumstances were favorable. . . . I lived in a country that embraced basic

freedoms and protected individual rights and the rule of law. I attended good public schools and had access to libraries that I did not have to pay for. I did not suffer from hunger, contaminated water, or lack of basic health-care. I was vaccinated against devastating childhood diseases. I had more than three thousand colleges and universities from which to choose, and scholarships and loans were available to make attendance possible, even for someone with no money. I entered an economy that was strong and grow-ing, with opportunities for me to put my education and God-given abilities to work productively. Best of all, I found that diligence and hard work were almost always rewarded. (p. 117)

Like Stearns, I too believed that people generally got what they deserved. I looked upon the cruel discrepancy between my life and the lives of oth-ers, only to conclude, blissfully, that inequalities existed largely because of cultural dysfunctions and moral misdeeds. Whatever complex of factors explained the misfortune of others, I could rest assured that my life was not implicated whatsoever. So, I kept telling myself that the world is essentially fair: As in baseball, people get what they deserve and deserve what they get. Since the afflictions of others had no relationship to my life, I had no moral responsibility to help correct them.

A dramatic reversal in my "it's a just world after all" worldview took place during a one-month stay in Haiti. There I witnessed hard-working but persistently poor people—a reality that didn't neatly fit my individual-ist ethos. What I absorbed impressionistically was confirmed empirically in the pages of Paul Farmer's *Pathologies of Power* (2005), a searching analysis of the health crisis facing the desperately poor. Farmer's analysis persuaded me that Haiti's brutal poverty and malnutrition had little to do with the behavior of individual Haitians. Rather, it was bound up with the break-down of subsistence living, lack of property rights, unemployment, and the nation's history as a slave colony, among other things. In short, economic and political *structures*, far outside the control of those affected by them, profoundly conditioned life chances.

A journal entry during those unsettling days in Haiti reveals my struggle to grasp the radical *dis*continuity between individual effort and the results one gets.

How successful would I be if I were raised in a place with a debilitating climate, prone to regular drought or flooding, and subject to widespread epi-demics? A place where clean water is a luxury; where one out of five children die before the age of five; where one is constantly weak and fatigued because of poor diet; where there is no reliable health care system to treat disease and parasites; where you can't go to school because you have to fetch water, beg or sell gum on the streets; where jobs, if you are lucky enough to find one, are low-paying and irregular; where criminal gangs terrorize your community; and where you and your family have a good chance of becoming one of the world's 10 million refugees or 24 million internally displaced persons. No matter how talented or ambitious you are there is little opportunity to fulfill your potential. Through no fault of your own, you stay poor, trapped by circumstances outside your ability to directly alter.

Haiti marked my journey out of individualization and into structuralization as a way of perceiving and interpreting the world around me. To think structurally is to ask below-the-surface questions: What's really going on here? How are relationships ordered? Who has economic and political power, and who does not? How is that power currently wielded, and with what consequences? And how are the configurations and operations of power connected to political history, among other things?

Individualization had coaxed me to explain human events in terms of discrete *personal* or *cultural* attributes. Structuralization shifted my attention to a host of *systemic* factors—like foreign relations, trade rules, corporate policies, environmental constraints, military actions, and technology transfers—as a basic framework for probing beneath surface symptoms to root causes. I began to think that maybe, just maybe, solutions to the world's most perplexing problems lay in changing not only the character of people but also the social institutions and roles available to them. The stage was set for me to consider how the crises that disproportionately afflict others might connect to my own life (interrogation), and how repairing the world might require fundamental changes in the institutions I have heretofore passively approved (reconstruction).

Move #4: Question Ourselves (Interrogation)

This fourth move spotlights our inward response to our outward journey. It is altogether possible to narrow the physical and psychological distance between "us" and "them," to empathically enter the circumstances of others, and to methodically analyze the structural forces and power brokers that influence a situation, and still *not see ourselves as being morally implicated in those conditions whatsoever.*

Today's high-technology global economy has made it possible for Earth-spanning corporations to affect lives everywhere, for good *and* for ill. For the vast majority of the world's haves, the implicit logic, policies, and consumer products of the global system are nigh irresistible. Most of us can hardly imagine life without Google, Apple, Amazon, and Walmart, or the less well-known agricultural giants (like ConAgra, Cargill, Monsanto, Syngenta, and Archer Daniels Midland) and energy corporations (like General Electric, ExxonMobil, Saudi Aramco, and Peabody Energy). Consequently, we rarely concern ourselves with any harms—social, psycho-emotional, or ecological—that may result from their activities.

"Hold it right there," you protest. "You and I didn't decide the system we were born into; neither can we be held responsible for whatever damages it produces." True, most of us, as individuals, do not actively participate in harming life. Moreover, advantage and disadvantage are not causally linked in some clear-cut way. Inequality of fortune is, to a great extent, the cumulative result of policies and actions spread out over generations and enacted by innumerable people—most of whom we will never know.

At the same time, in the course of our daily lives, we *consent* to the system, whether or not we consciously *approve* of the way the world system is structured. In fact, if I'm to be perfectly honest, most of the time I inwardly *do* approve of it, for the simple reason that I receive substantial benefits from it, whilst avoiding most of the costs. Recently, I completed a carbon footprint analysis of my current lifestyle, with a sobering revelation: The world would need 3.5 Earths if everyone consumed like me. What's more, the way I live exerts a heavy human slavery footprint (Slavery Footprint, n.d.). Somewhere between 20 and 30 forced laborers work on my behalf. They pick cotton for my shirts, harvest coffee and cocoa beans for my mochas, grow rice and tomatoes for my curries, and harvest rubber for my bicycle tires.

Nowhere are global justice connections and costs more apparent than in issues surrounding climate change. In 2004, 20 million people lost their homes and 800 people lost their lives due to devastating floods in Bangladesh, one of the poorest and most densely populated countries in the world. Some of the flooding was attributed to local deforestation and silted river channels. But according to climate experts, the excessive amounts of monsoon rain and Himalayan snowmelt that destroyed property and displaced millions of lives were the result of atmospheric concentrations of greenhouse gases (McGranahan, Balk, & Anderson, 2007). Most of the regional pollution came from tanneries, textile mills, and dyeing plants that produce the low-priced clothing sold to global consumers through companies like Walmart and Marshalls.

Unfortunately, the low prices enjoyed by Western consumers come at a high price for peoples of the Global South. Garment workers in places like Bangladesh, Sri Lanka, and Vietnam are among the lowest paid in the world. About 90% are female, often as young as 13 or 14, with sexual harassment a daily fact of work life. Moreover, workers lack any opportunity to organize or collectively bargain for better pay or health and safety standards. Those who dare to try are typically threatened, fired, blacklisted, or beaten. These injustices, again, do not result from malevolent bosses or poor work habits; they are a basic part of a global production system.

Suddenly, those of us who participate in that system through our lifestyle choices are structurally implicated in the flooding and abuses. From a distance, we might feel sympathy for the victims. But imagine that we are Nicole, and the affected garment workers include our host mom and two close friends. To the extent that we understand their hardships to be even remotely related to our patterns of consumption, pity alone becomes an inadequate moral response. The relevant question is not How much money can I send to the victims? but rather What does justice require of me?

Personal interrogation in the direction of doing justly requires that we do four things:

1. Recognize the disproportionate impact of our lifestyle on peoples and places elsewhere.
2. Acknowledge how we benefit from those conditions that burden others.
3. Accept a fair share of responsibility for the structural injustice we help sustain.
4. Interrogate the mind-set and related personal choices that harm, whether directly or indirectly, human and natural communities.

In short, we take pains to understand our obligations toward those with whom we share the planet. In the words of Franz Fanon (1963), we "decide to wake up, put on [our] thinking caps and stop playing the irresponsible game of Sleeping Beauty" (p. 62). To properly steward the uncommon truths revealed through world learning, merely seeing more *of* the world is not enough. We must learn to see it, and ourselves, *differently*. That requires conscious awareness and consistent self-scrutiny.

Over the years, hundreds of study away returnees have come back to the campus where I work with questions that doggedly disturb, confuse, or otherwise occupy their minds. The Addendum that follows this chapter synthesizes and presents the top 10. None of the questions are easily or immediately answerable. That's because, as Laurence Peter (1982) rightly observes, "some problems are so complex that you have to be highly intelligent and well informed just to be undecided about them" (p. 24). At the heart of transformative global learning is discovering, and living, the right questions, instead of forcing premature answers.

Move #5: Take Action (Reconstruction)

Living the questions is made practical by a final move: taking reconstructive action in the world. Stewarding the transformation, as we've said, calls for appreciative seeing, empathetic experience, and scrupulous thinking. Critical thinking, in particular, helps learners to see through the power arrangements and conformist habits that sustain existing conditions. This is preparatory for actually *applying* one's reasoning skills and ethical decision-making in real-world settings following graduation.

Action aimed at reconstructing the good that has either been lost, damaged, or yet unknown often emerges organically, experience-by-experience, step-by-step. The looming threats narrated in chapter 1 are the result of billions of individual choices. If it is possible to create a better world for our children's children, we will need billions of *new choices*, made by *new types of persons*, who find their moral and ethical grounding in a *new story*. We have arrived at a major fork in the road to creating a more inclusive and sustainable world. At this turning point, global learners are presented with two nearly opposite ways of understanding the world and the task before them.

One outlook insists that the present world represents the best of all possible worlds. Millions of families around the world have made a "great escape" from poverty. Life expectancy is rising and infectious diseases are retreating. Women's rights and girls' education are expanding. Democracy and freedom are spreading. The global population is stabilizing. Of course, this golden age has yet to reach everyone: Nearly a billion people still live in extreme poverty, mostly in the world's war zones and ungoverned spaces. Even in the United States, the world's richest country and homeland of freedom, citizens continue to be plagued by a cluster of cascading social, psycho-emotional, environmental, and geopolitical threats.

Despite the immensity of these challenges, techno-humanists like Ray Kurzweil (*The Singularity Is Near*, 2006), Johan Norberg (*Progress*, 2017), Hans Rosling (*Factfulness*, 2003), and Steven Pinker (*Enlightenment Now!*; 2018) trust unaided reason and science to solve them. Their message is this: Given the right incentives, humans are smart enough to deal with just about any problem that comes their way. Indeed, humanity is on the cusp of a new age of reason, one that will creatively bundle new STEM (science, technology, engineering, and mathematics) knowledge with GRIN (genetics, robotics, information, and nano) technologies. Energy from nuclear fusion and the sun will replace energy from fossil fuels. Machines that suck carbon dioxide out of the atmosphere will save us from climate-related disasters. Artificial, lab-grown meat will help revolutionize the human diet, providing a healthier and more environmentally friendly alternative to factory-farmed pork, beef, and chicken. Gene-editing technologies, combined with indoor farming, will grow crops to feed 10 billion (or more) of us. While robots efficiently perform routine human tasks, self-driving electric cars and trucks will provide the masses with safe, clean transportation. In short, humanity will solve incrementally, its present environmental crisis with new technologies and a new, green economy. Most importantly, they will do so without requiring any major changes to the dominant culture of global capitalism, or to the lifestyles of the world's privileged classes.

The alternative outlook and course of action is not nearly so upbeat. While the world's technological capacity is truly mind-boggling, it's also true that the planet is getting hotter, more crowded, more unequal, more ecologically degraded, and less biologically diverse every year. Decades of technological innovation and capital accumulation have *not* stabilized the climate or saved the myriad species and habitats that make Earth such an awe-inspiring place. In fact, those problems continue to worsen. What we lack is not brain power or adequate investment in technological or market solutions. We are simply asking money and machines to solve problems that are inherently *human*, and that require the restoration of certain ancient virtues—like reverence, humility, affection, self-restraint, fidelity, modesty, and solidarity.

There is no blueprint for a social and economic order that ensures that the Earth's abundance will be stewarded carefully and shared fairly. What engaged global learners do have is the ability to reimagine a manner of life that is measurably more inclusive, harmonious, healthy, productive, beautiful, and protective of biological and cultural life than it is today. In this restorative economy, communities are strong and vibrant. Social institutions are not too big to understand, appreciate, and meaningfully participate in. Public agencies are more responsive to the common good. Many enterprises are locally anchored and collectively owned. Residents have the opportunity to pursue meaningful, socially contributive work. Products are more durable and easy to repair. Prices reflect the true environmental and social costs. Waste is either eliminated or used as an input elsewhere. When people speak of "progress" and "growth," they immediately think about the capacity to produce collective well-being, not just short-term profits or conspicuous consumption. Quality of life replaces standard of living as the central indicator of the wealth of persons and communities.

Taking action to build such communities is the defining task of our times. While the cultural shift we need must ultimately be orchestrated by social movements on a very large scale, this fact should not lead us to conclude that individual actions don't matter. All great social movements were started by creatively maladjusted and determined individuals who refused to accept the prevailing social norms.[1]

Without the possibility of personal power, it makes no sense to talk about social or civic responsibility. Structural conditions do powerfully shape how persons desire, think, and behave. But the reverse is also true: Shifts in human consciousness, mobilized by masses of people, are what drive system reform. The personal *is* political. The solutions to the growing impoverishment of land and social life begin with ourselves: how we choose to feed, house, transport, work, play, and relate. Big changes in public policy and corporate practice are made in response to changes that are necessarily small, local, and personal. Concrete actions, taken by enough individuals, help create a cultural shift that begins to change systems and institutions. We need big solutions by companies and political leaders but they will surely fail if not accompanied by innumerable small solutions made by individual citizens, especially the wealthiest members of the wealthy countries. The ultimate responsibility rests on us, not upon miracle technologies or electoral politics.

Three small solutions stand out as primary moral responses to the sustainability predicaments we face.

Progressive simplification
The first solution involves restraining our overall consumption of energy. Virtually all of the goods and services that support humans require energy to produce. We might marvel at the low price of a Whopper sandwich at

Burger King, but fail to consider the sum total of embodied energy that was required to produce it. Embodied energy accounts for everything from raw material extraction and transport to the manufacture, assembly, installation, disassembly, and deconstruction and/or decomposition of products. The concept also helps us determine the total amount of greenhouse gases produced through our consumption activities, typically expressed as carbon dioxide equivalent or CO_2e. The Whopper's embodied energy includes not only the cooking of the meat but also the clearing of grasslands and forests to grow feed for the cattle; the slaughtering, freezing, and transporting of the beef patties; the management of packaging waste; and the associated health risks of eating high amounts of red meat. Since most of the social and environmental costs are "externalized," affecting other parties without being reflected in the cost of the Whopper, they remain largely invisible to us.

The average American's annual carbon footprint (CO_2e) is about 17 tons. To put it in comparative perspective, this is more than *four times* the worldwide average of 4 tons of CO_2e, and nearly 2,000 times that of a villager in the African nation of Chad (0.04 metric tons per year). In fact, the bottom three billion humans emit almost nothing, whereas the world's 500 million richest people (about 8% of us) are responsible for a shocking 50% of all global greenhouse gases. Culpability lies not so much with countries as with the global class of already satisfied super consumers—people like you and me.

The consensus among the world's scientists is that the planet must be kept below an increase of 2°C (3.6°F) in order to avert pervasive and dramatic ecological, social, and economic consequences. "The path we are on as a planet should terrify anyone living on it," writes David Wallace-Wells (2019) in *The Uninhabitable Earth* "It's only a matter of time until we, or our descendants, have our lives turned upside down, or even ended, by the devastating impacts of climate disruption." (p. 226). Rising temperatures change everything for everyone, everywhere. We might hope that some energy miracle, carbon tax, or worldwide smart grid will allow business as usual to continue indefinitely; yet no grand technological and political rescue is anywhere in sight.

The mandates of reality suggest that members of the global consuming class need to learn how to live within our fair share of the world's resources. At a minimum, those of us who can afford fossil-fuel-dependent comforts and conveniences should meet our basic needs for mobility, food, cooling, heating, lighting, and consumables with dramatically fewer resources. This doesn't mean we go back to riding horses, hunting and gathering our food, and living off the grid in log cabins. But it does mean we learn to need less, to waste less, to make things last longer, and to refuse to purchase fashion or glamour or prestige.

The goal of progressive simplification is not joyless austerity; it's a relation between humanity and habitat that is inwardly rich, outwardly simple, and publicly contributive. Those of us who have been privileged to *live an alternative* long enough to normalize a healthier, more convivial and conserving lifestyle are perhaps in the best position to advocate for real policy solutions back home. A global clean energy economy with a hard cap on resource use wait upon the future, and so are presently nonexistent. But a 50% reduction in our ecological footprints can be achieved right now, with rather painless personal changes in four areas: diet, mobility, housing, and product consumption.

- *Diet:* Substitute a mainly local and plant-base diet for a factory-farmed meat and dairy-based diet (-2.5 tons CO_2e per capita).
- *Transport:* Use trains or buses instead of planes for domestic travel, and a bicycle and/or public transport instead of a private car for 75% of all trips (-1.5 tons CO_2e per capita).
- *Housing:* Reside in a mixed-use development that utilizes renewable energy systems. (-3 tons CO_2e per capita).
- *Stuff:* Purchase 60% *fewer* new goods by buying secondhand, repairing, borrowing, or going without (-2 tons CO_2e per capita).

Relational diplomacy
The second solution, in addition to dealing with climate and ecological risks, personal action can also help create the a socially sustainable world. In this text we've emphasized how community-engaged global learning can help us think beyond the borders of our own cultural imprinting. Although large group sizes and short terms tend to discourage rich, abiding interactions with strangers, entrepanuerial learners do manage to burst the field bubble and to be profoundly marked by alternative stories and states of mind. The trick, as noted previously, is to make that mark indelible back home. Industrial society are facing a precipitous decline of social trust and cooperation. Most of us are strangers even to residents next door. Indeed, a good neighbor is no longer viewed as someone who trades recipes or watches the kids in a pinch; it's someone who leaves us alone and doesn't threaten our property values.

In our early years together, Leslie and I had to decide where we were going to live. We could either rent a loft in an upscale, ethnically homogenous neighborhood or move into an area where we were the minority among marginal, low-income families. We opted for the latter, not as a modern version of *noblesse oblige*, but because we were convinced that we had much to learn about building relational bridges with people we'd otherwise overlook or avoid. We joined one of the many gospel churches in the area and periodically visited a Nation of Islam mosque. Leslie opened up a free after-school tutoring center out of our studio apartment while I wrote a master's thesis on literacy development among residents of a large public housing project three blocks away. Local residents, naturally wary of outsiders, eventually opened up to us. By the end of our two-year stay, our social network of strangers-turned-friends included congregants, neighbors, local hairdressers, shopkeepers, coin laundry workers, and street vendors. We listened and laughed and sang together. We gave to and received from each other. Community was created out of previously separated people.

Relational diplomacy not only aims to turn strangers into friends but also seeks to create collaboration for the common good. Although action on a range of quality-of-life issues is needed at every level (global, national, regional, and municipal), it's the scaled-down community that provides something of a sweet spot for meaningful engagement. Small solutions thrive in small places. Effective action can include membership in a citizens' action group advocating for active (human-powered) transportation, running for local office, or engaging with local officials on issues of land use, affordable housing, open-space conservation, and redevelopment. Beyond the formal machinery of local politics, one can mentor youth or organize study groups and film showings. Local congregations with a missional focus also play a quiet yet vital role in civic life. Many address the social and spiritual needs of the faithful, while working with government agencies to provide better services for low-income residents. In short, opportunities abound for ordinary citizens to initiate grassroots diplomacy activities that enrich the commonweal.

Sounds simple enough. But crossing borders, listening carefully, and working cooperatively requires time and intentionality. Our natural impulse is to retreat into our own physical or virtual bubbles, surrounded by people who look and speak and think the same as us. Relational diplomacy challenges our reflexive tribalism by calling forth the humility needed to acknowledge our ignorance and prejudices, and to allow the Other to potentially prevail against us. True, forging friendships across political, racial, religious, and class divides will not mystically mitigate the harms that come to people as a result of unequal opportunities and life prospects. Nor will it substantially allay the global crises converging around us. But by depolarizing social life, ever so slightly, we strengthen the base of shared experience, mutual understanding, and cooperative action that underwrites the common good.

Vocational discernment

A third small solution entails the work we do—not merely to make a living, but to produce good in our world. By senior year, many college students are trying to figure out life after graduation. With only a short grace period for student loans, and under pressure to find a job that is meaningful, graduates are understandably restless. When I'm asked by unusually anxious students what they should do with their lives, I generally tell them that there is no neat formula. One's work depends on a variety of factors: who they are, what their passions are, where their talents lie, what their conscience demands, and what their life circumstances will allow. Not to mention how much effort they are willing to expend. A college degree may open up more work options and social privileges than not having one, but ultimately each person must decide how they will use their cultural power. Will the work they do simply pay the bills or instantiate what Hannah Arendt calls *amor mundi* (love of the world)?

In one of her poems, Mary Oliver (2005) asks: "Tell me, what is it that you plan to do with your one wild and precious life?" (p. 94). It is a question we need to continually ask ourselves, a fundamentally *vocational* question. Vocation conveys the old and honorable idea that work is not primarily a thing one does to live, but the thing one lives to do. Work gives us an opportunity to bring forth goods and services that conserve or expand, rather than diminish, the health of human and natural communities. Deep personal satisfaction ultimately derives from doing something that leaves a lasting legacy of good done for the world. Figure 7.2 portrays the world-serving character of vocation, famously summed up by Frederick Buechner (1973) as "that place where one's deep gladness and the world's deep hunger meet" (p. 95).

Vocation can't be reduced to a particular occupation. A prestigious career as a scientist, lawyer, professor, or doctor can be a natural response to our vocation, as well as a way to avoid it. Does that, then, leave us without any

FIGURE 7.2.   Discerning vocation.

objective measures of value? Might someone fulfill their vocation in *any* line of work? What does *productive labor* mean in moral and ethical terms?

Graduates rarely ask such questions, simply because it's difficult to determine whether certain types of labor actually produce social value. Steel working, for example, may be productive when used to add strength and durability to homes, but unproductive when used in a nuclear submarine. Which is why most people's natural default is to questions of *paycheck* ("How much will it pay?") and *prestige* ("How will my job increase my social status?"). Routinely sidelined are the more important questions of *purpose*:

- Does this work exercise my intelligence, skill, and moral sense?
- Is this work internally ennobling, causing me to feel alive, awake, and grateful?
- Are the products or services resulting from this work durable and useful (socially contributive)?
- Does this work help to positively reshape the structures of modern life?
- Does this work minimize ecological and social costs?

Purpose questions push us to discriminate between good labor and bad labor. Without this discernment, we might reasonably imagine using bad work as a means of doing good. A young graduate, for instance, might feel quite fortunate to land a job modeling expensive lingerie or lobbying for Big Tobacco, and actually find the job to be subjectively meaningful. The job can also make her oodles of money, with which to do good things, like supporting girls' education in Pakistan or clearing minefields in Angola.

However, those who adhere to this logic soon discover that work begun as a means to some relative life goal becomes, over time, an end in itself. Every hour spent in labor that is frivolous or absent of real value changes us, ever so slightly, in the direction of the products and people that surround us. Once the larger purpose questions evaporate, virtually *any* job can be seen as acceptable.

This generation has a collective vocation, a Great Work: to rebuild human existence into a thing of beauty, opportunity, prosperity, and livability. That's a really tall order, but one with vocational paths that include everything from architecture and land-use planning to social enterprise and food production. Our moment in history is breathtaking.

Conclusion

I'm reminded of the Rip Van Winkle allegory that Martin Luther King Jr. (1965) once referenced in a commencement address to Oberlin College students. In the story, a man ascends a mountain, sleeps for 20 years, and awakes to a world he hardly recognizes. After summarizing the tale, King exhorted the graduating class: "There are all too many people who, in some great period of social change, fail to achieve the new mental outlooks that the new situation demands. There is nothing more tragic than to sleep through a revolution."

In King's day, the necessary revolution was two-fold: to sweep away the old order of racial humiliation and segregation, and to end "the madness of Vietnam" (King, 1967b). Today's revolution is both social and ecological. Community-engaged global learning can serve the revolution by furnishing students with new insights, new outlooks, and new possibilities. But they must choose to remain awake and respond to the demands of their historical situation. Stewarding the transformation ultimately comes down to creating a more humane and resilient future. Global learners either find ways to convert their global awareness and conscience into a force of practical moral action, or they settle for sleepwalking into the future. Much depends on the choices they make in their personal lifestyle, their community relationships, and their chosen vocations.

Over the next several decades, the GRIN revolution will fundamentally transform our way of life. These technologies' convergence will empower vast smart cities, create apocalyptic weapons, help defeat illness and disease, and potentially make genetic cognitive enhancements available to low-income communities. If we collectively follow this transformation through to the future we want and need, I would be the first to declare the modern project a resounding success. If not, we will likely enter what Stanford historian Ian Morris (2011) calls "Nightfall"—an era marked by environmental catastrophe, famines, millions of climate migrants, global pandemics, and quite possibly all-out nuclear war. "The next 40 years," contends Morris (p. 608), "will be the most important in human history."

Notes

1. Examples include the abolition of slavery, women's right to vote, control of child labor, fair labor standards, civil rights, LGBT rights, resistance to apartheid, and, more recently, the youth-led climate justice movements like Sunrise and Extinction Rebellion.

ADDENDUM

Questions of Consequence

ONE OF THE sweetest fruits of global learning is for sojourners to discover the right questions, and then to subsequently wrestle with them until they stumble into truth. The following 10 questions are merely suggestive of the range of topics that can help them faithfully steward their transformation. They might be expanded to include work, play, waste, faith, sexuality, marriage, consumption, vocation, culture/media, technology, beauty, urban design, economy, governance, and more.

1. *Inequality:* Why are some despairingly poor and others lavishly rich? How does my relative affluence connect to poverty elsewhere? What is just in an economically divided world?
2. *Development:* What does real development look like? Are indigenous and traditional cultures failed attempts at being modern? Or are they unique expressions of the human imagination, just as valid as our own?
3. *Nationalism:* Is the United States exceptional in ways that Denmark or Bhutan are not? Are economic, military, cultural, and diplomatic power evidence of superior national character?
4. *"Stuff":* What do I think I need, and what do I *really* need? How much is "enough"?
5. *Food:* How should I eat, given the fact that animal agriculture is the leading cause of species extinction, water pollution, ocean dead zones, and habitat destruction?
6. *Mobility:* After not using a car for so many months, what would it take for me to substitute the train or bus or bicycle for my car in order to help reduce sprawl, congestion, and air pollution?
7. *Progress:* Is technological development in modern societies the truest sign of progress?

8. *Strangers:* What do I owe those whose land and labor have enabled me to live well? Having witnessed the desperate search by migrants for a better life, how will I relate to strangers at home?
9. *Privilege:* How do I use unearned life advantages in constructive and socially just ways, rather than wallowing in privilege guilt?
10. *Vocation:* How will my life contribute to the kind of world I want? How do I reconcile my desire to improve (save) the world with my desire to enjoy (savor) the world?

APPENDIX A

Global Competence

Global competence is . . .

- *A way of learning from the world:* The ability to skillfully investigate the world within and beyond one's immediate environment; to live and work and learn with people from different language, economic, and cultural backgrounds; to examine pressing issues from different angles, privileging the perspectives of those on the margins of power (the "view from below"); and to acknowledge moral wisdom embedded within alternative ways of life.
- *A way of thinking about the world:* The ability to interpret world realities through interdisciplinary lenses (e.g., philosophy, history, politics, economics, sociology, culture/religion, and ecology); to comprehend the cross-cultural and international dimensions of one's major field of study; to process discipline-specific questions from different cultural perspectives; and to consider ways to address specific issues in light of an ethical vision.
- *A way of seeing oneself in the world:* The ability to recognize all others, human and other-than-human, in *covenant* (interdependent) relationship; to affirm the intrinsic (versus merely instrumental) worth of all that participates in being; to exercise neighbor-love as intercultural understanding, economic justice, and environmental equity; to identify with the universalities of the human experience; to recognize global-justice connections between ourselves and others; and to become aware of the moral weight and consequence of those connections.
- *A way of behaving in the world:* The ability to recognize the call to love and safeguard human and natural communities; to value and respect human differences; to communicate effectively across those differences; to develop and sustain intercultural friendships; to

participate in the social and political life of local communities; to make responsible choices in one's personal lifestyle (e.g., related to how we eat and transport ourselves, what we purchase, who we befriend or exclude); to take action to improve local conditions through voting, volunteering, advocacy, and activism.

Global learners demonstrate their competence through . . .

1. *Self-limitation.* Learners narrow the distance between themselves and others by taking on some of the conditions and limitations of those radically different from themselves.
2. *Rootedness.* Learners demonstrate, through extended residence, a personal knowledge of particular places: their history, geography, groups, water and power sources, and native species.
3. *Interactive depth.* Learners engage with others across ethnic, linguistic, religious, socioeconomic, and national differences, enjoying the rewards of being and talking together.
4. *Social solidarity.* Learners form self-sustaining relationships with diverse others through active dialogue and collaboration.
5. *Cultural experimentation.* Learners try out new ways of thinking and acting within unfamiliar cultural settings.
6. *Perspective-taking.* Learners demonstrate the ability to see things through the eyes of others; to evaluate diverse perspectives in the face of conflicting positions; and to question the source of their own cultural assumptions, values, and judgments.
7. *Self-awareness.* Learners are able to describe themselves in terms of multiple, intersecting micro-identities (national, racial, social class, immigration status, etc.), and the power and prestige accorded them in their home and host societies.
8. *Intelligence.* Learners demonstrate growth in a range of "heart" qualities: enthusiasm, confidence, curiosity, initiative, humility, empathy, compassion, justice, flexibility, and perseverance.
9. *Foreign language development.* Learners demonstrate intermediate-level facility in at least one foreign language, with appropriate body language and sociocultural etiquette.

10. *Global awareness.* Learners articulate the interconnections—social, economic, political, and environmental—of the world community, along with the global conditions and systems that positively and negatively affect it.

11. *Social analysis.* Learners read back and forth from the local and national to the international, using various disciplines to analyze global-scale issues.

12. *Documentation.* Learners document field experiences through clear, cogent, and well-organized oral and written reports that integrate conceptual and experiential knowledge.

13. *Ethical reasoning.* Learners demonstrate the ability to make reasoned, evidence-based judgments on substantive issues involving diverse interests and competing claims. Learners decipher their basic moral obligations—in terms of time, talent, or treasure—in support of the common good.

14. *Perspective transformation.* Learners demonstrate a consciousness shift that exposes personally held myths (e.g., regarding superior race, chosen nation, progress, and worth by wealth) and imagines alternative ways of securing a more peaceful, just, and sustainable future.

15. *Cosmopolitan response.* Learners turn field lessons into concrete changes in their "being in the world" (e.g., social relations, consumption habits, vocational choices) as their fair share of responsibility for conditions that negatively affect the Earth and its inhabitants.

APPENDIX B

Program Features

THE FOLLOWING 20 program features explain fundamental differences in the design of global-learning programs. Consider the program you lead, manage, or hope to participate in. Then rate each feature on a scale of 1 (low representation) to 4 (high representation).

Features and Descriptions	Rating
1. *Dual purpose.* The program is intentionally organized to integrate community improvement outcomes with student learning outcomes. Both purposes receive equal attention and are held in symbiotic relationship.	
2. *Location.* The program prioritizes locations where the racial, cultural, and socioeconomic backgrounds of hosts and guests radically differ (to maximize the intercultural development of learners), and avoids destinations with high tourist-to-resident ratios (to minimize negative social and cultural impacts).	
3. *Community voice.* The program actively engages partner organizations in program planning and decision-making, ensuring that the locus of power and authority remains firmly rooted in the community. Common understandings are formalized in a nonbinding Memorandum of Understanding (MOU).	
4. *Duration.* The program is long enough for participants to acquire basic language and culture skills, and to support the formation of continuous, caring relationships supportive of the goals of partner organizations.	
5. *Size of group.* The program guards against creating a separate and self-sustaining foreign enclave that distorts local patterns of life and potentially destabilizes fragile ecologies. Ideally, host families and community organizations are limited to only one foreign guest.	

Features and Descriptions	Rating
6. *Diversity of group.* The program attracts a diverse student population (by gender, race, social class, and academic interests). Program participants are matched with community residents in ways that allow for a rich exchange of contrasting experiences and interpretations of local realities.	
7. *Student selection.* The program screens and selects participants based on established criteria, with primary consideration given to their desire to become a sympathetic, respectful, and contributing part of host communities.	
8. *Student preparation.* The program offers pre-field and in-field opportunities for participants to acquire essential contextual knowledge, along with the basic skills of cultural appreciation—structured observation, guided conversation, active listening, and field-note writing.	
9. *Housing.* The program places learners in living situations (e.g., local families) where, as guests, they provide direct financial assistance (via room and board payments) to host nationals, while cultivating empathetic cross-cultural bonds.	
10. *Language learning and use.* The program equips learners to communicate inside and outside the classroom in the local language, with appropriate body language and etiquette.	
11. *Community immersion.* The program seeks breadth from depth by embedding learners in local institutions—such as host families, service organizations, universities—where the primary emotional-social support system is formed with host nationals.	
12. *Environmental sustainability.* The program reduces negative environmental impacts through the purchase of carbon offsets for round-trip flights, and by not overconcentrating foreigner activity and waste production within ecologically sensitive areas. Learners reduce their water and power consumption toward the local standard.	
13. *Economic sustainability.* The program seeks to expand economic benefits to local residents by sourcing housing, food, transportation, and touring needs through indigenous entities—host families, local eateries and vendors, public forms of transportation, local guides, and national staff.	

Features and Descriptions	Rating
14. *Social sustainability.* The program entails the formation of mutually enriching relationships with host nationals. Program participants willingly adapt to local customs, interpersonal style, food culture, and language patterns.	
15. *Cultural sustainability.* The program guards against learner behavior deemed offensive or injurious by residents—such as stealth photography, bargaining below the fair price, substance abuse, and commercial sex.	
16. *Self-direction.* The program encourages learners to share responsibility for deciding *where* they will learn and serve, *with whom*, and *how* (e.g., the selection of academic materials and learning strategies).	
17. *Pedagogy.* The program moves beyond the classroom in arranging relevant content, contexts, and pedagogical tasks that investigate local phenomena related to learners' personal, academic, or professional interests.	
18. *Organization building.* The program aims to enhance native capability by involving learners as guests, interns, and investigators in respected families and organizations.	
19. *Instruction and mentoring.* The field support system includes purposeful direction and mentoring by able members of the host community—host family heads, service agency staff, language coaches, and research guides.	
20. *Sociocultural and disciplinary analysis.* The program involves learners in systematic in-field and post-field analysis of *sociocultural differences* and *discipline-specific issues*. Reflection on primary experience guides learners in constructing informed responses to the world.	

APPENDIX C

Community Health Indicators

1. **Material security**
   - *Employment:* Number and quality of jobs created and sustained by residents through business development.
   - *Economic opportunity:* The freedom to hold property (land and movable goods) and to seek employment on an equal basis with others.
   - *Income and investment:* Increase in personal, household, and business incomes, as well as savings and investments, leading to greater material security.
   - *Infrastructure:* Number of community facilities—roads, clinics, schools, water lines, and so on—built through resident and governmental actions, investments, and advocacy.
   - *Physical health:* Overall improvements in diet and medical services, leading to an increase in the number of people living a life of normal length.
2. **Psycho-cultural vitality**
   - *Imagination and thought:* The ability to imagine, think, and reason; to form a conception of the good; to engage in critical reflection about the planning of one's life; to exercise liberty of conscience and freedom of religious exercise.
   - *Self-confidence and efficacy:* Reduction in fatalistic perceptions and increased levels of self-esteem, community pride, and levels of initiative-taking.
   - *Life-enhancing education:* Increase in the percentage of school-age children (especially girls) enrolled in high-quality primary and secondary schools, leading to improvements in basic skills and human dignity.
   - *Cultural pride:* The protection and affirmation of religious or cultural traditions, occupations, and identities; the ability to laugh, to play, and to enjoy recreational activities.

3. **Sociopolitical equity:** Residents liberated from various forms of humiliation, oppression, marginalization, deprivation, and powerlessness in order to become agents of change within their communities.

   - *Social respect and freedom:* Formal establishment of the social bases of self-respect, non-discrimination, and security against sexual assault and domestic violence.
   - *Gender equity:* Increase in the number of women accessing and controlling assets (e.g., title to land, businesses), and enrolled in primary and secondary education.
   - *Sociopolitical participation:* Increase in the number of residents participating in grassroots and mainstream political organizations, local institutions, and various volunteer or advocacy activities.
   - *Political freedom:* Guarantees of freedom of expression (political opinion), of assembly, and of religious exercise, with enlarged choices to act together to improve the quality of community life.

4. **Moral-spiritual integrity:** Changes in vision, *telos*, values, affections, habits, and mind-set supportive of changes in the social, economic, and political dimensions of community life.

   - *Moral vision:* Increase in the number of community groups embracing a common and comprehensive conception of collective well-being.
   - *Support groups:* Increase in the number of community members involved in small groups focused on personal transformation and social betterment (e.g., support/recovery groups, family social service groups, youth development clubs).
   - *Faith communities:* Increase in the number of people gathered together as communities of mutual support, religious practice, moral development, and public action.
   - *Personal freedom:* Increase in the numbers of people freed from life addictions and destructive patterns, including greed, hatred, substance abuse, infidelity, and compulsive gambling.
   - *Just relationships:* Decline in the incidences of teen pregnancy, domestic violence, sexual abuse, divorce, crime, and environmental harm. Increase in community-wide levels of trust, honesty, fidelity, cooperativeness, and environmental care.

5. **Earth community**
   - *Land security:* Increase in the percentage of family units with security of tenure (as defined by residents).
   - *Rootedness:* Increase in the number of activities that safeguard the community's sense of history and culture, ecological processes, and biodiversity.
   - *Stewardship:* Increase in the number of community organizations acting to create clean neighborhoods, open spaces, access to safe drinking water, improved sanitation systems, and community gardens.

APPENDIX D

Organization Standards

THE FOLLOWING 15 queries indicate a framework of standards for evaluating and selecting organizations sponsoring global learners in community service and research activities. Rate each criterion on a scale of 1 (low representation) to 4 (high representation).

Conditions and Queries	Rating
1. *Credibility.* Does the organization and its leadership enjoy a reputation in the host community/region for being honest and sincere, without evidences of misconduct related to fund use and governance? Do experienced practitioners and scholars respect the organization?	
2. *Accountability.* Does the organization report to a functioning board or other recognized authorities? Is the organization transparent in the selection of board members, as well as the sources and uses of funds through financial disclosure statements? Are performance assessments available?	
3. *Size.* Does the organization have a minimum of two paid staff, plus volunteers and part-time staff, with the capacity to absorb more qualified volunteers? Does it sponsor various programs or projects within different localities?	
4. *Gendered.* Are women present in positions of leadership? Are they involved in planning, organizing, and decision-making? Are any of the organization's projects women-centered (e.g., women's savings and credit groups)?	
5. *Participatory.* Is the organization able to articulate the dreams and development priorities of local populations? Does the organization involve local residents in determining how the energies and ideas brought in by outsiders might be positively employed?	

Conditions and Queries	Rating
6. *Sovereign*. Does the organization see itself as active and empowered rather than passive and victimized ("poor me" syndrome)? Has it initiated people-centered solutions without becoming a surrogate vehicle for the funded projects of outside agencies?	
7. *Networked*. Has the organization developed forms of partnership with other grassroots organizations, as well as with researchers and multilateral agencies?	
8. *Welcoming*. Does the organization extend an invitation to qualified volunteers and external agencies to join them in community improvement efforts, while maintaining decision-making power over organizational goals, policies, and budget?	
9. *Solidarity*. Does the organization involve outsiders in tasks that place them in direct relationship with beneficiaries and local staff, without concentrating them at a given project site or merely using them as additional clerical help?	
10. *Empowering*. Does the organization maintain a respectful dialogue with the people they aim to help? Does it guard against *resource paternalism* (foreign funds or materials), *managerial paternalism* (foreign-driven initiatives), *knowledge paternalism* (foreigners instructing residents about how best to do things), and *labor paternalism* (foreigners working *for* residents rather than *with* them)?	
11. *Resource conservation*. Does the organization place foreign workers in living situations (e.g., local families, eco-villages) that don't disturb natural living patterns, and where they are expected to adjust their level of water and power consumption toward the local standard?	
12. *Appropriate scale*. Does the organization safeguard the social and natural environment by not overconcentrating foreigner activity and waste production within ecologically sensitive areas (e.g., small islands, high mountain regions, and tropical forests)?	
13. *Capacity building*. Do proposed service and/or research activities build upon the organization's internal strengths, contributing fresh energy and encouragement, alternative perspectives, new skills, and after returning home, continued advocacy?	

Conditions and Queries	Rating
14. *Mentored.* Does the organization include informed, bilingual local staff capable of providing workers on-site training, supervision, issue analysis, and performance feedback?	
15. *Equity.* Does the organization seek to distribute economic, social, and cultural/spiritual benefits to populations that are most disadvantaged? Can it guarantee that women and children are not exploited?	

REFERENCES

Ahmed, M. N. (2010). *A user's guide to the crisis of civilization*. London, UK: Pluto Press.

Alstete, J. W. (2014). Revenue generation strategies: Leveraging higher education resources for increased income. *ASHE Higher Education Report 41*(1).

Altbach, P. G., Berdahl, R. O., & Gumport, P. J. (2011). *American higher education in the twenty-first century: Social, political, and economic challenges* (3rd ed.). Baltimore, MD: Johns Hopkins University Press.

Appiah, K. A. (1997). Cosmopolitan patriots. *Critical Inquiry, 23*(3), 617-639. Retrieved from http://www.jstor.org/stable/1344038

Appiah, K. A. (2004). *The ethics of identity*. Princeton, NJ: Princeton University Press.

Appiah, K. A. (2006a). *Cosmopolitanism: Ethics in a world of strangers*. New York, NY: W.W. Norton.

Appiah, K. A. (2006b, January 1). The case for contamination. *New York Times Magazine*. Retrieved from https://www.nytimes.com/2006/01/01/magazine/the-case-for-contamination.html

Appiah, K. A. (2010). *The honor code: How moral revolutions happen*. New York, NY: W.W. Norton & Company.

Appiah, K. A. (2013, August 27). Sidling up to difference: Kwame Anthony Appiah on social change and moral revolutions. [Radio broadcast episode]. In Krista Tippett [Producer], *On Being*. Washington DC: National Public Radio.

Aristotle. (2004). *The Nicomachean ethics*. (J. A. K. Thomson, Trans., H. Tredennick, Ed.). London: Penguin.

Association of American Colleges (AAC&U). (n.d.). *What is a liberal education?* Retrieved from https://www.aacu.org/leap/what_is_liberal_education.cfm

Association of American Colleges (AAC&U). (2011). *The LEAP vision for learning: Outcomes, practices, impact, and employers' views*. Washington DC: Association of American Colleges and Universities.

Barr, R., & Tagg, J. (1995, November/December). From teaching to learning: A new paradigm for undergraduate education. *Change*. Retrieved from https://digitalcommons.unomaha.edu/slcehighered/60/

Bauerlein, M. (2009). *The dumbest generation*. New York, NY: Tarcher Perigee.

Bayles, M. (2014). *Through a screen darkly: Popular culture, public diplomacy, and America's image abroad*. New Haven, CT: Yale University Press.

Bennett, M. J. (1993). Towards ethnorelativism: A developmental model of inter-cultural sensitivity. In R. M. Paige (Ed.), *Education for the intercultural experience* (2nd ed., pp. 21-71). Yarmouth, ME: Intercultural Press

Berger, W. (2014). *A more beautiful question.* New York, NY: Bloomsbury.

Berry, W. (1993). *Sex, economy, freedom, and community.* New York, NY: Pantheon.

Berry, W. (2002). *The art of the commonplace: The agrarian essays of Wendell Berry.* Berke-ley, CA: Counterpoint.

Berry, W. (2003). *The long-legged house.* Berkeley, CA: Counterpoint.

Berry, W. (2007, May 12). Commencement address. Bellarmine College, Louisville, KY. Retrieved from http://www.bellarmine.edu/studentaffairs/Graduation/ berry_address.asp

Bhandari, R. (2013, March 14). Re-envisioning internationalization: International education for what? *Opening Minds Blog.* Institute for International Education. [Blog Post]. Retrieved from https://www.iie.org/Learn/Blog/2013/03/2013-March-Reinvisioning-Internationalization.

Birdsall, J. T. (2005). *Community voice: Community partners reflect on service learn-ing.* Retrieved from https://www.mesacc.edu/community-civic-engagement/ journals/community-voice-community-partners-reflect-service-learning

Bolen, M. (2001). Consumerism and U.S. study abroad. *Journal of Studies in Interna-tional Education, 5,* 182-199.

Bornstein, D. (2007). *How to change the world.* New York, NY: Oxford University Press.

Boyer, E. (1996). The scholarship of engagement. *Journal of Public Service and Out-reach, 1*(1), 11-20.

Brooks, D. (2016, May 17). One neighborhood at a time. *New York Times.* Retrieved from https://www.nytimes.com/2016/05/17/opinion/one-neighborhood-at-a-time.html

Brown, E. (2014, January 2). In Gallup poll, the biggest threat to world peace is . . . America? *International Business Times.* Retrieved from http://www.ibtimes.com/ gallup-poll-biggest-threat-world-peace-america-1525008

Brown, L. (2009). *Plan B 4.0: Mobilizing to save civilization.* New York, NY: W.W. Norton & Company.

Buechner, F. (1973). *Wishful thinking.* New York, NY: HarperOne.

Buffett, P. (2013, July 26). The charitable-industrial complex. *New York Times.* Retrieved from http://www.nytimes.com/2013/07/27/opinion/the-charitable-industrial-complex.html

Burkey, S. (1993). *People first: A guide to self-reliant participatory rural development.* New York, NY: Zed Books.

Butin, D. W. (2010). *Service-learning in theory and practice: The future of community engage-ment in higher education.* New York, NY: Palgrave Macmillan.

Caffarella, R. (1993). Self-directed learning. In S. Merriam (Ed.), *An update on adult learning theory: (New Directions for Adult and Continuing Education, no. 57, pp. 25-35).* San Francjsco, CA: Jossey-Bass.

Cannon, C. (2013). *Evaluating non-governmental organisations: An overview of* The Global Journal's *Top 100 NGOs methodology in 2013.* Retrieved from http://www.alnap .org/pool/files/evaluating-ngos-(methodology-paper)-en.pdf

Carey, K. (2015). *The end of college.* New York, NY: Riverhead Books.

Carnegie Foundation (2008). *Community engagement elective classification.* Retrieved from http://classifications.carnegiefoundation.org/descriptions/community_ engagement.php

Castells, M. (1998). *End of millennium.* Malden, MA: Blackwell.

Chambers, R. (1997). *Whose reality counts?* London, UK: Intermediate Technology Publications.

Champion, D. P, Kiel, D. H., & McLendon, J. A. (1990). Choosing a consulting role. *Training and Development Journal, 44*(2), 66–69.

Chomsky, N., & Nader, L. (1997). *The Cold War and the university: Toward an intellectual history of the postwar years.* New York, NY: New Press.

Cicero, M. T. (1971). *Cicero on the good life.* (M. Grant, Trans.). London: Penguin.

Cleverdon, R., & Kalisch, A. (2000). Fair trade in tourism. *International Journal of Tourism Research, 2,* 171–187. Retrieved from http://download.clib.psu.ac.th/ datawebclib/e_resource/trial_database/WileyInterScienceCD/pdf/JTR/JTR_5 .pdf

Clifford, J. (1998). *The predicament of culture: Twentieth century ethnography, literature and art.* Cambridge, MA: Harvard University Press.

Cohen, E. (1972). Toward a sociology of international tourism. *Social Research, 39*(1), 164–182.

Cole, T. (2012, March 21). The White-savior industrial complex. *The Atlantic.* Retrieved from http://www.theatlantic.com/international/archive/2012/03/ the-white-savior-industrial-complex/254843/

Collier, P. (2008). *The bottom billion.* New York, NY: Oxford University Press.

Collins, R. (1979). *The credential society: An historical sociology of education and stratification.* New York, NY: Academic Press.

Cornwell, G., and Stoddard, E. W. (1999). *Globalizing knowledge: Connecting international and intercultural studies.* Washington DC: Association of American Colleges and Universities.

Corrie, R. (2009). *Let me stand alone: The journals of Rachel Corrie.* New York, NY: W.W. Norton & Company.

Crabtree, R. D. (2008). Theoretical foundations for international service-learning. *Michigan Journal of Community Service-Learning, 15*(1), 18–36.

Crabtree, R. D. (2013). The intended and unintended consequences of international service-learning. *Journal of Higher Education Outreach and Engagement, 17*(2), 43–65.

Davidson, C. N. (2017, Oct. 22). A new education for our era. *The Chronicle of Higher Education.* Retrieved from https://www.chronicle.com/article/commentary-a-newer-education/241313

Davis, W. (1998). *Shadows in the sun: Travels to landscapes of spirit and desire.* Chicago, IL: Island Press.

Davis, W. (2007). *Light at the edge of the world.* New York, NY: Douglas & McIntyre.

Davis, W. (2013, January 9). Review of *The world until yesterday* by Jared Diamond. *The Guardian.* Retrieved from http://www.theguardian.com/books/2013/jan/09/history-society

Day, D. (1996). *The long loneliness.* New York, NY: HarperOne. (Original work published 1952)

De Bairacli Levy, J. (1979). *Travelers' joy.* New Canaan, CT: Keats.

De Botton, A. (2004). *The art of travel.* New York, NY: Vintage.

Deardorff, D. K. (2012). Intercultural competence in the 21st century: Perspectives, issues, applications. In B. Breninger & T. Kaltenbacher (Eds.), *Creating cultural synergies.* Newcastle Upon Tyne, UK: Cambridge Scholars.

Deardorff, D. K. (2013, Fall). Beyond ourselves: Embracing our global responsibilities. *IIE Networker.* Retrieved from http://www.nxtbook.com/naylor/IIEB/IIEB0213/index.php?startid=37#

Deardorff, D. K., & Jones, E. (2012). Intercultural competence: An emerging focus in post-secondary education. In D. K. Deardorff et al. (Eds.), *The Sage handbook of international higher education.* Los Angeles, CA: Sage.

Deresiewicz, W. (2014). *Excellent sheep: The miseducation of the American elite and the way to a meaningful life.* New York, NY: Free Press.

Dewey, J. (1997). *Education and experience.* New York, NY: Free Press. (Original work published 1938)

Diamond, J. M. (2012). *The world until yesterday: What can we learn from traditional societies?* New York, NY: Viking.

Dillard, A. (1989). *An American childhood.* New York, NY: Harper & Row.

Dostoyesvsky, F. (2005). *The brothers Karamazov.* New York, NY: Dover. (Original work published 1880)

Dunkelman, M. (2014). *The vanishing neighbor: The transformation of American community.* New York, NY: W. W. Norton & Company.

Durning, A. (1989). Action at the grassroots: Fighting poverty and environmental decline (Worldwatch Paper no. 88). Retrieved from https://web.uri.edu/mind/files/Reforming_-Development_-Assistance2.pdf

Easterbrook, G. (2018). *It's better than it looks: Reasons for optimism in an age of fear.* New York, NY: Public Affairs.

Easterly, W. (2007). *The White man's burden.* New York, NY: Penguin Books.

Edin, K., & Shaefer, H. L. (2015). *$2 a day: Living on almost nothing in America.* New York, NY: Houghton Mifflin Harcourt.

Ellerman, D. (2005). *Helping people help themselves: From the World Bank to an alternative philosophy of development assistance.* Ann Arbor: University of Michigan Press.

Emerson, R.W. (1841). Circles. *Essays: First series.* Retrieved from https://archive.vcu.edu/english/engweb/transcendentalism/authors/emerson/essays/circleshyp.html

Engle, L., & Engle, J. (2003). Study abroad levels: Toward a classification of program types. *Frontiers: The Interdisciplinary Journal of Study Abroad, 9*, 1–20.

Engle, L., & Engle, J. (2012). Beyond immersion: The AUCP experiment in holistic intervention. In M. Vande Berg, R. M. Paige, & K. H. Lou (Eds.), *Student learning abroad* (pp. 284–307). Sterling, VA: Stylus.

Eurlich, P. (2012). Solving the human predicament. *International Journal of Environmental Studies, 69*(4), 557–565. Retrieved from http://mahb.stanford.edu/wp-content/uploads/2012/02/2012_PRE_AHE_Solving-Human-Predictiment.pdf

Eyler, J., & Giles, D. (1999). *Where's the learning in service-learning?* San Francisco, CA: Jossey-Bass.

Eyler, J. S., Giles, D. E., Gray, C. J., & Stenson, C. M. (2001). *At a glance: What we know about the effects of service-learning on college students, faculty, institutions and communities, 1993-2000.* Nashville, TN: Vanderbilt University.

Fadel, C. & Trilling, B. (2014). *21st century skills: Learning for life in our times.* San Francisco: Jossey Bass.

Fanon, F. (1963). *The wretched of the earth.* New York, NY: Grove Press.

Fantini, A. (2006). *Exploring and assessing intercultural competence.* Brattleboro, VT: SIT Graduate Institute. Retrieved from http://digitalcollections.sit.edu/cgi/viewcontent.cgi?article=1001&context=worldlearning_publications/

Farmer, P. (2005). *Pathologies of power: Health, human rights, and the new war on the poor.* Berkeley: University of California Press.

Feinberg, B. (2002, May 3). What students don't learn abroad. *The Chronicle of Higher Education, 48*, B20. Retrieved from https://www.chronicle.com/article/What-Students-Dont-Learn/23686

Fish, S. (2012). *Save the world on your own time.* New York, NY: Oxford University Press.

Fitzgerald, F. S. (1993). *The crack-up.* (E. Wilson, Ed.). New York, NY: New Directions (Original work published 1945).

Forum on Education Abroad. (2011). *Code of ethics for education abroad*, 2nd ed. Carlisle, PA: The Forum on Education Abroad. Retrieved from https://forumea.org/resources/standards-of-good-practice/code-of-ethics/

Forum on Education Abroad. (n.d.). *Education abroad glossary.* Carlisle, PA: The Forum on Education Abroad. Retrieved from https://forumea.org/resources/glossary/

Friedman, T. L. (2005). *The world is flat: A brief history of the twenty-first century.* New York, NY: Farrar, Straus and Giroux.

Frey, C. B., & Osborne, M. A. (2013, September 13). *The future of employment: How susceptible are jobs to computerization?* Oxford, UK: University of Oxford. Retrieved from http://www.oxfordmartin.ox.ac.uk/downloads/academic/The_Future_of_Employment.pdf

Fromm, E. (1955). *The sane society.* New York, NY: Fawcett Books. (Original work published 1955)

Fromm, E. (1994). *Escape from freedom.* New York, NY: Holt. (Original work published 1941)

Fromm, E. (2010). *Pathology of normalcy.* New York: Lantern.

Frumkin, P., & Jastrzab, J. (2010). *Serving country and community: Who benefits from national service?* Cambridge, MA: Harvard University Press.

Funk, M. (2014). *Windfall: The booming business of global warming.* New York, NY: Penguin Books.

Geertz, C. (1983). *Local knowledge: Further essays in interpretive anthropology.* New York, NY: Basic Books.

Geertz, C. (1988). *Works and lives: The anthropologist as author.* Palo Alto, CA: Stanford University Press.

Giannetti, E. (2000). *Lies we live by: The art of self-deception.* London, UK: Bloomsbury.

Gibson-Graham, J. K., Cameron, J., & Healy, S. (2013). *Take back the economy: an ethical guide for transforming our communities.* Minneapolis, MN: University of Minnesota Press.

Gilbert, E. (2007). *Eat, pray, love.* New York, NY: Riverhead Books.

Glanzer, P. L., Alleman, N. F., & Ream, T. C. (2017). *Restoring the soul of the university.* Downers Grove, IL: IVP Academic.

Gochenour, T., & Janeway, A. (1993). Seven concepts in cross-cultural interaction: A training design. In T. Gochenour (Ed.), *Beyond experience: The experiential approach to cross-cultural education* (pp. 15–22). Yarmouth, ME: Intercultural Press.

Goffman, E. (1989). On fieldwork. *Journal of Contemporary Ethnography, 18*(2), 123–132.

Goleman, D. (2005). *Emotional intelligence: Why it can matter more than IQ.* New York, NY: Bantam Books.

Goulet, D. (1995). *Development ethics: A guide to theory and practice.* New York, NY: Zed Books.

Goulet, D. (2006). *Development ethics at work: Explorations 1960-2002.* New York, NY: Routledge.

Hall, E. (1959). *The silent language.* Garden City, NY: Doubleday & Company.

Hallowell, E. M. (1999, Jan.–Feb.). The human moment at work. *Harvard Business Review.* Retrieved from https://hbr.org/1999/01/the-human-moment-at-work

Harkavy, I. (2015, Winter/Spring). Creating the connected institution: Toward realizing Benjamin Franklin and Ernest Boyer's revolutionary vision for American higher education. *Liberal Education, 101*(1/2). Retrieved from https://www.aacu.org/liberaleducation/2015/winter-spring/harkavy

Hartman, E., Paris, C. M., & Blache-Cohen, B. (2014). Fair trade learning: Ethical standards for community-engaged international volunteer tourism. *Tourism and Hospitality Research, 14,* 108–116.

Havel, V. (1997, Dec. 9). State of the Republic. Presidential address to the Parliament and Senate of the Czech Republic. Quoted in J. B. Elshtain (2000), Families and trust: Connecting private lives and civic goods. *Chicago Studies 39*(1), 25-26.

Hawken, P. (1993). *The ecology of commerce: A declaration of sustainability.* New York, NY: HarperBusiness.

Hawken, P. (2008). *Blessed unrest.* New York, NY: Penguin Books.

Heclo, H. (2008). *On thinking institutionally.* Boulder, CO: Paradigm.

Hedges, C. (2012, November 11). Once again—death of the liberal class. *Truthdig. com.* Retrieved from https://www.truthdig.com/articles/once-again-death-of-the-liberal-class/

Hedges, C., & Sacco, J. (2012). *Days of destruction, days of revolt.* Toronto, ON: Alfred A. Knopf Canada.

Heinberg, R., & Lerch, D. (2010). *The post-carbon reader: Managing the 21st century's sustainability crises.* Healdsburg, CA: Watershed Media.

Helliwell, J. F., Layard, R., & Sachs, J. D. (2019). *World happiness report 2019.* New York, NY: Sustainable Development Solutions Network.

Holland, J., & Blackburn, J. (Eds.). (1998). *Whose voice? Participatory research and policy change.* Warwhickshire, UK: Practical Action.

Homer-Dixon, T. (2008). *The upside of down.* Washington DC: Island Press.

Hoopes, D. (1981). Intercultural communication concepts and the psychology of intercultural experience. In M. Pusch (Ed.), *Multicultural education: A cross-cultural training approach* (pp. 10–38). Yarmouth, ME: Intercultural Press.

Hovland, K. (2009). Global learning: What is it? Who is responsible for it? *Peer Review, 11*(4). Retrieved from https://www.aacu.org/peerreview/2009/fall/ovland

Howard, A. (2006). *The soil and health: A study of organic agriculture.* Lexington: University Press of Kentucky.

Hudzik, J. (2011). *Comprehensive internationalization: From concept to action.* Retrieved from https://shop.nafsa.org/detail.aspx?id=116E

Ignatev, M. (1984). *The needs of strangers.* London: Chatto & Windus.

Illich, I. (1968). *To hell with good intentions.* Paper presented at The Conference on Interamerican Student Projects, St. Mary's Lake of the Woods Seminary. Retrieved from http://www.uvm.edu/~jashman/CDAE195_ESCI375/To%20Hell%20with%20Good%20Intentions.pdf

Illich, I. (1971). *Deschooling society.* New York, NY: Harper & Row.

Institute of International Education. (2016). *Open doors report on international educational exchange.* Retrieved from https://www.iie.org/Why-IIE/Announcements/2016/11/2016-11-14-Open-Doors-Data

Intergovernmental Panel on Climate Change (IPCC). (2013). *Fifth assessment report of the intergovernmental panel on climate change.* New York, NY: Cambridge University Press.

Irie, E., Daniel, C., Cheplick, T., & Philips, A. (2010). The worth of what they do: The impact of short-term immersive Jewish service-learning on host communities. *Repair the World.* Retrieved from http://werepair.org/blog/short-term-volunteering-can-have-long-term-positive-effects-on-communities/4387

Ivanova, D., Stadler, K., Steen-Olsen, K., Wood, R., Vita, G., Tukker, A., & Hertwich, E. G. (2015, December 18), Environmental impact assessment of household consumption. *Journal of Industrial Ecology, 20*(3), 526–537.

Iyer, P. (2000, March 18). Why we travel. *Salon Travel.* Retrieved from http://picoiyerjourneys.com/index.php/2000/03/why-we-travel/

Iyer, P. (2005). *Sun after dark: Flights into the foreign.* New York, NY: Vintage.

James, W. (1961). *The varieties of religious experience: A study in human nature.* London, UK: Collier Books.

Jameson, J. K., Clayton, P. H., & Jaeger, A. J. (2011). Community engaged scholarship as mutually transformative partnerships. In L. M. Harter, J. Hamel-Lambert, & J. L. Millesen (Eds.), *Participatory partnerships for social action and research* (pp. 259–277). Dubuque, IA: Kendall Hunt Press.

Kaplan, R. (1998, August). Travels into America's future. *The Atlantic.* Retrieved from http://www.theatlantic.com/magazine/archive/1998/08/travels-into-americas-future/377147/

Kaplan, A. (2002). *Development practitioners and social process: Artists of the invisible.* London, UK: Pluto Press.

Kelly, G. (1963). *A theory of personality: The psychology of personal constructs.* New York, NY: Norton.

Kezar, A. J., Chambers, T. C.; Burkhardt, J. C. & Associates. (Eds.). (2005). *Higher education for the public good: Emerging voices from a national movement.* San Francisco, CA: Jossey-Bass.

Kiely, R. (2004). A chameleon with a complex: Searching for transformation in international service-learning. *Michigan Journal of Community Service Learning, 10*(2), 5–20.

King, M. L., Jr. (1964, December 11). The quest for peace and justice. Nobel Peace Prize Lecture, Oslo, Norway. Retrieved from https://www.nobelprize.org/prizes/peace/1964/king/lecture/

King, M. L., Jr. (1965, June). Remaining awake through a great revolution. Commencement address for Oberlin College, Oberlin, Ohio.

King, M. L., Jr. (1967a). *Where do we go from here: Chaos or community?* New York, NY: Harper & Row.

King, M. L., Jr. (1967b, April 4). Beyond Vietnam: A time to break silence. Retrieved from https://kinginstitute.stanford.edu/sites/mlk/files/a_time_to_break_silence_curriculum_guide.pdf

King, M. L., Jr. (1968a). Letter from a Birmingham jail. Atlanta, GA: Martin Luther King Jr. Center for Nonviolent Social Change. Retrieved from https://kinginstitute.stanford.edu/king-papers/documents/letter-birmingham-jail

King, M. L., Jr. (1968b, March 14). The other America. Speech delivered at Stanford University. Retrieved from http://www.gphistorical.org/mlk/mlkspeech/

King, M. L., Jr. (2010). *Strength to love*. Minneapolis, MN: Augsburg Fortress Press. (Original work published 1963)

Kolb, D. A. (1984). *Experiential learning: Experience as the source of learning and development*. Upper Saddle River, NJ: Prentice Hall.

Kolbert, E. (2015). *The sixth extinction: An unnatural history*. New York, NY: Picador.

Korten, D. (2007). *The great turning: From empire to Earth community*. San Francisco, CA: Berrett-Koehler.

Kuh, G. D., & Schneider, C. G. (2008). *High-impact educational practices: What they are, who has access to them, and why they matter*. Washington DC: Association of American Colleges and Universities.

Kurzweil, R. (2006). *The singularity is near*. New York, NY: Penguin Books.

LaBrack B., & Bathhurst, L. (2012). Anthropology, intercultural communication, and study abroad. In M. Vande Berg, R. M. Paige, & K. Hemming Lou (Eds.), *Student learning abroad: What our students are learning, what they're not, and what we can do about it* (pp. 188–214). Sterling, VA: Stylus.

Lasker, J. (2016). *Hoping to help: The promises and pitfalls of global health volunteering*. Ithaca, NY: Cornell University Press.

Lecky, W. E. H. (1955). *History of European morals from Augustus to Charlemagne*. New York, NY: George Braziller.

Lee, H. (1960). *To kill a mockingbird*. Philadelphia, PA: Lippincott.

Lempert, D. H., & Briggs, X. S. (1996). *Escape from the ivory tower: Student adventures in democratic experiential education*. San Francisco, CA: Jossey-Bass.

Lévi-Strauss Claude, Weightman, J., Weightman, D., & Wilken, P. (2012). *Tristes tropiques*. New York, NY: Penguin Books. (Original work published 1955)

Lopez, R. (2013, June 17). Most workers hate their jobs or have 'checked out,' Gallup says. *Los Angeles Times*. Retrieved from http://www.latimes.com/business/la-fi-mo-employee-engagement-gallup-poll-20130617-story.html

Lough, B. J., McBride, A. M., Sherraden, M. S., & Xiang, X. (2014). The impact of international service on the development of volunteers' intercultural relations. *Social Science Research*, 48–58.

Louv, R. (2005). *Last child in the woods: Saving our children from nature-deficit disorder*. Chapel Hill, NC: Algonquin Books.

Lugones, M. (2003). *Pilgrimages/peregrinajes: Theorizing coalition against multiple oppressions*. Lanham, MD: Rowman & Littlefield.

Lupton, R. (2007). *Compassion, justice, and the Christian life*. Ventura, CA: Regal Books.

Lutterman-Aguilar, A., & Gingerich, O. (2002). Experiential pedagogy for study abroad: Educating for global citizenship. *Frontiers: The Interdisciplinary Journal of Study Abroad, 8*, 41–82.

Malinowski, B. (1922). *Argonauts of the Western Pacific: An account of native enterprise and adventure in the archipelagoes of Melanesian New Guinea*. New York, NY: E. P. Dutton.

Marcus, G. E. (1995). Ethnography in/of the world system: The emergence of multi-sited ethnography. *Annual Review of Anthropology, 24*, 95–117. Retrieved from http://www.annualreviews.org/doi/abs/10.1146/annurev.an.24.100195.00 0523?journalCode=anthro

Mayer, S. (1994). *Building community capacity: The potential of community foundations.* Minneapolis, MN: Rainbow Research.

McBride, A. M., Lough, B., & Sherraden, M. S. (2012). International service and the perceived impacts on volunteers. *Nonprofit and Voluntary Sector Quarterly, 41*(6), 969–990.

McGranahan, G., Balk, D., & Anderson, B. (2007). The rising tide: Assessing the risks of climate change and human settlements in low elevation coastal zones. *Environment and Urbanization, 19*(1), 17–37.

McKibben, B. (2010). *Eaarth: Making a life on a tough new planet.* New York, NY: Henry Holt.

McKinnon, K. (2011). *Development professionals in northern Thailand: Hope, politics and practice.* Singapore and Copenhagen, Denmark: National University of Singapore Press and Nordic Institute of Asian Studies.

McNamee, S., & Miller, R., Jr. (2009). *The meritocracy myth.* New York, NY: Rowman & Littlefield.

Mezirow, J. (1978). Perspective transformation. *Adult Education Quarterly, 28,* 100–110.

Mezirow, J. (2000). *Learning as transformation.* San Francisco, CA: Jossey-Bass.

Mill, J. S. (1867, Feb. 1). Inaugural address delivered to the University of St. Andrews. Retrieved from https://en.wikisource.org/wiki/Inaugural_address_ delivered_to_the_University_of_St._Andrews,_Feb._1st_1867

Mills, C. W. (1951). *White collar: The American middle classes.* New York, NY: Oxford University Press.

Mills, C. W. (1956). *The power elite.* New York, NY: Oxford University Press.

Moore, M. (Director). (2016). *Where to invade next.* [DVD]. Toronto: Mongrel Media.

Morris, I. (2011). *Why the West rules—for now.* New York, NY: Farrar, Straus & Giroux.

Morton, K. (1995). The irony of service: Charity, project and social change in service-learning. *Michigan Journal of Community Service Learning,* Fall, *2*(1), 19–32. Retrieved from http://quod.lib.umich.edu/m/mjcsl/3239521.0002.102/1/– irony-of-service-charity-project-and-social-change

Mortenson, G., & Relin, D. O. (2007). *Three cups of tea: One man's mission to promote peace, one school at a time.* London: Penguin.

Mumford, L. (1951). *The conduct of life.* New York, NY: Harcourt, Brace.

Murphy, D., Sahakyan, N., Young-Yi, D., & Magnan, S. S. (2014). The impact of study abroad on the global engagement of university graduates. *Frontiers: The International Journal of Study Abroad, 24.* Retrieved from https://frontiersjournal.org/wp-content/uploads/2015/09/MURPHY-SAHAKYAN-YONGYI-MAGNAN-FRONTIERSXXIV-TheImpactofStudyAbroadofTheGlobal-EngagementofUniversityGraduates.pdf

Musil, C. M. (2003). Educating for citizenship. *Peer Review, 5*(3). Retrieved from https://www.aacu.org/publications-research/periodicals/educating-citizenship

Narayan, D., Chambers, R., Shah, M., & Petesch, P. (2000). *Voices of the poor: Crying out for change.* New York: NY. Oxford University Press for the World Bank.

Narayan, D., Patel, R., Schafft, K., Rademacher, A, & Kock-Schulte, S. (2000). *Voices of the poor: Can anyone hear us?* New York, NY: Oxford University Press for the World Bank.

Nettle, D., & Romaine, S. (2000). *Vanishing voices: The extinction of the world's languages.* Oxford, UK: Oxford University Press.

Neuwirth, R. (2004). *Shadow cities: A billion squatters, a new urban world.* New York, NY: Routledge.

Niebuhr, R. (2001). *Moral man and immoral society: A study in ethics and politics.* Louisville, KY: Westminster John Knox Press.

NOAA National Centers for Environmental Information. (2017, January). *State of the climate: Global analysis for annual 2016.* Retrieved from https://www.nasa.gov/press-release/nasa-noaa-data-show-2016-warmest-year-on-record-globally

Norberg, J. (2017). *Progress: Ten reasons to look forward to the future.* London, UK: One World.

Notz, D., & Stroeve, J. (2016). Observed Arctic sea-ice loss directly follows anthropogenic CO_2 emission. *Science, 354*(6313), 747–750. Retrieved from https://science.sciencemag.org/content/sci/354/6313/747.full.pdf

Nussbaum, M. (1997). *Cultivating humanity: A classical defense of reform in liberal education.* Cambridge, MA: Harvard University Press.

Nussbaum, M. (2001). *Upheavals of thought: The intelligence of emotions.* Cambridge, UK: Cambridge University Press.

Nussbaum, M. (2011). *Creating capabilities: The human development approach.* Cambridge, MA: Harvard University Press.

Nussbaum, M. (2013). *Political emotions: Why love matters for justice.* Cambridge, MA: Harvard University Press.

Nye, J. (2004). *Soft power: The means to success in world politics.* New York, NY: Public Affairs.

Ogden, A. (2008). The view from the veranda: Understanding today's colonial student. *Frontiers: The Interdisciplinary Journal of Study Abroad, 15*, 35–55.

Oliver, M. (2005). The summer day. In *New and selected poems* (Vol. 1). Boston, MA: Beacon Press.

Olson, C. L., & Peacock, J. (2012). Globalism and interculturalism: Where global and local meet. In D. K. Deardorff et al. (Eds.), *The Sage handbook of international higher education.* Los Angeles, CA: Sage.

Olson, C. L., Evans, R., & Shoenberg, R.F (2007). *At home in the world: Bridging the gap between internationalization and multicultural education.* Washington, DC: American Council on Education.

Orr, D. (1990). Liberal arts, the campus, and the biosphere. *Harvard Educational Review, 60*(2), 205-216.

Orr, D. (1991, Winter). What is education for? *In Context*. The Context Institute. Retrieved from http://www.context.org/iclib/ic27/

Orr, D. (1994). *Earth in mind: On education, environment and the human prospect*. Washington DC: Island Press.

Oxfam. (2015, December 2). Extreme carbon inequality: *Why the Paris climate deal must put the poorest, lowest emitting and most vulnerable people first*. Retrieved from https://www.oxfam.org/sites/www.oxfam.org/files/file_attachments/mb-extreme-carbon-inequality-021215-en.pdf

Oxfam. (2017, January). *An economy for the 99%*. Retrieved from https://www.oxfam.org/sites/www.oxfam.org/files/file_attachments/bp-economy-for-99-percent-160117-en.pdf

Paige, R. M. (Ed.). (1993). *Education for the intercultural experience*. Yarmouth, ME: Intercultural Press.

Paige, R. M., Fry, G. W., Stallman, E. M., Josic, J., & Jon, J. (2009). Study abroad for global engagement: The long-term impact of mobility experiences. *Intercultural Education, 20*, S29-S44.

Palmer, P. (1993). *To know as we are known: Education as a spiritual journey*. New York, NY: HarperOne.

Parenti, C. (2011). *Tropic of chaos: Climate change and the new geography of violence*. New York, NY: Nation Books.

Park, R. (1925). *The city*. Chicago, IL: University of Chicago Press.

Pérez-Peña, R. (2014, December 26). Colleges reinvent classes to keep more students in science. *The New York Times*. Retrieved from http://www.nytimes.com/2014/12/27/us/college-science-classes-failure-rates-soar-go-back-to-drawing-board.html

Peter, L. (1982). *Peter's almanac*. New York, NY: William Morrow & Company.

Pietsch, T. (2013). *Empire of scholars: Universities, networks and the British academic world, 1850-1939*. Manchester, UK: Manchester University Press.

Piff, P. K., Stancato, D. M., Côté, S., Mendoza-Denton, R., & Keltner, D. (2012). Higher social class predicts increased unethical behavior. *Proceedings of the National Academy of Sciences, 109*(11), 4086-4091.

Pimentel, D., & Pimentel, M. (2008). *Food, energy, and society* (3rd ed.). Boca Raton, FL: CRC Press.

Pinker, S. (2018). *Enlightenment now: The case for reason, science, humanism, and progress*. New York, NY: Viking.

Pimm, S. L., Jenkins, C. N., Abell, R., Brooks, T. M., Gittleman, J. L., Joppa, L. N., . . . Sexton, J. O. (2014). The biodiversity of species and their rates of extinction, distribution, and protection. *Science, 344*(6187), 987-997.

Pitzer College. (2014). *The Pitzer College 50th anniversary engaged faculty collection: Community engagement and activist scholarship*, 69-71. Claremont, CA: Pitzer College Community Engagement Center.

Pogge, T. (2008). *Global poverty and human rights* (2nd ed.). Cambridge, MA: Polity.

Pope Francis (2015). *Encyclical letter Laudato Si' of the Holy Father Francis on care for our common home.* Rome: The Vatican. Retrieved from http://w2.vatican.va/content/francesco/en/encyclicals/documents/papa-francesco_20150524_enciclica-laud-ato-si.html

Pope, J. (2011, September 11). American students abroad pushed out of 'bubbles'. *USA Today.* Retrieved from http://usatoday30.usatoday.com/news/education/story/2011-09-25/study-abroad/50550430/1

Porritt, J. (2009, March 23). Perfect storm of environmental and economic collapse closer than you think. *The Guardian.* Retrieved from http://www.theguardian.com/environment/2009/mar/23/jonathon-porritt-recession-climate-crisis

Prahalad, C. K. (2009). *The fortune at the bottom of the pyramid.* Philadelphia, PA: Wharton School.

Pratt, M. L. (1991). Arts of the contact zone. *Profession, 91,* 33–40. Retrieved from https://www.jstor.org/stable/25595469

Quinones, S. (2015). *Dreamland.* New York, NY: Bloomsbury.

Reardon, K. & Forester, L. (Eds.). (2015). *Rebuilding community after Katrina: Transformative education in the New Orleans planning initiative.* Philadelphia, PA: Temple University Press.

Remarks at the First European Conference of the Forum on Education Abroad: President of Ireland. (n.d.). Retrieved from https://www.president.ie/en/media-library/speeches/remarks-by-president-higgins-first-european-conference-of-the-forum-on-educ.

Rhodes, F. H. T. (2006). Sustainability: The ultimate liberal art. *The Chronicle Review, 53*(9), B24.

Rischard, J. F. (2003). *High noon: 20 global problems, 20 years to solve them.* New York, NY: Basic Books.

Rogers, C. (1994). Personal thoughts on teaching and learning. Reprinted in *Freedom to learn: A view of what education might become.* Princeton, NC: Merrill. (Original work published 1969)

Rohr, R. (2003). *Everything belongs: The gift of contemplative prayer.* New York, NY: Crossroad.

Rosenthal, J. (2009, July 18). Patriotism and cosmopolitanism. *Policy Innovations.* Carnegie Council for Ethics in International Affairs. Retrieved from http://www.policyinnovations.org/ideas/briefings/data/000141

Rosling, H., Rosling, O., & Rönnlund Anna Rosling. (2019). *Factfulness: ten reasons we're wrong about the world - and why things are better than you think.* London: Sceptre.

Ryan, E. (2015, March 27). Remarks on education abroad. The Forum on Education Abroad annual meeting. Retrieved from http://eca.state.gov/speech/assistant-secretary-state-evan-ryan-remarks-education-abroad

Sacks, J. (2013, August 13). Covenant and conversation—Tzedakah: The untranslatable virtue. *Torah.* Retrieved from http://www.ou.org/torah/article/covenant_and_conversation_tzedakah#.Uh5I4rxKk7A

Sagan, C. (1998). *Billions & billions: Thoughts on life and death at the brink of the millennium.* New York, NY: Ballantine Books.

Saltmarsh, S. & Hartley, M. (Eds.). (2011). *"To serve a larger purpose:" Engagement for democracy and the transformation of higher education.* Philadelphia, PA: Temple University Press.

Sample, I. (2009, March 18). World faces 'perfect storm' of problems by 2030, chief scientist to warn. *The Guardian.* Retrieved from https://www.theguardian.com/science/2009/mar/18/perfect-storm-john-beddington-energy-food-climate

Sanders, S. R. (1993*). Staying put: Making a home in a restless world.* Boston, MA: Beacon Press.

Sanford, N. (1967). *Self and society: Social change and individual development.* New York, NY: Atherton Press.

Sapolsky, Robert M. (2017). *Behave: The Biology of Humans at Our Best and Worst.* Penguin Press.

Saunders, D. (2012). *Arrival city: How the largest migration in history is reshaping our world.* New York, NY: Vintage.

Sayers, D. (1949). *Creed or chaos?* London, UK: Methuen.

Schattle, H. (2007). *The practices of global citizenship.* Lanham, MD: Rowman & Littlefield.

Schneider, C. G. (2003). Liberal education and integrative learning. *Issues in Integrative Studies, 21,* 1–8.

Schrecker, E. (2010). *The lost soul of higher education: corporatization, the assault on academic freedom, and the end of the American university.* New York: New Press.

Schumacher, E. F. (1975). *Small is beautiful: Economics as if people mattered.* New York, NY: Harper & Row.

Sen, A. K. (1999). *Development as freedom.* New York, NY: Oxford University Press.

Sertillanges, A. G. (1998). *The intellectual life: Its spirit, conditions, methods.* Washington DC: The Catholic University of America Press.

Sexton, J. (2006, Dec. 6). Interview by Stephen Colbert. *Colbert Report* [Television Series].

Shaull, R. (2000). In P. Freire, *Pedagogy of the oppressed.* [Foreword]. New York, NY: Continuum.

Simon, J., & Ainsworth, J. W. (2012, July 19). Race and socioeconomic status differences in study abroad participation: The role of habitus, social networks, and cultural capital. *ISRN Education, 2012.* Retrieved from https://www.hindawi.com/journals/isrn/2012/413896/

Sinclair, U. (1985). *The jungle.* New York, NY: Penguin Books. (Original work published 1905)

Singer, P. (2004). One atmosphere. In *One world: The ethics of globalization.* New Haven, CT: Yale University Press.

Singer, P. (2010). *The life that you can save.* New York, NY: Random House.

Slavery Footprint. (n.d.). *How many slaves work for you?* Retrieved from http://www.slaveryfootprint.org

Slimbach, R. (2016). Deschooling international education: Toward an alternative paradigm of practice. In B. Streitwieser and A. Ogden (Eds.), *International education's scholar-practitioners: Bridging research and practice.* Oxford, UK: Symposium Books.

Smith, P. (1997). *Killing the spirit.* New York, NY: Viking Books.

Sobania, N. (Ed.). (2015). *Putting the local in global education: Models for transformative learning through domestic off-campus programs.* Sterling, VA: Stylus.

Sobania, N., & Braskamp, L. A. (2009). Study abroad or study away: It's not merely semantics. *Peer Review, 11*(4). Retrieved from https://www.aacu.org/publications-research/periodicals/study-abroad-or-study-away-its-not-merely-semantics

Speth, J. G. (2008). *The bridge at the edge of the world.* New Haven, CT: Yale University Press.

Standing, G. (2015, June 13). A new class: Canada neglects the precariat at its peril. *Globe and Mail.* Retrieved from http://www.theglobeandmail.com/report-on-business/rob-commentary/a-new-class-canada-neglects-the-precariat-at-its-peril/article24944758/

Standish, A. (2012). *The false promise of global learning: Why education needs boundaries.* New York, NY: Bloomsbury.

Stearns, R. (2010). *The hole in our gospel.* Nashville, TN: Thomas Nelson.

Stefanko, K. (2015, Jan. 21). *Should I volunteer abroad?* Retrieved from https://blog.travel-peopleandplaces.co.uk/should-i-volunteer-abroad-an-article-we-contributed-to/

Stephens, D. (2013). *Hacking your education.* New York, NY: Perigee Books.

Stiglitz, J. E. (2016). *The great divide: unequal societies and what we can do about them.* New York, NY: Norton & Company.

Stoeker, R., & Tyron, E. (2009). *The unheard voices: Community organizations and service learning.* Philadelphia, PA: Temple University Press.

Stoeker, R., Beckman, M., & Boo Hi Minn. (2010). Evaluating the community impact of higher education civic engagement. In H. E. Fitzgerald, C. Burack, & S. Seifer. (Eds.), *Handbook of engaged scholarship: The contemporary landscape. Volume two: Community-campus partnerships* (pp. 177–198). East Lansing, MI: Michigan State University Press.

Streitwieser, B., & Light, G. (2016). The grand promise of global citizenship through study abroad: The student view. In E. Jones, R. Coelen, J. Beelen, & H. de Wit (Eds.), *Global and local internationalization.* (pp. 67–74). Rotterdam, Netherlands. Sense.

Taleb, N. N. (2012). *Antifragile: Things that gain from disorder.* New York, NY: Random House.

Tavernise, S. (2016, April 22). U.S. suicide rates have surged to a 30-year high. *The New York Times.* Retrieved from http://www.nytimes.com/2016/04/22/health/us-suicide-rate-surges-to-a-30-year-high.html

Taylor, C. (2003). *Modern social imaginaries.* Durham, NC: Duke University Press.

The Newsroom (2012, October 21). *America is not the greatest country in the world anymore.* [Video File]. Retrieved from https://www.youtube.com/watch?v=q49NOyJ8fNA

Thoreau, H. D. (1919). *Walden: Or, life in the woods.* New York, NY: Houghton Mifflin.

Theroux, P. (1975). *The great railway bazaar.* New York, NY: Houghton Mifflin.

Theroux. P. (2014). *The last train to Zona Verde.* New York, NY: Mariner Books.

Tonkin, H. (2010). A research agenda for international service learning. In R. Bringle, J. Hatcher, & S. Jones (Eds.), *International service learning: Conceptual frameworks and research.* Sterling, VA: Stylus.

Tourism Concern. (2017). *Fair trade tourism principles.* Retrieved from https://www.tourismconcern.org.uk/about/who-we-are/ethical-fair-trade-tourism-principles/

Tulane University. (2015, July 30). *Final report: 2013/14 survey research on child labor in West African cocoa growing areas.* School of Public Health and Tropical Medicine, Tulane University. Retrieved from http://www.childlaborcocoa.org/index.php/2013-14-final-report

Turner, V. (1969). *The ritual process: Structure and anti-structure.* New York, NY: Penguin.

Twelve-Step Program. (n.d.). *Twelve Steps.* Retrieved from http://en.wikipedia.org/wiki/Twelve-Step_Program#Twelve_Steps

Twenge, J. M. (2017). *iGen: Why today's super-connected kids are growing up less rebellious, more tolerant, less happy—and completely unprepared for adulthood (and what this means for the rest of us).* New York, NY: Atria Books.

Ubels, J., Acquaye-Baddoo, N.A., & Fowler, A. (2010). *Capacity development in practice.* London, UK: Earthscan.

Unger, P. (1996). *Living high and letting die.* New York, NY: Oxford University Press.

UN Habitat. (2011). *Hot cities: Battle ground for climate change. Global report on human settlement 2011.* New York, NY: United Nations.

UN Habitat. (2016). *The city we need 2.0: Towards a new urban paradigm.* Nairobi, KE. Retrieved from http://www.worldurbancampaign.org/sites/default/files/documents/tcwn2en.pdf

University of California, Los Angeles (UCLA). (n.d.). *Transforming L.A. through cutting edge research.* Retrieved from http://grandchallenges.ucla.edu/sustainable-la/

U.S. Department of Education, National Center for Education Statistics. (2018). *Digest of education statistics.* Retrieved from https://nces.ed.gov/programs/digest/2018menu_tables.asp

Urry, J. (1995). *Consuming places.* London, UK: Routledge.

Uslaner, E. (2012). *Segregation and mistrust: Diversity, isolation, and social cohesion.* New York, NY: Cambridge University Press.

Vande Berg, M., Paige, R. M., & Lou, K. H. (Eds.). (2012). *Student learning abroad: What our students are learning, what they're not, and what we can do about it.* Sterling, VA: Stylus.

Vygotsky, L. (1978). *Mind in society: The development of higher mental processes.* Cambridge, MA: Harvard University Press.

Wallace-Wells, D. (2019). *The uninhabitable Earth: Life after warming*. New York, NY: Penguin Random House.

Wegner, N., & Weidman, T. (2015). *Mustang: Lives and landscapes of the lost Tibetan kingdom*. New York, NY: Goff Books.

Weisman, A. (2013). *Countdown: Our last, best hope for a future on earth?* New York, NY: Little, Brown and Company.

Weissman, N. (2012). Sustainability and liberal education: Partners by nature. *Liberal Education, 98*(4). Retrieved from http://www.aacu.org/liberaleducation/le-fa12/weissman.cfm

Wheatley, M., & Frieze, D. (2011). *Walk out walk on: A learning journey into communities daring to live the future now*. San Francisco, CA: Berrett-Koehler.

Williams, R. (2009, November 12). Closing keynote lecture. New Perspectives on Faith and Development. [Video File] Retrieved from https://www.youtube.com/watch?v=lNiu4PDGBSw

Wilson, E. O. (1999). *Consilience: The unity of knowledge*. New York, NY: Vintage Books.

Wise, T. (2008). *Tim Wise on White privilege: Racism, White denial and the costs of inequality*. [Video File]. Retrieved from https://www.youtube.com/watch?v=9AMY2Bvxuxc

Woolf, M. (2010). Another *mishegas*: Global citizenship. *Frontiers: The Interdisciplinary Journal of Study Abroad, 19*. Retrieved from http://frontiersjournal.org/wp-content/uploads/2015/09/WOOLF-FrontiersXIX-AnotherMishegas.pdf

World-o-Meters. (2019). Current world population. Retrieved from https://www.worldometers.info/world-population/

World Bank. (2012). *Turn down the heat*. Retrieved from http://climatechange.worldbank.org/sites/default/files/Turn_Down_the_heat_Why_a_4_degree_centrigrade_warmer_world_must_be_avoided.pdf

Worrall, L. (2007). Asking the community: A case study of community partner perspectives. *Michigan Journal of Community Service Learning, 14*, 5–17.

Zemach-Bersin, T. (2009). Selling the world: Study abroad marketing and the privatization of global citizenship. In R. Lewin (Ed.), *The handbook of practice and research in study abroad: Higher education and the quest for global citizenship* (pp. 303–320). New York, NY: Routledge.

ABOUT THE AUTHOR

Richard Slimbach, raised and educated in California, is currently professor of Global Studies at Azusa Pacific University. He created Azusa's Los Angeles Term and Global Learning Term programs, and co-created the Transformational Urban Leadership program (focused exclusively on the planet's one billion slum dwellers). A graduate of UCLA (Ph.D. in comparative and international education), he is the author of *Becoming World Wise* (Stylus, 2010). He lives with Leslie, spouse of 36 years, and their two children (Justus and Destinae) in Monrovia, California.

INDEX